Penguin Books

PIECES OF BLUE

Kerry McGinnis was twelve when her father decided to leave the city and go droving with his four children. The family roamed widely before eventually settling in the Queensland Gulf Country. Kerry has worked as a shepherd, droving hand, gardener, and a stock-camp and station cook. Together with her brother and sister she now operates the family property Bowthorn, which is also a tourist destination.

Kerry is the author of the best-selling *Heart Country*, and has published articles and short stories in various publications, including the *Sydney Morning Herald*, the *Herald & Weekly Times*, *Meanjin* and the *Bulletin*.

Also by Kerry McGinnis

Heart Country

KERRY McGINNIS

PIECES OF BLUE

PENGUIN BOOKS

For the MTZ mob

Penguin Notes for Reading Groups are available at www.penguin.com.au

Penguin Books

Published by the Penguin Group
Penguin Books Australia Ltd
250 Camberwell Road,
Camberwell, Victoria 3124, Australia
Penguin Books Ltd
80 Strand, London WC2R 0RL, England
Penguin Putnam Inc.
375 Hudson Street, New York, New York 10014, USA
Penguin Books, a division of Pearson Canada
10 Alcorn Avenue, Toronto, Ontario, Canada M4V 3B2
Penguin Books (NZ) Ltd
Cnr Rosedale and Airborne Roads, Albany, Auckland, New Zealand
Penguin Books (South Africa) (Pty) Ltd
24 Sturdee Avenue, Rosebank, Johannesburg 2196, South Afric
Penguin Books India (P) Ltd
11, Community Centre, Panchsheel Park, New Delhi 110 017, India

First published by Penguin Books Australia Ltd 1999
This edition published by Penguin Books Australia Ltd 2000

13 12 11 10 9 8 7 6

Design by Marina Messiha, Penguin Design Studio
Typeset in Granjon by Midland Typesetters, Maryborough, Victoria
Printed and bound in Australia by McPherson's Printing Group, Maryborough, Victoria

National Library of Australia
Cataloguing-in-Publication data:

McGinnis, Kerry.
Pieces of blue.
Includes index.
ISBN 0 14 029530 5.
1. McGinnis, Kerry. 2. Country life – Australia – Biography. 3. Australia – Rural conditions – Biography.
I. Title
307.72092

This project has been assisted by the Commonwealth Government through the Australia Council, its arts funding and advisory body.
[it0,0]

www.penguin.com.au

ONE

The day she died I called my mother wicked. I was six, big enough
to lift baby Patrick as he tottered, crying, across the green kitchen
linoleum. I jogged him in my arms, feeling the cold of his wet
nappy, nuzzling my nose into his soft neck. He opened his mouth
and roared. He was hungry.

'Birdie.' I pointed to the calendar. 'Pretty birdie!' But he went
on sobbing for his mother.

'Wicked old Mummy's not up yet,' I said. 'We'll tell Dad.'

But Dad was at the Gladstone hospital watching her die, and it
was Mrs Patterson from next door who changed Patrick's nappy
and heated his milk, then got breakfast for the rest of us.

'Has the new baby come yet?' Sian asked. The question, which
astonished Judith and me ('Are we getting another one?') seemed
to confuse our neighbour.

'I don't know, dear. You'd better ask your dad – only not today, eh? You can come over to my place later to play, and choose your own lunches too.'

'Is today special?' I was puzzled. 'We only do that on special days.' But Mrs Patterson started clattering the crockery together and didn't answer.

It was a week before we learned that both the new baby and our mother had died. They were very sick, Dad said at first, so we couldn't see them. Instead, he told us, we'd pack the caravan because we were all going to visit Gran and Grampy in Adelaide.

This was a great adventure. We ran willingly from room to room, collecting books and shoes and favourite toys, while Dad, in desperation, defaced the van's various cupboards with painted signs: 'Pants', 'Singlets', 'Socks'. His fingers were too big for Patrick's buttons, his grief too numbing to remember which of us had the red shoes, or that I couldn't plait my own hair. We were too young to help him – Patrick only two and Judith five, I was six and Sian, the eldest, eight.

In the car he told us baldly, gripping the wheel while the white guide posts with their magic eyes that lit up at night, flashed past.

'Your mother's not sick,' he said. 'She's gone to Heaven with the baby. You know what that means, don't you? You'll never see her again.'

'She's not at Gran's?' Judith voiced our bewilderment. We had settled it among ourselves that she would be waiting there when we arrived.

'She's gone,' Dad said. The car swerved and slowed. Horrified, we heard him sob, then he thrust the door open and lurched away.

We sat frozen, listening. It had never occurred to us that grown-ups cried. Heaven must be a terrible place to have this effect on Dad.

In the back seat Patrick slept, cushioned by pillows and rugs, while Sian, Judith and I, terrified into silence, stared ahead through the windscreen.

Dad was wiping his face when he returned. Our eyes, stretched wide, swung to him as if pulled by a single string. 'Well,' he tried to smile. 'It's all right now. Everything will be all right – you'll see. We won't talk about her again.'

Perhaps he didn't mean it as a taboo but we took it that way, and from then on everything to do with our mother vanished from our conversations. Judith, gabbling the post-meal ritual of 'Mummy, may I leave the table?', was told to say 'Dad' instead. And my red and green rosebud dress, made from remnants of a pattern my mother had sewn for herself, disappeared. By the time we reached our destination the name we must never speak was locked inside us – as if she had been ten years, rather than ten days, dead.

∽

Every year until I was nine, we spent the holidays in Adelaide at Gran and Grampy's place, at Flora Street, St Peters. They were my mother's parents, and lived in an old stone house with a grape arbour shading its morning side and the branches of an almond tree moving above the woodshed at the back.

Everything at Gran's was different: the papered walls; the florid, rose-patterned thunder-mugs under the beds, the chip heater roaring like a captive dragon in the bathroom. I loved the beautiful bottled fruits in the store cupboard – queenly containers of red cherries, purple plums and peach halves nested together like spoons. I loved the red and gold tea caddy with the picture of the King, and the colourful rag cushions on the horsehair sofa under the window. It was a homely but exciting house, cluttered with a lifetime's possessions and very different from our own. I loved every part of it except the dark passage connecting the front rooms to the kitchen. I always ran its length to bed with a prickling nape and shoulders hunched against unseen horrors in the dark.

My early memories were filled with vignettes of Flora Street; of noisy arrivals there, of laughter and cake in the kitchen followed by interrupted games with my siblings, and sleepy departures under streetlights like hazy yellow moons. The almond tree frothing its blossom over one such picture and, in the very next, me sitting with Grampy on the wash-house steps, cracking nuts with a broken stick.

Then a space without pictures until the new ones started on that terrible day the year I was six, in 1951, when Dad stopped the car before the old house and, carrying baby Patrick, herded the rest of us through the gate and up the steps to the opening door. I heard Gran's surprised cry, 'Why, it's Mac!' and ever after I would remember the way her glance skipped over us to the empty car, and hear her sharp question, 'Where's Anne?'

From that day onward nothing was ever the same at Gran's. The King George caddy remained, the seed cake, the sofa and the terrors of the dark passage, but the feeling of security had vanished.

That first night I stared about bewildered, for all through the endless miles of our coming I had clung to the belief that, once within those safe, familiar walls, everything would somehow come all right again, and be the way it always had.

My sense of betrayal never lessened. By the time I was nine, holidays there had become an ordeal to dread, despite treats like tram rides, matinées and visits to the beach. To be sure, these were rarer events that summer as Gran had had an operation for breast cancer. In spite of my tender years I knew about this, understanding from an overheard conversation that Gran had gone to a hospital where a doctor in a white coat had cut away part of her body. The nature of that cutting haunted me. Suppose, besides being held and cried over, as usually happened, I was forced to view this mutilation as well?

Thereafter, on the days we left for Gran's, I would wake reluctantly with a sick coldness inside and a heaviness like wood in my limbs. While the others shouted and squabbled in the car, I sat silent and apart, as if in preparation for the days I would spend tensed in order to repudiate Gran's advances – the tears and cakes and special treats. It was of course wasted effort, for though I might wriggle free of her arms and pretend not to recognise pictures of my dead mother, nothing would stop Gran speaking of her.

The trouble was that everybody in my grandmother's world had known my mother. The old lady at the back, the one we met by chance at the tram stop. The friends, corsetted and powdered, who came to afternoon tea. Their eyes all peered at me as they smiled and questioned and filled the kitchen with their gusty sighs. The aunts who came on Sundays were not much better, speaking sharply enough to their own children but lavishing endearments on me. I hated them all.

Only with Grampy did I feel safe. He never pried. There was more balm in the clasp of his thin, veined hand than in all Gran's kisses and cakes. A bent, gentle man with a persistent sniff, a legacy of German mustard gas, he shepherded us through outings, twisted bits of paper into animal shapes for us, and whistled marching tunes on the way to the tram, to shorten the distance for weary feet.

Between the lions' and the monkeys' cages at the zoo that year I was nine, I asked quickly, while courage lasted, 'How long are you dead for, Grampy?'

He didn't fail me. 'For always, Kerry. Didn't your father tell you?' I shook my head, whispering my fearful secret to him. 'He cried.'

'It doesn't matter,' Grampy said gently, and some of the awful weight I had carried so long lifted from me. The others were racing back towards us and Grampy took my hand. 'Let's feed the ducks, shall we? I used to take another little girl to do that.' And without minding at all I knew he was speaking of my mother.

Before her operation, Gran had worked mopping and dusting in a little gift shop on Payneham Road, a penny ride from the tram stop. It was filled with a myriad of dainty things – fragile teasets, glassware, painted fans of lace and ivory. I loved being there while Gran worked, to wander between the shelves and admire the flounce of a porcelain lady's skirt, to breathe on the hanging chimes and make them sound, or tickle my chin with dyed ostrich plumes. There was pure pleasure in the shapes of the soap and scent bottles – and in the knowledge that Gran was too busy to have time, just then, for the past.

Then, one morning, walking home from the tram stop, past the

6

blank wall of the Wheaties factory where the king of the wheat strode ten feet high across the bricks, Gran, twitching her beret straight, said suddenly, 'The lady I work for has a grandson about your age. He'll be in the shop tomorrow, love, so you can meet him. But mind, you mustn't stare. Polite ladies never do when they meet disfigured people.'

I stopped dead. A clammy sickness rose inside me. 'Is he ... horrible?'

'Of course not! But he was in a fire. I want you –'

I heard no more. I never returned to the shop and, ever after, the strange boy lurked, hideously twisted and scarred, in the dark passageway leading to bed.

Fortunately I didn't sleep alone. I shared what had been an uncle's room with baby Patrick whom I could cuddle against my night terrors. The room was crammed with bolsters, furniture and fire irons, the only sign of its former occupant being a model boat and a cloth-bound book of school life entitled *Something Like a Hero*.

An even older volume I found in the tallboy caused me endless despair, even while it drew me on to read more of its alarming contents. *Ten Thousand Things That Every Woman Should Know* (and that I would some day be a woman Gran never tired of telling me) symbolised for me the distance separating children from the perfect freedom of adulthood. Dimly I recognised that growth and knowledge went together, but with that book in my hand the path out of childhood seemed hedged about with as many difficulties as the passageway to bed.

Of course there were other days, untouched by troubles at Gran's, when the sun shone and we chalked hopscotch on the pavement

7

out front, when I helped Gran turn out and wash the contents of the china cupboard – the gold-rimmed cake plates and quaint figurines. And always, set back in my mind like a jewel in velvet, there was the parlour.

This was a show room, never used, a shrine to my grandmother's tastes and values. Drawn by its sheer gorgeousness, I loved to sit on the brocaded sofa amid the gilt and plush simply to savour its splendour. It was as dim as a church. Even on sunny days, the light came filtered by heavy crimson drapes, and the cream wallpaper with its dark green dado was well hidden by heavy furniture. There were no pictures or books, only sepia photographs in wooden frames. I knew them all by heart – my mother and uncles as children, Grampy in soldier's uniform, and a buxom young woman in a long dress with a curtain over her head. I was nine before I recognised Gran as a bride.

There was also a grandfather clock, a fireplace guarded by a brass fender, tall vases, a teak elephant, and a lowboy containing scraps of my mother's girlhood – useless, pretty things left behind when she married. An evening purse, a tea cloth worked at school, a shimmery blue dress missing part of the beaded pattern on the bodice. These relics drew me irresistibly, and when I knew myself safe from observation I explored the drawers, catching in the faint fragrance and slithery feel of satin against my cheek echoes of what had been.

I was occupied in this way on the day the drawer stuck. In a sudden panic to free it, I jerked too hard and the brass ring-pull sailed across the room, missing a vase by a whisker, and clattered onto the hearthstone. Faint with fright, I scampered behind the fender to retrieve it, and there paused, my eye caught by the knob of a little hatch, set like a magic door in the bottom of the chimney.

My fear of discovery temporarily overcome, I took hold of the knob, lifted, and found myself staring at a large glass jar stuffed full of five-pound notes. I never paused to wonder why they were there. Dismayed, as if I had broken something precious, I fumbled the hatch back into place, jammed the ring in the drawer, and crept with thumping heart from the room. Secrets were sinister things. My mother's departure had been a secret without farewells, surrounded by lies and evasions. An echo of the terror I had felt on first finding her gone rose in me now.

I told nobody of the discovery I had made, the unseen presence of which now tainted the parlour. I did not sit there again that summer, or ever; that was to be our last visit to the old house. Despite the surgeon's efforts, Gran's cancer had stealthily returned to claim its victim before my next birthday. Overnight Grampy became a shuffling wraith, and he lingered only a season longer. He was briskly buried by his youngest son, who made a bonfire of unwanted possessions before selling the old house, and with it memories of hopscotch and almond blossom and the secret hoard in the chimney.

I forgot about it myself until I came, at thirteen, upon the information that old-age pensioners could not receive both a wage and a pension cheque. Not, that is, unless they copied Gran with her undeclared earnings taken in cash and hidden away like a talisman against want.

I was in the bush then – a world away – but suddenly I was crouched again in the shadowy parlour, staring at what I had uncovered. Not the actual money, but the anxious fears of an elderly woman who had broken the law to buy piece of mind.

The old familiar sickness clogged my throat, and thronging around me like bats came again the monstrous, tenebrous things from the passageway which I had implicitly believed belonged to, and would stay in, childhood. For until that moment of discovery, when innocence died, I had never imagined that adults too could be afraid.

TWO

After our mother's death Dad got rid of the caravan, but from the time Patrick started school we always had a tent and trailer. We used them for camping holidays, the only sort of holiday a man with a tribe of kids could afford, Dad said. The trailer was also useful for carting firewood on Sunday afternoons whenever the supply was low, or when moving house. That was something we did often at first. We were forever packing up and moving on, losing old friends and joining new schools.

When we first arrived in Adelaide we went to school for a few months while Dad was sorting out things like a job and a place to live. The danger of Payneham Road had lain between school and my grandparents' place. Grampy had walked us the two blocks to where the traffic roared, and with Judith's and my hands in his own, and Sian close behind, taken us across. Each afternoon he'd be sitting on the low stone wall of the umbrella factory, waiting for us to turn the corner so he could take us back.

'Why don't you have a car, Grampy, like Dad?' Judith asked one day.

'I wouldn't know how to drive it, pet.'

He walked slowly – to get his wind, he said – and we had to remember, as Gran had told us, to take small steps and not bustle him.

'Didn't you ever have one?' Sian looked astonished. 'How did you go places, then?'

'On the train. You can get most places by train.'

'No you can't, Grampy,' Sian said earnestly. 'We've been to heaps of places – the beach and the mountains, and funny little towns even – where there aren't any trains.'

'Is that so?' He sniffed and dabbed at his eyes, which ran when his chest was bad. 'Well they run where your Granny and I want to go. And that's never very far. Unlike some.'

It was the first criticism I'd ever heard him make of Dad.

At Kadina, where we moved in 1952, the school, a grim collection of stone buildings asphalted into its block, lay diagonally across the street from our rented house. There was no escape from its presence. On weekends we would look up from play in our yard and see it there, waiting for Monday.

At Paringa we caught a bus to school, or at least to the stop at the bottom of the hill on which it stood. And at Sedan, where we lived with Aunty Mary and Uncle Dave, we trailed the entire length of the town, passing my uncle's hardware shop, then the 4 Square store, the Imperial Motel, the post office, Marshall's Bakery, the garage and the police station, before reaching our destination. It was one of those towns that trains didn't go to. There was no picture theatre, library or park, just the swimming hole in a creek five miles distant, the playground at the school, and endless paddocks of wheat behind dry stone walls.

In Melbourne we lived for a while with Dad's sister, who had two grown-up sons and a daughter. Uncle Ted took us mush-rooming along the edges of the Essendon airfield. I liked him. He looked like a big ungainly bird with his long legs and habit of walking bent forward with his hands behind him. Patrick cried a lot when Dad was away at work, and I heard Aunty Dale tell her daughter, who wore earrings and worked at a place called Med-school, that she'd forgotten how noisy children were.

I knew then that we wouldn't stay long, even though we'd just been enrolled at St Mary's Primary.

We went to Gran's again for the holidays in the summer of '53 only this time she was cross with Dad. Grampy was mostly silent, but one day when Dad came back from wherever he'd been I heard Gran crying in the kitchen. She ran up the passage with her pinny to her face and Dad yelled after her, 'Jesus, woman! I'm doing it for the best.' Then the back door slammed behind him.

Grampy was hiding behind his paper on the horsehair sofa, but I could tell from the stillness of him that he wasn't reading it. I pulled at his arm. 'What's wrong with Gran? Why's she crying?'

'She's just a bit upset, pet,' he said. 'She'll be all right.'

Later Dad told us we'd be getting a new mother. 'I'll take you to meet her this afternoon.'

We were silent, as much from bewilderment as surprise – how could such a thing be possible?

Dad said, 'Jesus, Mary and Joseph! Not you too! I thought you'd be pleased.'

He strode from the house banging the door again, and we heard him drive away.

Gran, still teary, came to hug us and make us promise that we wouldn't tell anyone – by which she meant the Bennet and Murray children from the houses across the street – what Dad had told us. We would understand when we were older, she said. She started to cry again, gulping angry sobs. 'They'll think he never loved your mother. But there's one comfort,' she sounded spiteful, 'it'll never last.'

～

It was after Dad married our new mother that we went to Renmark, on the River Murray in South Australia. It was the first place we really settled – not just stopped at, like the dozens of other towns I could remember. Dad had been born on the goldfields, way back in 1907, and Gran had once told me that he had a digger's restless blood in him. It was why he moved around so much, she said. In Renmark he drove a red and white Gilbarco van to work, and it was there that Patrick started school.

We lived in a Soldier's Settlement house, which Dad said would take him the rest of his life to pay off. Grown-ups seemed obsessed with money, and with insisting that kids should keep their clothes clean. The latter, obviously impossible, wasn't worth bothering with, but I really thought I'd found the answer to the money problem when I learned that the cheque Dad wrote for the new furniture was the same as money.

'So why don't you write one for a thousand pounds? Then you could pay for the house too.'

'Because you have to have the money in the bank first, Kerry. Otherwise it's stealing.'

'But –'

'It's like a promise, stupid,' Sian said. 'You can't make a promise to give something you haven't got.'

'You can,' I said, just to be contrary.

'You can't!' Then Judith slammed the car door on Patrick's finger and the day dissolved into screams.

We walked the two miles to school at Renmark, plodding through winter rain in our gumboots and hooded macs, and loitering bare-headed along dusty summer roads. Hopkins Street, where we lived, was a dead end. The last house in it butted up against a two-acre market garden owned by an irascible bearded man we called Old Moses. Moses hated trespassers and had two savage black dogs to discourage them. He fed the dogs, we all knew, on little kids caught on his land, so although it would have saved half a mile to make a short cut across his paddock, only Sian ever did. The thought of Patrick's chubby body providing dinner for the dogs turned Judith and me pale.

Gran had been right when she said, back when Dad told her he was remarrying, that it wouldn't last. We had only been in Renmark a year when the marriage ended. I never knew why our new mother left, but we were glad she had. At least there were no more fights. A truck came to collect her piano and some boxes of glassware and pictures, and we never saw her again.

'Well, it's just us, now.' Dad was terse about the change. 'But if everyone pulls their weight, we can manage the load.'

It meant a lot of work. Weekends and evenings were filled with chores which had to be done, Dad said, and done right. When it came to motherless children, there were busybodies aplenty, only too happy to trot off to the welfare people with stories of neglect. Our floors were going to be cleaner than anyone else's, our shoes shinier, and our clothes had to resemble Rinso ads. Saturday mornings were given over to the weekly wash. Dad was always bumping his head on the clothesline, which had to be wound low when we hung out the washing. I was tall for eleven but Judith, who hung out the socks and hankies, did it on tiptoe.

Dad and I managed the cooking between us – and most of it was more or less edible, he said. He always cooked the Sunday roast while we went to Sunday School, but the rest of the week was usually sausages, mince or fish.

One winter evening I blocked the sink by pouring a saucepan of melted fat down it, on the assumption that, once melted, it wouldn't again solidify. Another day, finding a recipe for apricot tart, I plunged into pastry making, then discovered, after I'd lined the roasting dish, that we didn't have any fruit. I used jam instead, emptying three large bottles into the piecrust before floating half an inch of crust over it. It was a good try, Dad said, the bloke who invented electricity probably didn't get it right first time, either.

We were well acquainted with bath brick and floor polish – even Patrick could dab that on by the time he was six. Sian, then twelve, split the stove wood and cleaned the shoes each night, and both Judith and I, who were learning basic stitches by sewing samplers in school, could cobble the holes together in socks.

The only free time was Sunday afternoons. We went fishing with Dad, squatting under the willows dangling homemade rods in the turbid Murray while the Sunday craft went by. There were houseboats, occasional paddle-steamers with side or stern wheels, and determined men in dinghies with rods braced under the thwarts. Sometimes Dad hitched the trailer to the Standard Ten and we went out, beyond the town and the blocks of vines and fruit trees, to gather wood. We shot rabbits too – at least Sian and Dad did, with the long-barrelled Harrington Richards shotgun Sian got for his birthday. It was nearly too heavy for him to aim, and he'd screw his face up against the kick every time he pulled the trigger. We ate rabbit stew after these outings, and rabbit pie. They were the curse of Australia, Dad said, and he got impatient when Patrick cried because they were dead.

After Christmas the year Sian got the shotgun, we went camping along the Ovens River. There were half a dozen other families at the spot we chose, so we had plenty of company. The first day I was devastated to lose the new gold bracelet I'd got for Christmas. Mrs Fields had given it to me, and she was my favourite person. Her husband Bob had been in the war with Dad, and we often visited them. She had said that school shoes (which Dad gave both Judith and me) were all very well, but girls needed pretty things too. I searched the riverbank every single day, but never found my bracelet.

Dad went bushwalking and fly-fishing, but the only trout we

saw was the one Judith scooped from the river with her bare hand. The tent blew down in a thunderstorm, and the day we went hiking at the foot of Mt Buffalo, Patrick slipped on a rocky ledge and fell ten feet into an enormous tangle of blackberry.

I was in grade six that year, and when I returned to school after the holidays I wrote a composition about it. Mr Snell, who was given to yelling at the kids while his face filled up with blood, just like a turkeycock's wattle, was impressed. He gave me twenty out of twenty for it and got me to read it to the class, prefacing this command with the observation, 'Well, McGinnis, we have at last found something you can do.' He called the girls by their surnames and threw bits of chalk at inattentive students. I was frequently targeted because I read library books in class, holding them flat on my knees under the desk. He kept those he caught me with, so I was forever starting books I couldn't finish.

'Why don't you read at home, McGinnis?' he yelled one day, plucking *Venture to the Main* off my lap.

'Oh, please!' My heart plummeted. 'It's Sian's, sir. Don't take it – please! He said I have to give it back tonight.'

'Then why risk it? You know the rules. Reading's a leisure activity you do at home.'

'But I can't, sir – truly. There's always cooking and dishes and washing, and I'm not allowed to stay up late. There's never any time to read.'

'Well, you'll have to wait for the holidays, won't you?'

He took the book but returned it at lunchtime, telling me gruffly to have it back on his desk when school resumed. He wasn't nearly as fierce as he sounded, old Snell.

Walking home that day of the essay with my friends Kay and Val, I moved in a blaze of happiness, knowing what my future held. We often talked about it. Kay (with no very clear idea how) was going to have babies, Val would be a teacher. She often imitated Miss Jewell, a very pretty primary teacher the big boys whistled after, by twisting her skirt into a knot at the knee and swaying her hips as she walked. All I had been able to decide was what I didn't want, which was housework and children. But now I knew. When I grew up, I would own a café (so I never had to cook again) and write stories everyone could read.

～

In 1956 the floods came to Renmark. The biggest, the wireless said, in the history of the white man. Women, children and old and non-essential men were evacuated from the town, the shops closed, and everybody's fridge and furniture was lifted up onto benches. The army was sent in. Dad stayed because his job made him responsible for the fuel depots and service stations, and somehow Sian, then thirteen, stayed with him. Patrick was sent back to Aunty Dale in Melbourne, Judith and I to Bob and Mrs Fields, who lived in a safe area, beyond the reach of the water.

The floods lasted forever. The men saving Renmark built the levee banks higher and higher, but the mighty Murray just kept spreading and rising. Patrick got his photo on the front page of the *Advertiser*. It showed him standing beside his suitcase at the airport with his golliwog under his arm. Dad had tied a label to a buttonhole of his coat, in case he forgot where he was going.

Many of the orange orchards died during the floods – those on the low ground from too much water, those higher up from the lack of it, because the irrigation system no longer worked. We saw some of the blockers – as the orchardists were called – harvesting bobbing oranges with fishing nets, and other men rowing out to tiny islets of high ground to kill the rabbits crowding there. They'd become marooned as the water rose and were starving to death before they could drown. From the Paringa rail bridge you could see the crowns of great willow trees, floating like mermaids' hair in the water.

When it was finally over, we returned to a town slowed and changed by disaster. Kay's father, who was a blocker, had lost his house and all his trees, and they were moving away. Old Moses' two acres had a hole cut in the fence and a vehicle track across it – the rest was all thistles and weeds. He'd been shovelling dirt on the levee one night, Dad told us, and dropped dead in mid-swing. It was more impressive than being ruined, like Kay's father. We walked to the end of the street and stared at the overgrown paddock, aware we could make a short cut to school now, because the police had taken the black dogs away.

'As long as there isn't a ghost,' Judith whispered, and my heart jumped. We looked at the old hut, at the clutter of kennels and railings and dray, shadowy under the gums, and knew we'd still take the long way round. Old Moses had been scary enough living – he'd be a monster dead.

Our Sunday School was closed because the church hall, where it was held, had had its foundations washed away. Not knowing this, we had gone along anyway, then found ourselves with a free morning to fill. We couldn't do much dressed in our Sunday best, so we passed the time skipping stones at the river's edge, watching the ferry come in. We took the long way home round the levee bank, because if we got back too soon Dad would only send us off to the Methodists or Lutherans instead. He didn't care about religion himself, but going to Sunday School was just as important as having clean socks, he said, and for the same reason.

'We'll have to go next week,' I said, but I was wrong. When we told Dad about the hall, he just grunted.

'Doesn't matter. We'll be leaving soon, anyway.'

He'd had a sickener of floods, he said, and we weren't waiting round for the next one. We packed our clothes and crockery and schoolbooks, the camping gear, saucepans, Sian's shotgun, and Patrick's golliwog, and left the rest. All the roses, the fountain Dad had built in the garden, the quince tree I'd planted, Sian's aviary of budgies – even Creamy Nylon, our big ginger tomcat – were left behind.

~

Sydney was different from everything we'd ever known, and we hated it. The house we rented had no yard, and there was too much traffic to play in the street. You had to be allocated a place in a school, so we wound up at three different ones. It was hardest on Patrick – there were bullies at his school, and he came home the first day with his pencil case smashed and his arms red from Chinese burns. Sian would have beaten them up, but he was catching the train to Homebush every day, while Judith and I struggled with the rules of our first all-girls school, where you weren't even allowed to run.

Dad wasn't any happier. He'd been his own boss in Renmark and hated the rush-hour scramble to work and fighting the traffic home again. Money was a constant preoccupation. We needed a new stove, and then the school sent a note saying that Judith and I would require uniforms next year.

'Jesus, Mary and Joseph!' Dad held his head. 'A man's already paying enough hire-purchase to make a sheep cocky think.'

A few days later Judith and I, who got home from school first because Patrick had to wait for Sian to collect him, found a stream of water pouring down the paved area between the house wall and the fence. The kitchen was flooded too, and the door of the bathroom – which was really only a converted woodshed at the back of the house – was smashed open. Somebody had broken in and stolen the gas heater and the taps, only they hadn't bothered to turn the water off first. Sian did it when he got home, then we tried to clean up the kitchen by bucketing water into the sink.

'There must be a zillion gallons run away,' Sian said. 'When the bill comes Dad'll hit the roof.'

'You don't have to pay for water!' I scoffed.

'Course you do!' The conviction in his voice silenced me. Mopping at the mess, I hated the unknown thief for the worry he was bringing Dad.

It must have been the final straw, because that was our last week at school. Dad said nothing at the time, but on Saturday morning, when we'd started out to the beach and were inching along in bumper-to-bumper traffic, he suddenly slammed his hand down on the wheel.

'I've had it!' he said. 'I'm fed to the teeth with this rat-race. What about it, kids? Shall we head for the bush and a bit o' freedom? Look at 'em out there. Like ants! I can't live this way – and you lot shouldn't have to. What d'you say?'

The three oldest of us drew simultaneous breaths to speak, but Patrick, who'd got very quiet lately, beat us all to it.

'Can we go soon, Dad?'

The following Monday afternoon we brought our books home from school, and a couple of days later – only two nights after watching the Russian Sputnik pass in its lonely orbit across the sky – Dad pulled the last rope tight on the trailer and tied it off. Then he got behind the wheel, winking at Patrick as he slammed the door. 'All set, champ?'

Our old life was over, and another, different one about to begin.

THREE

Billy Conway's place lay in the embrace of the hills on the outskirts of Alice Springs. He ran a few horses there, breeding and dealing as a sideline, but lived in town. Dad found him, by whatever means horsemen find each other, and got permission for us to camp at the bore on the property.

Dad had a temporary labourer's job on a new road being built not half a mile across the hills from our camp. Judith and I used to take him his smokos, with the lid jammed tight on the billy to keep the tea hot. We'd trudge down the cleared line, past the water trucks, rollers and graders, envying the near nakedness of the men who wore only shorts and helmets. It was baking hot. The heat reflected off the stony hills and torn earth, splintering against our eyes, making us squint, and pulsing, a shimmery veil, in the middle distance.

Nobody took much notice of us for the first few weeks. But when the holidays ended, Dad told us to keep out of sight or we'd find ourselves in school. 'You'll be right once we're out in the bush,' he said. 'Nobody to bother us there. But they'll bang you up, quick smart, in town.'

So from then on he boiled the billy on the job. And to fill our days we scrambled over the hills, or went down to lie on the rocks above the bore and watch the horses come in. None of us, not even Sian, had ever touched a horse, but now Dad was going to buy some and we'd all learn to ride, and go droving, he said, when we were older. It was a future that school couldn't hope to compete with.

Before the war, Dad had been a drover. Sian and I knew he was a fitter and turner by trade, so it was intriguing to suddenly learn of this other life. He'd used a wagonette back then, he said, and we'd do the same now because the car we had was unsuitable, and there was no question of affording a truck. Billy Conway had a four-wheel trailer we could buy and convert, and some old harness lying around, which was all we'd need to start.

Lying kicking our legs on the rocks, watching the horses, we talked of nothing else. We could hardly wait for the road job to end so that our odyssey might begin. Beyond the folds of ochre and purple hills the bush lay waiting. We envisaged brumbies, dingoes, campfires burning on frosty nights, a narrow brown road running on ahead. And horses. Horses to name and ride and own. It beat the city where, only three months before, Dad had worked at Nuffield's Engineering, clocking on and off like a bit of machinery, he said, and fighting his way through streets roaring with cars and people.

The days dragged by until the road job cut out, then, at last, we were free to leave. We went after dark, Sian, Judith and I sitting up among the gear and rations on the big four-wheel trailer, while nine-year-old Patrick rode in the vehicle with Dad and Mr Conway. The trailer wasn't registered – as a wagonette it didn't have to be – and moving it at night was just practising courtesy towards the cops, Dad said.

We were towed twenty-five miles north up the bitumen to a drovers' spelling paddock, which had a dam and a yard, and there we camped. Dad made a fire and pulled our swags off the load. Patrick had climbed up there when we stopped and was already asleep. It was strange to be without the car. Sian, squatting on his heels in the red fire-glow said, 'How're we gunna get to the shops when we need more food?'

'We aren't.' Dad kicked his swag open and sat on the nap, pulling off his boots. 'There's six months' supplies there. After that we'll buy off the stations. Off to bed, now! The horses'll be here tomorrow.'

After lunch next day, the man Dad had bought the horses from drove up to the paddock. He was lanky and brown, with big-knuckled hands and brawny arms. A drover, Dad said. He called him Mort. Dad boiled the billy and they squatted together in the shade, on their heels, drinking tea and waiting for the plant – that's what a collection of working horses was called. Around mid-afternoon, Dad said, 'They're coming,' and got to his feet. We heard it too, then, a repetitious clanging, but we couldn't see anything.

'Up there, above the timber.' He pointed, as Mort pulled the yard gate wide. Mystified, we stared above the tree line, then saw the dust, like red talcum powder against the blue. Moments later they came jogging into view, eleven horses led by a big chestnut mare with a wide, white face. A black man was driving them, feet thrust forward in the stirrups, on a tall brown.

Mort had only come to pick up the rider and his gear. When the man and his saddle were both in the back of the landrover, Mort waved, slammed the driver's door and left. With a whoop, we raced to the rails – and the horses snorted and took off for the far side of the yard.

'First lesson,' Dad said. 'Move slow and speak soft. And the second one – they kick. Remember it. Don't get behind 'em, ever.'

There were four horses that had been broken in. The quietest of these, Polly and Wadgeri, we'd learn to ride on, Dad said. The blackish brown, which he called Maori, was a buckjumper that he'd got cheap. He'd deal him away, later on. The one the black man had ridden was a pacer, about twelve years old, but good for a few years yet. We'd call him Rambler, Dad said, for the way he could cover the ground. For the rest there were two yearling foals and five unbroken horses. Three were to be team horses, the other two saddlers. They trotted away from us in the yard, tails high, muscles sliding easily under shiny coats. Dad stood watching them, hands on hips, and then it was time for us to get off the rails and learn to catch and hobble a horse.

Next morning we started breaking in. Over breakfast we learned the difference between a headrope and a halter, and by smoko the big half-draught we called Todd was on the end of the rope.

We had never imagined horses could be so violent. Dad dropped the loop over Todd's head, whipped the rope's end twice around a post and told us to haul him in. Standing in line, Sian first and Patrick last, we heaved with a will, hanging back with our heels dug in when the horse plunged. We got him within a few yards of the post, then he reared, screaming, forefeet flailing the air. We let go and ran, until we were stopped by the roar behind us.

'Jesus, Mary and Joseph! I said pull the bloody rope, not let go of it! He's in the yard – how can he hurt you there? Now get back here, and this time hang onto him.'

Shamefacedly we did so. We watched Dad get the headstall on and the collar-rope and hobbles. We saw Todd bagged and taught to face up on the rope, and watched Dad pull his tail. By lunchtime he could be led, and had learned to shuffle about in the hobbles. It was a good start, Dad said. He'd do a bit more with him that arvo, and maybe catch one of the others tomorrow.

∽

It was a crowded introduction to our new life: riding out each day with Dad through thickets of whipstick mulga, following the sound of the bells. Learning the different tones of them. And the names and uses of the harness pieces. Learning to drive the plant and to catch the newly broken colts on the open camp. Dad insisted on that. You might as well not own a horse you couldn't catch without the help of a yard, he said.

One by one the horses were roped and worked, until only Grace, the big chestnut draught mare, was left. She was going to be trouble, Dad thought, and we wondered how he could tell. Todd and Polly were pulling the wagonette by then. Dad had started them off towing logs and tyres in the yard, with two of us balanced on top for more weight. Then came heavier logs, around the paddock, and finally the wagonette.

That first trip he drove them alone, harnessed to either side of the long pole he'd fitted over the tow-bar. We'd cut down a straight gum tree for the pole from behind the dam wall and Sian, trying to shape the butt with the adze, had almost taken his foot off. The horses' chains hooked on to the swingle bar, which in turn was fixed to the body of the vehicle. The pole straps buckled onto their collars so the pole turned with them, and because of the turntable the vehicle followed the pole. There was no brake, which was something that needed seeing to, Dad said. When the pair bolted that first day, he steered them into a patch of dense whipstick, and a chastened Todd came home with mulga splinters hanging from the soft flesh of his nose.

Then it was Grace's turn in the yard. She was a Clydesdale, bred for harness work. From the start she'd been quieter than the others, plodding where they raced, standing her ground while the rest were crowding the rails. She was big and solid. Hair feathered her heavy limbs and she had feet like dinner-plates. She stood quietly on the far side of the yard as Dad shook out the loop. He kicked at the dust to make her run, and she flattened her ears and came at him like a thunderbolt.

Somebody – I think it was Judith – screamed. We scattered from the rails like rabbits, and Dad sort of rolled through them a second before the mare's massive hoof smashed into the lower one. She pulled up in a long slide, big yellow teeth gripping the bit of cotton she'd ripped from his sleeve.

'Oh, you would, would yer?' Dad said. He buttoned the fallen pipe back into his pocket and swiped dust from his pants.

'You better shoot her.' Sian looked as scared as I felt. 'She's an outlaw!'

'Nah, just spoilt. And I'm not shooting anything that cost three quid. Besides, she don't get the better of me that easy.'

He went back to camp, then we heard chopping among the gums down on the dam bank. When he returned, he carried a springy six-foot sapling, trimmed of leaves. We waited tensely while he dropped over the rails into the yard with it. Grace came at him again and he let her have it up the side of the face, a full-armed swing that stopped her in mid-career. She wheeled away blindly, throwing her head high, then gave a piggy squeal and charged again.

She seemed to come in slow motion. I could see her flattened ears and the knots in her flying mane. White showed in her eyes, and her great feet thrust at the earth, which plumed into dust behind her. She was roaring through her open mouth and distended nostrils, the noise adding to our own cries of warning and horror. Then Dad slammed the sapling across her nose and she went down like a poleaxed steer.

'That'll give her something to think about.' He propped the stick against the rails and filled his pipe. Grace got up again, shaking her head and walking in circles. Blood dripped from her nostrils, and there was a raised swelling where the blow had landed. Dad smoked his pipe. Then he knocked it out against a post and picked up the rope. This time she let herself be caught.

It was the first of many problems with the big mare. She'd been caught before, Dad said, and let go. He told us to keep away from her, particularly her back end. She kicked with calculation, knowing her reach to an inch. Nor was she above striking with her great front feet. For the first few days, he got the hobbles on and off by pushing Polly up alongside and using her body as a shield. She was a copper-plated bitch, he said, who'd be dear at five bob. He left the winkers on her, which meant she could only see forward, but she could still hear where we were, so it didn't help much.

'What's being copper-gated mean?' Patrick asked next day. We were in the yard. Grace and Todd were harnessed to a load of old posts and tyres and Dad had been teaching them to work in tandem, until a rein slipped under Todd's tail.

'What's it mean, Dad?' Patrick persisted just as the bay gave a flying leap that tightened the rein, snapping it in three places. Sian ran to catch him while Grace started kicking the load apart. Dad swore. He sent Judith for the coil of cotton rope in the camp and Patrick, red in the face, stamped and cried, 'What does it mean?'

'Being a bloody nuisance – like Grace,' Dad grunted. Then Judith came running back, swinging the rope around her head, and he let out a yell, 'Jesus, Mary and Joseph, girl! How many times have I told yer.' He grabbed at the bit rings of the horses to stop them taking off, and Grace's yellow teeth chomped down on his hand.

The crunch was plainly audible. Dad swore again, then we were all goggling, horrified, at the little finger of his left hand. Blood spurted from its foreshortened end, and Grace wrinkled back her lips and let fall the thing she'd mouthed.

'Jesus!' Dad grabbed his hand, Todd's long face looming over his shoulder. 'She bit it off! She bit clean through me bloody finger!'

Crimson spattered the dirt near his boots. Grace, top lip peeled back, shook her head, flapping the winkers. You could have sworn she was laughing.

Sian had been good at manual art subjects at school, so when the bleeding had stopped he got the tin snips and cut a metal cover out of a flattened milk tin to slip over the bandage as protection. In the meantime, Patrick, Judith and I sifted the yard in a widening circle until we found the bit of missing flesh.

It was a gruesome sight, pallid and rubbery, with the complete nail affixed – but it was Dad's. We wrapped it in a piece of silver paper taken from the tea chest, then buried it under the gums at the back of the dam. Patrick wanted to sing a hymn, but Judith and I decided a prayer would do. God, after all, wouldn't expect a fuss for a mere half-inch of finger.

Next day Dad took the wagonette up the bitumen to Hennessy's bore and back. Twenty-odd miles. It was slow work harnessing Grace with his bad hand, but it had to be done, he said. He took Sian with him. We watched them go: Todd, high-headed, already marked with nervous sweat; Grace, clomping dourly, heavy fetlocks flashing white below the chains. The sun winked on Dad's tin finger-guard, then a bend took them out of sight round a dark island of scrub.

They were late back. The sun was low and the shadows long under the mulga when they plodded into view again. Both horses were soaked with sweat, chest and shoulders lathered, legs streaked with it. They stopped at the first call, and Sian jumped down to chain the wheel, but you could see there was no need. Grace laid her ears flat but didn't move as the harness was pulled off. Todd, once let go, fell to his knees with a groan and rolled in the sand, kicking his legs to get right over.

'Nothing like an honest day's work to bring 'em to their senses,' Dad said. His hand must have been hurting because he held it curled against his body. He looked at the bright fire and brimming water bucket. 'Didja find all the horses?'

'Yep,' Judith said proudly.

'We couldn't catch Maori,' I said. 'But we drove him in, real slow. And Patrick caught some yabbies in the dam.'

'Didja, champ?' Dad sat down. He propped his elbow on the table and rested his bandaged hand against his shoulder. His face was strained and pale, but you could tell he was happy. He was smiling. 'Seems like I'll make bushies of you yet.'

FOUR

They were halfway through the mustering at Yambah station when the big mick got the head stockman in the yard. A mick was a young cleanskin bull, Dad told us. This one put a horn through the man and broke his leg – and so, because he was there, Dad took over his job. We'd left the Alice six weeks before but had travelled only seven days from the spelling paddock to Yambah.

It was there that we met Alcoota Dick. He was one of the seven blackfellas in the stock-camp, spoke fair English and was a man of property. Unusually, for that era, Dick owned his own saddle and half a dozen horses.

Dad was working our colts on the job, getting them a bit of stock savvy, he said. Dick admired them all, but really lost his heart to Maori.

'Proper flash fella, that one, old man.'

'Proper cheeky fella. Put yer longa ground, quick smart, bloody oath,' Dad said.

Dick, however, fancied himself as a rider and was undismayed. 'Might be make it swap?'

'Might be,' Dad agreed. ''Nother fella yarramun.' Yarramun was the word they used for horses.

Dick grinned and shook his head, the merriment dancing in his eyes. 'Little fella big ears,' he said.

This turned out to mean donkeys. There were three of them: a jack, a jenny and a yearling female foal. Dad threw a greenhide whip and a pair of spurs into the deal – about twice what the donkeys were worth, he reckoned afterwards. We never thought so, though. They were the best fun we'd had in years.

We called the old male Jack, the jenny Korai, after the morning star, and the foal Wongan, which Dick had said meant pretty girl. The morning star we were now all well acquainted with. It was when it glowed in the east above the gums, dwarfing all its neighbours, that Dad woke us to help get the horses in. We could use the donkeys for this, he said, only they never ran together and we usually found them last.

They were so small-bodied we had to shorten the girths to make the saddles fit, so it was easier to ride them bareback. And you could pull until the reins broke before they turned or stopped. We steered them by leaning forward and clapping a hat over one eye. This made them shy off in the opposite direction. Stopping them was more difficult – in an emergency, if they were heading for a fence or a creek-bank, it was best to jump off.

Judith, Patrick and I were riding them down to the trough at

Snake Well one day when Sian brought the horses up behind us. The two big foals, pricking inquisitive ears, broke into a canter and soon they were all chasing after the donkeys. All three took off. Then Wongan, with Patrick astride her, jumped a gully. He shot up her neck, got both arms around it, and wound up hanging underneath until his grip broke.

'Look out!' Judith screamed, then Jack was all over the top of him as well.

'Whyn't you watch where yer going?' he yelled, scrambling up, only to have Korai barge him off his feet again. We were never hurt by the donkeys – but it wasn't for want of trying, according to Dad.

The head stockman job went on for weeks. We camped at Snake Well for the duration, tailing the horses into water, playing in the sandy creek-bed and exploring the country around on donkey back. I found a strange horse track one day, where the open country ran into low foothills. It lay clear as print in the sandy soil, superimposed over the scurry of beetle feet, and my heart leapt. It had to be a brumby. But I couldn't judge when it was made and dared not follow it far, for fear of getting lost. We had been warned about this possibility. He would be seriously displeased, Dad said, if, for the want of a little forethought, he had to knock off work to come and find us.

Later, when the muster was over, we were going brumby running. It was the quickest way to build up the plant, Dad said. Brumbies cost nothing but the labour of yarding them, and they belonged to whoever did so. But the closest any of us had yet come to seeing one was my set of tracks in the sand.

One day Dad took me out with him to bring cattle back from a yard at the Four Mile Hole. I rode Wadgeri and stood in the irons most of the morning to keep up with Rose's brisk walk. Dad never waited, and he wasn't much for talking on the move. If you kept your tongue still, it was marvellous what you'd see and hear, he said, so I tried it.

I heard the slap of hooves and the creak of saddle leather, the buzz of flies and the comfortable snorts of our mounts. Birds called, the bit bars jingled, and roos thumped somewhere out of sight. I saw sunlight gleam on ropy strands of web strung between trees, the papery skin of an itchy grub's nest, and pearls of amber sap fused to grey mulga trunks. And at noon, across a wide expanse of plain, half a dozen horses.

'Brumbies,' Dad said.

I stared, mesmerised, watching the wild heads rise, then dip again as they saw us. They floated away, hooves skimming the grass, long tails streaming. My breath caught at the beauty and freedom of their being.

'They're just horses.' Dad sounded impatient. 'Rubbish stock – average looks, no breeding. There's nothing special about 'em.' But I knew better.

We boiled Dad's quart pot for lunch beside a gravel hole in the mulga, next to the main road. The water was red, but perfectly clean, Dad said. The colour came from the clay in the ground. Dad slipped the bits on the horses to let them graze, and while we ate a bush turkey stalked into the hole. He sank to his hocks at the water's edge to drink, then started back, wings up and neck feathers hackling, as a whirling cloud of budgerigars dimpled the surface in front of his beak. I looked at Dad to see if he'd seen, and he smiled as our eyes met. The birds hadn't noticed us sitting motionless under the mulga. And they were used to horses.

There was a tin shining in the grass. As we were leaving, Dad toed it with his boot.

'Look at that!' He picked it up. 'They're putting beer in cans now. Solid ones too. Stick it in your saddle pouch, Kerry. Might be useful.'

We got the cattle back to Snake Well, but I was worn out and my legs rubbed raw from the saddle by the time we reached camp. Dad shot one of the cows that same evening and butchered it, sharing the meat with the stock-camp. He'd put up a rail and made a lot of wire hooks, and we hung the fresh meat overnight, to cool. The corned cuts were rubbed with coarse salt, then stacked to drain. There were rib-bones for tea, grilled on the camp-oven lid over a bed of coals, and liver as well. We sat on our heels around the fire, chewing bones and sucking the meat juices from our fingers. Nothing had ever tasted so good.

A few days later the boss sent for Dad to do some welding repairs at the station. And while he was there he brazed a handle onto the beer tin to produce a quart pot, and made me a pair of spurs with rowels cut from two pennies. There wasn't much Dad couldn't do. Even the boss said so. He wanted him to stay on, but Dad said we had to see after our own business first, and right now that meant building up the plant. So we moved camp to Ladysmith bore, to get among the brumbies.

∽

There was an old steam engine at Ladysmith. It had been dragged aside, maybe twenty years before, to make room for the diesel engine that had supplanted it.

'How'd they ever get it here?' Sian marvelled. The great iron wheels must have been eight inches wide and the boiler, made of heavy plated metal, stood taller than Dad. Sian knocked his knuckles on the iron. 'Whew! Imagine old Grace hooked onto that!'

I peered past the stubby funnel at the flat sheet of the overflow. 'Look, there's ducks on the water.'

Patrick jumped off the wheel he'd been climbing. 'Bet there's yabbies!'

'Don't be stupid – it's too shallow.' Sian was scornful.

''Tisn't! Is it, Kerry?'

'It's bore water. How would they get there? Yabbies don't live in bores.'

'They might.' Patrick stuck out his chin. 'Dad said fish do. So I don't see why yabbies can't. I'm gunna ask him.'

He ran off across the gum flat, floundering into the boggy edges of the overflow and frightening the ducks into flight.

We'd camped out of sight of the bore behind a rocky outcrop, its slopes spiky with spinifex rings. A mill and tank stood on a gum flat, with a wide sheet of shallow spillage water between us and the trough. The yards were half a mile distant, on the edge of the open country. Red gravelly ridges rose behind them. There was broken rock, gullies and some scrub. Not too bad, Dad said. Enough open country to turn a mob and good visibility for shooting.

It was very quiet in the camp that evening. Dad had pulled the bells off the plant. No sense in scaring the brumbies, he said. Push 'em too hard and they'd clear off to another bore. We kept a small fire for the same reason, hardly needing it now for warmth or light because the moon was full. Once its silver disc rose above the scrub line, you could see everything except colour. We'd have to keep away from the trough, Dad told us, and get under cover if we spotted horses coming in during the day. We had just six riding horses, so only Sian would be riding with him. The rest of us must take care of the plant and camp, and keep a tally of the brumbies coming in during the day. There was plenty of cover because we had camped behind a rocky mound overlooking the trough. He showed us how to make a tally sheet using the end of a burnt stick in place of a pencil, then sent us off to bed so we'd be fresh in the morning.

Sleep was a long time coming. The moon was too bright and I felt too restless to settle. I watched the fire sink slowly to coals that faded to ash, and listened to the regular breathing of Judith and Patrick, whose swags lay on either side of mine. Sian was on the far side of the wagonette, and Dad snored by the dead fire. A little wind walked about. Not much, just enough to creak the mill vane around, and flutter the leaves on the branch hanging between me and the moon.

I punched my pillow and wondered where the ducks had gone. Perhaps there was a dam somewhere, or another bore with a permanent overflow. It wouldn't rain again before mid-summer, Dad said, and maybe not even then. Some years it didn't rain at all. A curlew wailed, sending a little rush of goosebumps over my skin, but it was only a bird. I knew there wasn't anything to be afraid of in the bush, except snakes, and they mostly left you alone, according to Dad, if you didn't bother them first.

The moon had moved over, the leaves I'd been watching were no longer silhouetted against it. I lay squinting upwards, trying to count them, while listening to the faint thud of my heart. I got muddled twice, then sat bolt upright, counting forgotten, as a horse snorted shockingly close at hand. Then I realised it wasn't my heart-beat I'd been hearing, but the thud of unshod hooves. There were brumbies on the trough.

Breathless with excitement, I pulled on my boots and crept from the camp. I saw them first from the rocky outcrop – a half dozen black shapes trotting in from the west, the dust like pale mist about their knees. A screen of bush hid them momentarily from sight, and on a sudden impulse I leaped headlong through the boulders and pelted for the bore. I could see every stick and leaf underfoot, and the boggy tongue of ground where the mud began. I jumped over it, and then, as the first head reappeared, cautious but un-alarmed, I dropped to the ground.

The cover of the steam engine was only tw   feet away. I crawled to it in little rushes, eyes fixed on the ho   't noticed me. In the shadow of the engine I s   I could see them – seven head, led by a lo   half-grown foal at her side. She halted for   and I heard the soft blast of air from he

42

Satisfied, she walked to the trough and the others followed, crowding the black steel sides, necks stretched to drink.

They all looked black by moonlight, save the grey at the end of the trough whose hide gleamed silver. It finished first, and squealed as the next horse nipped it, wheeling away and kicking up. The other one followed, nickering, and they splashed into the overflow, biting at each other in a ring of silver ripples. The curlew cried again and the five at the trough jerked their heads up, but the other two took no notice. They were circling each other, splashing and whickering, then the black one squealed on a harsh, urgent note and reared, and I saw, under his belly, the long, rigid shaft of his sex.

In amazement and fascination I watched them mate in the shining pool, the mystery at last unfolded. Dad had told me about it last year, when I was eleven, but I hadn't understood all his talk of sexual organs and had been far too embarrassed to ask. It had sounded awful – furtive and rather nasty – but this was different. The black horse and silver mare under the moon, and the white-trunked gums and the rippling pewter pool. It was beautiful. I could see the shine of moonlight reflected off the water's surface in his dark eye, and the wild flare of his mane as he reared. He grunted as he surged into her. I shared her trembling excitement and felt, in the tumult of my own breathing, the heaving effort of his.

When they broke apart, the others were leaving the trough and they joined them. I had watched for a moment? an hour? I couldn't tell. The moon leaned slightly to the west. Out along the horse-
d one of them snorted, the sound sharp and loud as a trumpet
was followed instantly by the thunder of galloping hooves.

They faded into distance and then there was only the curlew again and the intermittent gush of water through the float valve.

～

Next day, Dad and Sian yarded the first mob of brumbies a little before noon. There were only five of them, one a broken-in station mare, which was handy, Dad said. He'd ride her when the two colts, Rose and Mort, gave out. I was glad we had no more saddlers, because it wasn't how I thought it would be. Even from the camp we could hear the boom of the .303, and I didn't want a closer view because Dad was shooting more than he ran. He shot the leaders, the young foals, the stallions. He shot them as they streaked away, taking out the older, experienced ones first. Then he rode the rest down until they slowed and Sian could turn them back past where he lay waiting, with the rifle, to shoot again.

We didn't need foaly mares, he said, or anything over four years old. I hoped the mob I'd seen the night before stayed away. I didn't want the grey mare and her mate shot.

On the second day a baby foal wandered into the trough without its mother and he shot that too. Patrick screamed, 'No! No!' as he raised the rifle, then burst into tears when the foal fell. Dad looked at him, and at our mutely accusing faces, then slapped the rifle breech closed with his open palm.

'Jesus, Mary and Joseph! Did yer want it to starve? I shot its mother round noon yesterday. It hasn't had a feed since.'

I said tremulously, 'Why do you have to kill so many?'

'Because we want the colts.' He put his hand on Patrick's shoulder but he jerked away; Dad sighed and I could see him take hold of his patience. 'This is the quickest way o' getting them. Be nice if you could magic 'em into the yard by kindness, Kerry, like the storybooks say, but you can't. That's the facts of the game and you might as well learn 'em now as later.'

By noon of the third day there were twelve colts in the yard. Not a bad effort, Dad said. It was, anyway, all we had time for. The first horses yarded were now desperate for a drink and had chewed to sticks all the prickly bushes they could reach through the rails. They rushed the gate when Dad opened it, but only as far as the trough, then dropped their heads immediately to feed.

Tomorrow, Dad told us, we'd head back to Snake Well and set about breaking in. We'd accomplished what we'd come to do, and could repeat it, anytime. I hoped we wouldn't. And I was glad there was no grey mare among the twelve colts.

That night, our last at Ladysmith, I lay wakeful once more, but listened in vain. There were no hooves on the wind. Only the creeping scent of death from the bloated carcasses and the eerie wail of the curlew, crying like a dead soul through the white gum trunks.

FIVE

We'd had the wagonette a month before Dad named her the Territory Queen. She was heavy and shabby and old, but no irony was intended. Back in the thirties all the turn-outs, which was what you called a drover's vehicle, were named, he said. He'd known a Lady Jane, a Mulga Duchess, and several Queens. One day we'd get a bit of paint, pick out the wheels and railings in green and yellow, with maybe glossy black on the swingle bar and pole.

But in the beginning, the Queen was bare – just a trailer, really. Dad added the pole first, then the driving seat, and a table slung on chains at the back which folded up for travelling. He put on the water tank at Yambah, slung a greenhide between the axles to carry extra harness and the spare tyre, and finished the job with jarrah side-rails, two inches thick.

The brake was an afterthought. It was adequate for stopping

tired horses but useless when fresh ones decided to bolt. This happened pretty frequently because most journeys in the Queen were training exercises for colts. There were usually one or two needing work, or some of the string Dad was breaking for others. He'd tie unmouthed youngsters onto the polers' collars, just to keep them in hand. They had chains to pull with, but he had no way of steering or stopping them when things got lively.

Theoretically this wasn't a problem because when that happened Dad would roar, 'Jump!' and we were supposed to tuck our heads in and go over the side. But of course we never did. The emergency was always too thrilling to miss. We'd huddle breathlessly out of view behind the seat while Sian, who modelled himself on *Boys' Own Annual* heroes, clung stoutly to the brake handle.

Sometimes exhaustion stopped them, sometimes the scrub. It all depended on the terrain and the cause of the original trouble. Colts, Dad would say, giving us all the eye, were about as hare-brained and short-sighted as kids in the matter of foreseeing consequences. We couldn't argue – there were always too many recent follies we were waiting for him to forget to make rebuttal feasible.

But occasionally things went wrong independently of us, like the day we carted the bushes home for the bough shed. We were building a semi-permanent summer camp at Carmencita bore on Dneiper Downs, and the only foliage Dad would pass as a roofing material was from the gums growing at Entire Creek.

We had a saddle horse along with us that day which Sian and I took turns riding behind the turn-out. Dad was driving five horses – three colts in the lead, and two older stalwarts, Jean and Todd, on the pole. It was a blue, blowy day with the dust puffing underfoot and the gusting scent of wattle. There were gum sticks on the dinner fire, crisp curls of gum bark snapping underfoot along the creek-bank, and the shrill of cicadas. We kids dragged the sappy branches to the wagonette where Dad loaded them high as a green haystack. Then, in a discard of chips and lopped boughs, we yoked up and started back.

About mid-afternoon we neared the wide sandy crossing of Eastern Creek which, like the Entire, was an anabranch of the Plenty River. Trooper, the saddle horse, was jogging with the team by then, his reins tied to the nearside leader's chains. We kids nested half asleep on the load, lulled by the tread of hooves, senses saturated with the smell and feel of gum. So Dad was the only one to see the winkers slip on Mort, the offside leader.

They were an ill-fitting pair anyway. Our harness was made for draught horses, and Dad drove everything from Clydesdales to ponies, with a folded corn bag or a bit of twine to take up the slack. Now Mort's winkers suddenly reverted to their original shape and he got his first look at the load – the very thing winkers are designed to prevent. His terror inflamed the team and they bolted.

Dad, feet braced on the foot-rail as he hauled uselessly on the reins, yelled, 'Hang on!' The boughs were a slippery uncertain platform, certainly no footing to jump from. We grabbed hands, struggling through the green mass towards the anchor of the seat. The team had speared off the track, but the ground was mercifully open except for the line of timber a little way ahead, which marked the bank of Eastern Creek.

Sian, on the brake, shrieked the obvious into the wind of our passage. 'They'll smash over the creek-bank!'

'Get back!' Dad bellowed and to our amazement plucked the fifteen-foot driving whip out of its socket in the brake handle. The pony mare, Amunga, was the nearside leader. She was bolting with her ears flat and her tail jammed, head hauled sideways by the rein. Dad flung the whip forward right-handed, cracking it like a cannon six inches from Mort's ear.

Without slowing, the brown shied left, crashing Alice sideways into Amunga who perforce yielded to the insistent rein. Their pace was unchecked, but their swerve had brought them back onto the track just in time to swoop down the bank like a runaway train, into the tricky crossing. It was wide and sandy with a steep pull up the far side. And when we hurtled into it, the sand immediately began to tell, dragging inexorably at the wheels. The load swayed beneath our clinging hands, the slippery mass threatening to slide away beneath us as the Queen crashed and bounced. Dad had the whip out in earnest, cracking it like gunshots over the racing backs, creamed now with soapy lather. He called to them in stentorian tones: 'Hup, Jeanie! Put yer back into it, Todd! Ho, Mort! Pull, yer idle bastard!' We also yelled with excitement, urging them on, and we might have made it across if Trooper, galloping recklessly outside the team but still tethered to it, hadn't suddenly lost his head. You could tell by the set of his ears and the curl of his tail that he wasn't liking things much, but they only got worse when he lunged into the space between Todd and Amunga, tangling himself in the chains.

We stopped then, slewed half off the track in a sand drift at the foot of the rising pull up the far bank. The horses stood blowing and heaving, Todd turning his long face anxiously about, for he hated uncertainty. Amunga's checkrein had snapped and she'd twisted right about in the chains, squealing and humping at Trooper, himself kicking like mad at the trace around his hock.

Dad cursed him comprehensively as he sorted the tangle out. We listened in a respectful silence broken only by Judith making a suggestion.

'Maybe, if you took the winkers off the polers, they'd bolt?'

'Don't be bloody daft,' Dad said. 'Get the shovel, Sian. The rest of you start pulling the bushes off. We'll have to pack 'er out of the drifts.'

We carpeted a track through the sand with the gum foliage. Then Dad hooked Jean and Todd to a snig chain looped around the back axle. Judith and I hung onto the leaders (harness hooked up and reins removed) while the two polers towed the vehicle backwards onto the road again.

After that we reloaded the bushes, wilting a bit now from the handling they'd had, the pungent smell of them mixed with the gritty feel of sand. The team had cooled by then, the polers backing sluggishly into position, Alice, in the centre lead, snapping bad-temperedly at little Amunga. The bank looked awfully steep and from the moment they hit the collars without budging the load we all knew we were in trouble.

On the third attempt, Dad pulled the whip, striping Mort to tighten his chains, then thundering it over the polers' backs. The threat of it sent them lunging half-heartedly into the collars – an unsynchronised effort that rolled the Queen forward a few feet until the front wheels hit the gradient, when they chucked it in.

'Crack it again!' Sian urged. 'They were shifting it.' But Dad was already climbing down over the wheel.

'They've quit, boy. Look at 'em.' The leaders were sideways across the track and Todd, whom he'd long stigmatised as a Sunday horse – all show and no go – was trembling with a jammed tail. He looked pathetic, like a soppy giant in tears, the collar riding on his neck because he'd backed up in it from sheer funk.

'What'll we do, then?' Sian asked, and Dad sighed, eyeing the sun to judge how much daylight was left.

'Give 'em a spell and try again. We'll get Todd out of it and stick Alice in his place. And bring Mort back, hook him on alongside Jean – the bugger's not pulling a tap where he is.'

The new arrangement worked no better. Todd and Amunga, an incongruous pair in the lead, reared at the starting call, blocking the horses behind them. We kids flung our weight into the battle, and though Sian was ready with a chock at the back wheel he never got to use it.

Judith and I gathered gum sticks to boil the billy while Dad and Sian scraped away at the foot of the slope and shovelled sand from around the back wheels. The team sulked in the harness, Todd flinching and starting at every sound.

'Gutless wonder,' Dad said. He slung the shovel onto the toolbox under the seat and the big bay trembled. Sian, coming to the fire for tea, paused to pat his face and Todd leaned his head against him like a baby looking for comfort. Sian, scratching his ears, cried suddenly as if the horse had just spoken. 'That's what's wrong! He thinks you're mad at him.'

Dad snorted. 'Well, he's got that right, any road. Damn great ox could shift it himself if he wanted to.' His pannikin stopped halfway to his mouth, then slowly travelled on again but all he said was, 'Get your tea.' He drained his own in one long swallow without taking his gaze off the bay poler.

Afterwards, fire out and the tuckerbox packed again, Dad settled his hat then pulled the leaders out of the team and told Sian to stand by with the chock.

'The rest of you push,' he said, and walked over to Todd. He patted him, fussed with his collar and murmured to him, rubbing his ears the while. Todd appeared to grow with the attention. His head lifted and his shoulders seemed to swell into the collar as confidence flowed back into him. Dad tugged him straight in the chains, then he cried, 'Hup, Todd!' and the big bay leaned forward, bowed his back, and, rising to the very tips of his hooves, heaved the Queen forward.

'That's my beauty!' Dad crooned. 'You can do it, boy! Keep 'er going!' Conversationally he added, 'Clout Jean, one of you. Pull, me fine fella!'

Sian's chock slammed home at regular intervals, and when Todd's hoof skidded, Jean held the weight as the bay momentarily faltered. Dad kidded him forward again, crooning praise, a hand on his neck, and so the top of the bank was won.

∽

There was only an axe-handle of daylight left, but Dad said we'd water the team before going on. The mill of Chalmers Soak was among the gums at our right, and the track ran past the end of the trough. The afternoon had cooled but the horses, hides spiked with dried sweat, were thirsty. The winkered colts shied from the trough and Amunga backed into it. Judith, who was leading her, let go the reins when she bounded forward and they hooked themselves over the hames. At the same time her chains slipped free, and like the skittery, silly thing she was, Amunga took off, anti-clockwise around the trough.

Judith ran to get out of her way, and Amunga chased her. They went twice around the trough before Judith, shrieking with fright, jumped into the water and the splash brought Amunga to a snorting halt.

'Jesus, Mary and Joseph!' Dad bellowed. 'I dunno which is worse – kids or colts. Sian, grab that damn pony before she takes off again. And Kerry, find me a bit o' wire we can hook onto the back to tie Trooper to.'

'We could use the pannikin hook,' I said. He grunted assent and so we wound up jogging into the dusk with the grey secured to the loop where the pannikins normally hung. The evening star, which was the same as the morning one, shone pale above the dying pink where the sun had gone. And after that there were just the clopping hooves and the swaying load and Dad singing his travelling song into the dark: '"Oh, get along, pony, there's work to be done/ Got to be home by the setting of sun/There's nobody waiting to welcome me back/Save an old cow and a tumbledown shack/So roll along, pony ..."'

We were luckier, I thought drowsily. We were home all the time in the Queen, like sailors in their ship. And rocking on the billows of green we fell fast asleep.

SIX

I never learned what had become of my mother's belongings. A single glove lay for years in Dad's old tin deed-box along with her wedding ring, which they must have removed and given to him at the hospital. Nothing else remained – no clothes, or books, or photos. Sometimes I'd try to remember her – how she'd looked, what she'd said – but my mind pictures were already fading, like whispers in the wind.

When people asked, and they often did, we'd shrug, 'Oh, she died, ages ago.' And if they persisted, we'd lie through our teeth. 'I was too little to remember.' If we couldn't speak of our mother ourselves, nobody else was going to, either.

Soon after we had got the house at Renmark, the year I was eleven, Dad brought home a plaque enscribed with a poem, which he mounted at eye level in the hall. It had fancy lettering looped about with curly ribbons managed by bluebirds, and was entitled 'Our Mother'. We all knew it by heart but never spoke the words aloud.

Sometimes I'd stand in front of it, particularly when things went wrong in the kitchen. 'She gave advice so lovingly – Our Mother' ran one of the lines, only dead people couldn't give that sort of help. Poetry didn't help cakes rise, and the one I'd made for Patrick's seventh birthday was as flat as squashed rubber. It should have been a rainbow cake but it was just a gluggy mess and the only colour you could see was brown.

Dad said it was a good try, but I locked myself in the toilet and cried while the rest of them ate the fairy bread and frankfurters. Afterwards, meaning it as comfort, Dad said, 'Don't feel bad, your poor mother couldn't cook, either.'

I received this information in silence, constrained by habit and shyness from pursuing the subject. For whatever I might pretend, I did want to know about my mother, and the more so when I observed my friends with theirs. Val Ransome's mother wore pants and smoked cigarettes, which she screwed into a long black holder. She was tall and sallow-skinned, with bold red lips and snapping eyes. She was fun, Val said, and you could ask her absolutely anything.

'Was yours like that?'

I shrugged helplessly. 'I don't know.'

'Bet she was,' Val said loyally. 'Don't you remember?'

'No, only ...' Something struggled in my head – lamplight on a dressing table and Sian and I stroking the folds of a frock that hung against the wall. It shone silvery in the dim light and we spread the skirt of it, shimmering and lovely, half as wide as the room.

'Ooh, pretty!' Sian said. Or I did. And somebody (my mother?) laughed.

'I remember a dress she had – for dancing, I think. It was gorgeous.'

'There you are, then!' Val was positive. 'She would've been fun. My mum jives. Surely your father must have a picture of her?'

'No.' There was only a studio photo of the four of us, sepia-toned and solemn, taken a week before her death.

'Your poor mother arranged that,' Dad had said when he hung it in the new house. Patrick had had a lump on his forehead. He'd tumbled off the stool he was sharing with Judith and screamed the place down. How could I remember that, and not the shape of my mother's body in the final week of her pregnancy? She'd had five babies in nine years. I pictured her, faceless, but dumpy and big-bellied, holding her back like Mrs Gunn, who had twins already and a third child on the way. But it was like drawing a camel – no matter how you tried, you knew the real thing could never have looked like that.

Dad and my mother had got married during the war, before he was discharged from the army. I had discovered it was possible to glean information about my mother by questioning him about his life. He never spoke naturally about her, so neither could I. All I knew was that he had been a bushman, a product of dusty space and wide skies, and she had been born and bred to city living.

'Your poor mother never understood the bush life,' he told me once. 'She couldn't get the hang o' tracking, and you could lose her in the house paddock.' Yet she had gone with him – dam-sinking, roo-shooting, boundary-riding – to some of the loneliest country on the map, travelling in the side-car of his Harley Davidson motorbike at first, then in the old Star racer, and finally the tip-truck he bought for the Burra Council contract.

Before the war, he'd come within a whisker of breaking his back when a polo pony he was exercising put her forefeet in a rabbit warren, and somersaulted with him. The damage never really mended, and while he had the tipper he had spent three months encased, from his chest to just below his hips, in plaster of Paris. My mother had driven the truck (with seven-year-old Sian and Judith and me on the seat beside her), with Dad, unable to sit, standing on the running board, shouting the gear changes at her. Driving, it seemed, was something else she had no talent for.

Out of nowhere memory surfaced – a paddock in drizzly rain. 'I remember!' I cried. 'Picking mushrooms in the rain. There was a big dog . . . and . . . and party hats. And cake by the fire.'

'Your sixth birthday.' Dad said. 'The dog was a St Bernard puppy your mother picked up somewhere. Damn thing grew to the size of a yearling colt after a couple o' years. Ate its weight in tucker every week, too.'

'What happened to it?'

'Gave it away when we went to Queensland.' He fell silent, as if tired of the subject, and I said no more. It was in Queensland, the following April, that she had died. Aged thirty-three, I worked out a few years later, when I accidentally came upon their marriage certificate. It gave her real name too: Edith Carol. Gran had always called her Anne.

There was not a great deal more to be gleaned from Dad, or anyone else who had known my mother. Gran and Grampy were dead, and my mother's two brothers had become strangers. And because we had moved so much there were no old neighbours, or friends from her girlhood, to talk to.

〜

We had taken the wrong way through the ranges, got ourselves stuck in a gully during a storm, and were working our way back when we met the old man.

We'd had to leave the wagonette tilted across the gully while Dad and Sian took the horses on to water somewhere ahead. We'd already been there forever, trying to get out. It was bad to let the team quit on a pull, Dad said, but worse to bust their hearts if they really couldn't shift it. Besides, the daylight was going and he still had to get the plant a drink.

There was water in plenty by the time he got back, with the thunder bellowing over us, and brown Maori skidding on the wet rocks. The gully had run a banker, foaming over the jammed wheel. Dad roared at Judith and me for leaving the harness in the wet as we turned out in the cold to help hobble up.

Next day dawned like a clean page. The hill crests stood sharp against the sky, and every pebble showed clear in the silvered puddles. The horses played and nipped each other coming onto camp, sleek in their washed hides.

Dad took a crowbar to the edge of the little creek where the rain had loosened the rocks, and soon tumbled them out. There was no room to turn the wagonette, so we towed it backwards up along the gully. He led the horses while we rolled the loose stones aside. Then we swung the turntable around by pushing on the pole. When the Queen stood facing the way we'd come, we hitched up and started back.

The rain had taken the sameness from things. Swinging our legs over the side, Judith and I watched the country pass, eyes caught by the glitter of washed stones, the shiny carapaces of flighting beetles. The team's feet crunched satisfyingly on the gravel, their chains pulled taut against the spreaders. The backbands danced when the horses trotted, but slid slow and heavy across their quarters when Dad used the brake to ease the weight going downhill.

It was very quiet under the silvery-blue of the clean sky. Just the birds and the crunch of hooves. And Dad's voice, surprised. 'Hello, someone foot-walking.'

We hadn't noticed the tracks, but sure enough, beyond the next bend, we saw the old man. He plodded steadily, carrying a lidded billy, with a sugar bag slung over his back. He had a shapeless hat, a collarless vest, and long trousers with the knees out which he'd turned back to front. The holes flapped as he moved, showing bony shanks. His boots were laced with soft wire.

The team snorted at him and shied, but he just kept plodding until Dad drew level and pulled up. 'Want a lift, mate?'

The stranger grunted assent and climbed aboard.

'Where you headin'?' He stowed his billy beside the seat.

'Just travelling,' Dad said. 'My lad's behind with the horses. How about you?'

'Caroline Soak.' The stranger pointed with his chin to where the tumbled face of the range bent south. 'Mile or so in there.'

His name was Wal, and he and his mate were mica miners. The ranges were full of the stuff, he told us. Up close he was dirty, with stringy arms and grey hair that curled onto his shoulders. His faded eyes had yellowish whites and one side of his face was pushed in as though his cheekbone had been broken. Judith, too curious to worry about manners, asked him why he wore his pants backwards. 'Beats mendin',' he wheezed.

When Dad swung the leaders into the turn-off, he protested – but not very hard – that he could walk the rest.

''S no trouble,' Dad said.

We left a green bough over our tracks to let Sian know we'd be returning and followed the narrow road into the fold of the range.

Caroline Soak was in the bed of a narrow creek squeezed between the track and a rocky outcrop. There was a tiny mill about twelve feet high and a tank, half hidden by a green thicket of garden – the first one we'd seen for months. There were beans, tall green tomato plants, bright yellow peppers. And where the overflow spilled from the tank a real garden tree, glossy-leaved and laden with bright globes of fruit.

Patrick pointed suddenly. 'Look, a house!' I couldn't see one – then I could. The strangest house ever. It was small and built entirely of stone, its back end dug into the hill behind it. And it seemed to be growing out of the rocks there like a fairytale house, with a door no taller than I was, and half-sized window squares. A cat was sitting in one of them washing his ears as we pulled up.

Wal climbed down over the wheel calling out, 'Joe! Swing the billy, we got visitors,' in his hoarse, wheezy voice. Dad tied the reins and got down too. He said you never refused camp hospitality; it was insulting to do so. He chained the back wheel to the axle and detached the checkreins, using them to tie the leaders to the tree we'd stopped under.

Wal called, 'Joe!' again, then went to a pile of ash behind a hoop of tin where a log smouldered. He dropped sticks onto it from a nearby heap and hung an already filled billy on a hook above the flames. There was lots of ash raked back behind the fire, great mounds of it, so they'd obviously been camped here a long time.

A voice said, 'Hello,' (only it was more like ''Ello') and Joe, a pick over his shoulder, suddenly appeared. He was young, big and strong-looking, with dark, curly hair and a gold chain around his neck. His teeth were very white in his brown face when he smiled at us.

'Ninos,' he said, looking at us. Then he shook hands with Dad. 'I am Joe. I am Italy man. Here they cannot speak my proper name, so I am Joe.' His teeth flashed, 'And sometimes bloody wog.' He was looking at the horses, there were five in the team that day. 'You drive so many?' He poked his hand, too quickly, at Skimpy's face, and she snorted and jerked back. So did Joe. Patrick giggled and Dad frowned at him, but Joe didn't seem to mind. He shrugged, smiling his dazzling smile at us.

'Me, I am gardener, not a man of horses. You wish to see my garden?'

Dad was talking to Wal, so we three followed him down to the mill where he waded into the riot of tomatoes and returned with handfuls of the juicy crimson fruit. We bit into them, admiring the golden peppers and red flowering beans which swarmed up the tank, while he showed us his tangle of pumpkin vines and the okra bed.

'You know okra?'

We didn't. 'Who put the mill here?' Judith asked, and he shrugged, palms up, like a real foreigner. His skin was smooth and very brown, even the neck of his shirt didn't show any paleness. He wore ordinary clothes, dirty from digging. Stout boots, pants patched at the knees and a cotton shirt. It was only the gold chain that made him different. And his hat, which wasn't felt but made of raggedy cloth.

'Come, I show you somesink,' he said, leading the way to the dark tree at the edge of the overflow. Every now and then he mispronounced words. We could still understand them, but it made him seem exotic, like the chain around his neck. I saw now that a tiny gold cross hung from it, gleaming against his tanned skin.

'What is sat, eh?'

'An orange tree,' I said. My mouth watered looking at the abundant crop it held.

'True for you, little miss.' He gave us one each then led the way around the tree.

'And sat?' He was grinning as we stared in amazement at the lemons growing on a branch next to one laden with oranges.

'Is gardener magic, no?' His eyes danced, and Patrick crowed with delight and caught his hand.

'Oranges and lemons,' he sang. 'Can we see inside your house, Joe?'

'If you show me to pat your horse.'

The house had only one room, but it was bigger than it looked from the outside because it ran back into the hill, which also formed the back wall. And the floor had been dug out, so that although Joe had to bend to get through the door, he could stand upright inside. He had built it himself. In Italy, he said, people did not live under trees. That was for sheep.

It was cool inside. The walls were thick, the stones fitting into each other like the rails I'd seen Dad morticing into the posts of yards. Two squares, like shelves, had been let into the wall opposite the one with the windows. They had tucker stacked in them. There was a table, oil-drum seats, a stretcher in one corner, tools – and in the window a bunch of whitewood flowers stuck into a sun-blued bottle.

I stared, seeing the way the sun's rays pierced the glass to make a lovely splash of light on the grey stones. Gran had had a vase that colour – sort of bluey-green. It had been shaped like a basket with a pretty twisted handle and had stood on the sideboard in the parlour, flanked by family pictures. On Saturdays I was allowed to fill it with the big white daisies Grampy grew in the tub at the back of the house.

Memory ached in my throat and I jumped when Joe spoke. I hadn't noticed him come to stand beside me. 'Is pretty, no?' he said softly. I looked up and saw that all the brightness had gone from his face. He dipped his finger in the light as if he could scoop it up.

'In Italy,' he said slowly, as if struggling to remember the right words, 'is different, you know? Is 'ppy place for me. Friens, pretty girls, little childs. Ev'rywhere is growing bright flowers – big like my hand.' He spread it to show me how big. 'I drink the wine, I am singing –' he broke off. 'Is far away now, all gone. So I am picking sis flower to be 'appy.' He shook his head suddenly. 'Is like dream. And me, I am sad, sorry wog, no? Now we ask Papa for the bucket. We are picking se fruit to send home.'

Judith said hopefully, 'For us, you mean?'

Joe nodded briskly. 'Is too much for us. Your home is far?'

'Right outside the door,' I said, but we had to explain it twice before he understood.

'No house?' He looked astonished. 'Where is Mama then?'

'She went dead when I was little,' Patrick said importantly, and Judith gave him a shove.

'You're still little!'

'Am not!' They started to fight, but Joe stopped it by reminding Patrick that he wanted to be shown how to pat the horses.

We took him to the quietest, which was Clancy, and Patrick, showing off, said, 'Whoa, old man!' in a gruff voice and caught the rein. He spread his hand and ran it up the bay's face, then got Joe to do the same.

'You have to talk to them, too,' he said. 'Dad does, all the time. And you mustn't shove your hand at them – just sort of slide it, like this.'

Joe followed his example, patting by turn Clancy, Skimpy and Jean. Then he turned towards Grace and with one voice we shrieked, 'No! Not her!' Only Dad handled Grace.

Before he could ask, Judith said, 'You watch.' She grabbed a stick, said, 'Whoa, girl!' and leaning forward, gingerly tapped the chestnut mare's bit ring with it. Quick as a striking snake Grace's big yellow teeth snapped sideways, and we all jumped back.

'She kicks, too,' Patrick said. 'She kicked Dad once.'

'She didn't. She struck him,' Judith said, 'with her front foot. That's not kicking.'

'Me, I do not like to be kicked with the front feets or the back,' Joe declared. 'I sink we pick fruits instead.'

So we filled the water bucket with oranges and our pockets with lemons and by the time we got back Dad was unchaining the wheel. Joe and Wal stood watching us climb aboard and stow the bucket behind the seat. Dad had untied the leaders and was standing on the foot-rest, craning his neck for a place to turn, when Joe suddenly cried, 'Momento!' and dashed away.

'What'd he say?' Dad asked.

'Wants you to hang on a tic,' Wal said. ''Ere he comes now.'

Joe was carrying something. He ran back as if fearing to hold us up and thrust the blue bottle into my hands. 'A pretty for you,' he said.

His fingers were wet and warm. I could feel their pressure when they had gone, and the bright warmth of his sudden smile.

The team was moving. Wal lifted a hand in salute then turned away, but Joe stood waving his raggedy hat until we'd completed the turn and jogged on out of sight.

Sian would be wondering where we'd got to, Dad said. He stuck his pipe in his pocket and half turned on the seat to eye the bucket. 'You can chuck us one o' them over. I hope you thanked him for 'em. What've you got there, Kerry?'

I lifted my bottle, turning it slowly to make the colours spill on my hands. 'He gave it to me.'

'What would you want with that?' Dad spat a chunk of skin out and bit into the fruit, making the juice spurt over his beard. 'Sun must've got him! They make pretty good gardeners though, Eyeties. Couldn't have grown a better orange meself.'

SEVEN

William's Well was one of Kidman's waters. The cattle king had owned most of the country for hundreds of miles around, and the only thing he'd done for it, Dad said, was to sink the odd well or bore-hole. This one had been pumping water for half a century – brackish, mineralised stuff that only stock could drink.

Our camp was a couple of miles out, in the timber fronting Entire Creek. The feed was better there, so was the shade. And we had protection from the winter wind. We watered the plant at the Well but carted our own supplies from the Ten Mile. Sometimes, if Dad had colts to work in harness, we'd make a day of it and go as far as Mt Mary bore. The three waters formed a rough triangle across a vast expanse of claypan, sandflats and mulga scrub. From our camp you could see the Hartz Ranges away to the south. And nothing much but gum trunks and scrub in any other direction.

Dad was breaking for Jack Taylor at the Well yards and doing a few of our own too. It was unfenced country and there were plenty of brumbies about, but we kept the plant hobbled and tailed them into water each day at the Well.

The station was generous with both beef and hides, so when Dad wasn't working the colts he made catching ropes from greenhide, and headstalls and hobble-straps too. Greenhide was the battler's friend, he said. It might have been, but it made very stiff straps – which was no excuse, he told us, for driving the horses in hobbles. So we learned to carry a bit of eight-gauge wire with us to help undo them.

Taylor's horses were different – quiet but tricky to catch. They'd been handled and fed and had little fear of man. There were two white-eyed skewbalds, ugly, coffin-headed brutes, and a pair of brown thoroughbreds called Cattleman and Bridget.

'Handsome is as handsome does,' Dad said, when we first clapped eyes on the thoroughbreds. But we were all too busy wishing they were ours to listen. We admired their pasterns, the delicate curve of their hairless fetlocks, the depth of their shoulders, and their fine, aristocratic heads. Never had our own nags, with their sturdy bones and shaggy legs, loomed so ordinary in our sight. The absolute best we had was Rambler – three-quarters thoroughbred at most, twelve years old if he was a day, and with a quartered front hoof to boot.

Taylor had sent feed and leather hobble-straps for his blood-stock, which we considered no more than their due. We vied for the privilege of feeding them, and were jealous of Sian when Dad gave him Bridget to work.

Most days saw us hanging over the weathered rails of the

stockyard, hauling on ropes or running errands for Dad. He usually caught three colts at a time, and while he worked on one, would let us flop a bag over another, or lunge a third in the big yard. It was a very old yard but a sturdy one. The posts leaned, the mortices gaped where the wood had shrunk, and the gates dragged, but it was good for years yet. Sitting on the top rail you could see the black cockies floating into the dead bloodwood behind the mill, and the thin ribbons of cattle-pads spoking away from the trough.

We had to carry drinking water to the yard, as well as lunch, and the ropes, rollers and halters we needed. Mostly we loaded the donkeys up, then left them tied to the prickly bushes, which they ate, spikes and all. Each week we harnessed the team and went after a load of water. And it was on these trips that we first became acquainted with Humpy's mob.

Humpy was a black brumby stallion, shaped something like a camel. He bossed a huge mob – close to thirty head – and was often seen in the country bounded by the three waters. He was wild, tough, and intractable, but mostly tough. Years before, some-body, trying to run him, had pumped three .38 pistol slugs into his body. The resulting deformity had given him both his name and his notoriety. But whatever his shape, there was nothing wrong with his legs. You couldn't get near him with a rifle, and the full stock-camp had tried without success to yard him. He ran free with his motley band and might have continued to do so for years, if Sian and I hadn't lost the Taylor colts.

Until it happened we couldn't believe how easy it was. Dad was away somewhere working Alice, our bad-tempered bay mare, in the chains. Late afternoon, when he hadn't returned, we put the horses together and drove them, as we had many times before, to the Well for a drink. They jogged easily through dappled whitewood shade, forming their own little groups within the plant. The Taylor colts, being newcomers, clung to the flank of the mob, swerving aside when the others lunged at them with laid-back ears.

Then the emus appeared, racing back and forth with outstretched necks and shaking bustles, like it was some game. They ran across the lead of the plant, then straight through it, and the horses began to snort and kick up. Six of them broke into a canter, heads high, bells jangling; then Taylor's four hit the lead – and that's when the brumby colts shot out of the scrub. They tore off again at once, as though scorched, and after them, like mad dogs, went Taylor's breakers. We didn't have a hope of stopping them. Sian tried, but the plant was strung out chasing the emus, and we had to stop them first. Back at camp again we hobbled up with our hearts in our boots.

Dad arrived soon after, standing astride the log Alice was towing. She came at a canter with the lather foaming over her chest and her neck arched to the reins. Dad sang out, 'Whoa, girl!' and sprang off. He went to her head and called Patrick to come and unhook the snig chain. Then he saw our faces and his own changed. 'What's happened, now?' he asked.

Next morning he took after the truants with the rifle, without success. He went again the following day, and on the one after that came home driving both skewbalds. He'd seen neither hide nor track of the two browns, he said, but they wouldn't run alone for long. They'd pick up with Humpy – and that would be that.

～

Over the next week Sian and I moped about, wishing the world unmade. Dad said nothing more about it, but while he sat splicing rings onto greenhide ropes, or whittling pegs for hobble straps, we knew what he was thinking: that Jack Taylor, who'd made pets of those horses, had trusted them to him, and now they were gone. Never mind that it was our fault, the responsibility remained his.

He continued to work on Alice, towing quantities of firewood into the camp with her. And when he harnessed the team that week, she was in it, as was Grace's big colt, Clancy. It was to be a Mt Mary day. Ten miles into it, with the horses jogging to the sound of slapping back-bands and the crunch of wheels over sand, the brumbies cantered across our front.

'Humpy,' Sian said, and there he was, legs flowing, tail cocked, in a thunder of brown and bay and chestnut bodies.

'There!' I pointed. 'Cattleman!' And beside me Judith was yelling and pointing too.

'That's Bridget! Behind the bally chestnut – see?'

Clinging to the seat back, for the team had broken into a canter, we watched them pull away, wild hooves skimming the earth. Then the checkrein guiding Clancy snapped. He drifted sideways, got the wrong side of an ironwood and was suddenly in danger of being crushed between tree and wagonette. Dad grabbed the whip. He hauled the polers' heads to the right and the old Queen slammed into the tree, taking it squarely on the end of the jarrah side-rail. The impact stopped the horses in their tracks, and a second later the ironwood toppled beside them. By the time we'd led Clancy round the obstruction and refastened the rein, Humpy's mob had vanished.

'Well, they're no longer lost,' Dad said into the silence that had fallen on us. 'In a manner o' speaking, that is. Nothing's lost if you know where to find it.'

Next day we saw why Dad had been so busy with the ropes. He'd buckled one to each of the skewbalds' neck straps, and Alice's too. It would stop them galloping, he said. Then, just after midday, he went off alone on Rambler. He hadn't returned when it was time to take the horses down, so Sian and I put them together and set off.

There were no emus this time, and the colts kept treading on their ropes and pulling themselves up. The cockies were shrieking restively in the dead bloodwood as the leaders trotted in, and a dust haze hung above the prickly bushes at the yard. I squinted into the sun to see why. The yard was full of horses. Then a familiar shape shot between a gap in the green and wheeled, snorting, from the rails. Sian yelled and I stared, recognising Humpy.

We saw Dad then, coming slowly between the bushes, spurs dragging the dirt as he walked. He led old Rambler, whose head was on a level with his knees, which seemed likely at any moment to give way. He was as hollow as an empty drum, streaked white with dried lather, and rocking on his feet. When Dad pulled the saddle off, he just folded his legs and collapsed, not flat, but with his jaw propping his head, so that each breath blew little circles in the dust. Sian and I stared at him in awe, at his bony wither and shrunken rump. Dad rode twelve stone, and eight men on thoroughbreds had twice failed to run old Humpy.

Sian said stupidly, 'You got 'em. How'dja do it?' which only irritated Dad. He was always annoyed by the things we didn't know.

He had been angrier, it seemed to me, about us letting the emus start the plant off than he was about losing the colts.

'I used me head,' he said. 'Any man oughta be smarter than a horse. You stick with 'em, that's all. And when they've worn 'emselves out, you yard 'em.'

He threw his gear on Rose and returned with us to camp, leaving Rambler where he lay. Later, with the horses hobbled, he mellowed enough to describe the run, starting from the country just south of the Well, where he'd found them.

'They were coming into water. Must have been really dry, because they made a beeline for the Ten Mile. I took a punt on 'em fetching up there and cut across, just where that tongue of mulga sticks out into the scalded country.'

He sketched a map for us as he talked, and we listened breathlessly, reliving it all with him. He had beaten the mob to the bore and waited, hidden in the scrub while the wild ones drank their fill. Then he'd jumped them again, pounding in their dust as they streamed away south-east, water-heavy and beginning to panic. He plotted their course by their dust, cutting corners, sparing his horse but drawing up with them again whenever they started to slow.

The foals dropped out first. Then an old mare had plaited her legs and gone down in a sliding fall. Another, swag-bellied with foal, had somersaulted on a creek-bank as the brumbies suddenly doubled back.

He thought he'd lost them then, Dad admitted, that they'd beat him to the scrub, but gutsy old Rambler had managed to head the break, and Humpy, his nerve cracking, plunged into the dry sand of the creek-bed.

Inside five minutes, the mob was down to a canter in the strength-sapping sand. They'd have got out of it given the chance, but the far bank was too steep, and Rambler paced them on the near one for half a mile, until the channel widened and they burst suddenly from it. Then they slogged west again through broken patches of whitewood and supplejack, and Dad knew he had them. The pressure was breaking them – they were fanned out, trying to split up, the tailers down to a lagging trot.

He let some three or four drop out and crowded the rest, forcing them on. The Mt Mary mill sails were a glint in the distance behind him, the Well yards still seven or so civilising miles ahead. And by the time they reached them, with Rambler staggering under him, Humpy had trotted through the gates, only too happy to stop.

It was a great victory. The station men came down next day to see for themselves, along with the grader driver, and Quent the dogger. They all wore cotton shirts and big hats, and propped brown forearms on the yard rails to stare at Humpy. The boss had brought his rifle and gave Dad a hand to draft.

'Ugly old bugger, ain't he?' somebody said.

It was true. Humpy had big feet, a big head, and legs like old Grace's. His misshapen body was covered with battle scars. He wasn't even black, more a dirty brown, with a ropy mane that hung to the bottom of his neck.

The boss shot him as he was racing from the yard. And most of the others too. One by one they galloped through the gate, only to check and fall in mid-stride as the rifle spoke. Dad didn't want them killed in the yard, where the smell of death would upset the colts. He'd already drafted off eight young 'uns to keep, a brown, saddle-marked gelding with a symbol brand on the shoulder, and the runaway colts. Those went straight back into work, but they got little benefit from Jack Taylor's bag of feed. We kids were too busy sneaking it for Rambler.

There was no paddock to hold the new colts, so before they left the yards Dad ran them through the crush and buckled a three-foot length of greenhide to each near front foot. It was called a shin-flapper and effectively prevented them getting out of a trot. When he'd finished Taylor's horses, Dad said he'd be moving on to a pumper's job. There'd be a paddock so we could bush the plant until we were ready to catch the new colts. But for now, the daily handling and tailing about would do them a power of good.

～

Rambler wasn't ridden again that winter, and Dad told us to leave the hobbles off him. It would take green feed to build back the condition he'd lost, he said, but not even a bony frame could dim his magnificence in our eyes. We showed him off to every visitor, including the Hartz Range copper who, it turned out, had come not to admire one horse, but to arrest Dad for being in illegal possession of another.

He meant Tony, the branded gelding from Humpy's mob. Dad shook his head as if he couldn't believe it.

'Stolen, is he?' he asked. 'Who stole him, then?'

'You did, Mac,' the copper said. He had a beaky nose and light-coloured eyes as hard as stone. 'Under the Stock Act –'

'It's Mr to you, or McGinnis,' Dad said frostily. 'Mac's for me mates. Under the Stock Act – which I've been familiar with, by the way, since you was pulling your mother's tit – any person or persons finding lost, strayed or stolen animals is obliged to publicise the fact, and surrender said animals to owners appearing to claim them within three calendar months of the date of publication.' He rattled it off without drawing breath. 'So what's stolen? Because you've checked with your boss, in the Alice, haven't you? And the stock and station agents I wrote to? Prob'ly even dropped in to see Bennett about it, back at the station?'

The policeman let his hands slide off his hips and spread them instead. 'Well, not exactly. I –'

'Then, by Jesus!' Dad roared so loudly we all jumped. 'Until you have, don't you come here calling me a thief!'

We heard no more about it after that. Nobody ever claimed Tony so, six months later, Dad stuck our brand on him. We were at Carmencita by then, with the saddles hung up in the bough shed for the summer. We had a new camp, new colts to break after the rains. William's Well was behind us, along with Humpy. They were just the bones of an old story scattered in the grass.

EIGHT

No camp, according to Dad, was complete without a dog – we'd have to see about getting one. A cattle pup. Something useful that could earn its keep with the horses.

'Buy one off the stations,' Sian suggested, but Dad shook his head. Of all the dogs he'd owned during his years in the bush, the best had been freely given. We'd wait a bit, he said. One would turn up.

Larry did, but only after Patrick had first taken matters into his own hands. The night we camped at Huckita, he went off by himself as soon as the hobbling up was done. The rest of us carted wood and got the fire going, then the station boss came across to yarn to Dad. He was still there, squatting on his heels drinking tea in the shade, when Patrick returned, dragging a skinny, cringing mongrel on a length of chewed red-hide. It was a swap, he explained.

He'd given his last three marbles for it to a black kid in the blacks' camp behind the bore.

Dad said, 'Mother 'o God!' The hand holding the pannikin had frozen halfway to his face. He stared at the sorry spectacle – the dog's rump was covered in mange sores and its ribs stuck out like fenceposts. 'You can take that right back where you got it from.'

'But I swapped my marbles for him, an' one of them was an alley.'

'Then you made a bad bargain, son, but we're not keeping that.' You could tell he meant it. 'Just be patient. The right pup'll turn up one o' these days.'

The Huckita boss was watching, his wrists hanging over his thighs. He broke Patrick's sulky silence. 'You looking for a dog? I've a half-grown Smithfield collie, last of the litter. Pedigree long as yer arm. Stop by tomorrow and take him, if yer want.'

'Right,' Dad said, like it was the sign he'd been waiting for, and next morning we picked up Larry.

He was a gangly dog with a rough blue coat and a short tail. He had big feet, a big sloppy tongue, a whiskery face and eager eyes. Dad gave him his name. It had a good Irish ring to it, he said.

'He looks a bit unfinished.' Sian eyed him disparagingly, but Patrick, an arm around the wriggling blue body, was happy enough, and we heard no more of his lost marbles.

Dad taught Larry camp manners, and the rest, he said, he'd pick up as he grew. Dogs were smarter than horses, and this one bore the hallmarks of a sagacious animal.

'What's that mean?' Patrick looked blank.

'He's got his head screwed on straight,' Dad said. Puzzled, Patrick squatted in front of Larry, and we all shrieked as we realised he was checking to see if it was true.

Dad tied him up that night. Dogs, he said, had no business near the fire, the table, or people's swags.

Patrick rolled his out as close as he could to Larry – in case he got lonely in the night and cried, he told us – but it was Patrick himself who, shortly after the fire had sunk to rosy coals, woke screaming.

'Godalmighty!' Dad was up in an instant. I saw him as a black shadow jumping the coals, bending over Patrick who was thrashing about, sobbing in his blankets. Larry barked as Patrick shrieked again.

I ran over, bare feet wincing from the stubbly ground. 'What's wrong with him?'

'Jesus, I don't know! What is it, son? Get the light, Sian!'

Patrick let out another cry. 'It walks! It walks!' He was holding his right ear, his head turned sideways, rocking back and forth on his knees.

'It's all right, champ.' Dad squatted beside him. 'You've got an insect in your ear, but we'll get it out. Just hang on.'

Patrick took him at his word, gripping the cloth of Dad's pants, his tears shining in the glow of the carbide lamp that Sian had lit.

'I can feel it walking,' he hiccupped.

'I know. We'll drown it in two shakes.'

I ran for some water, but Dad sent me back for the golden syrup instead, mixing a spoonful of it with a little water warmed on the coals. He dribbled this mixture into Patrick's ear, and gradually the tension went from his body and his grip on Dad eased.

'Whyn't you just use water?' I asked as we waited.

'Syrup's denser. It'll float out – water just makes it stick to the flesh inside the ear.'

He was right. When Patrick tipped his head over and the syrup mixture ran out into a cloth, the body of a tiny flying insect came with it.

We all went back to bed then, but not before Patrick had tied up his head in his towel to protect his ears from invasion. He kept up this practice for months, waking each morning at daylight turbaned like a Turk.

～

Next day we moved on to Hope bore, which was on a pebbled flat in the Hartz ranges. The cattle-pads snaked in through narrow valleys between the hills, and the horses had to forage far back in these for grass. They'd had three dry years straight on Huckita, Dad told us, so you couldn't expect clover.

The only reason we stopped there at Hope was that Dad had a few days' work on the station, helping the boss pull a bore. That meant getting up several hundred feet of rods to find out why it wasn't pumping.

The boss came by the camp each morning in the landrover to pick Dad up, and he was gone all day. Sian went with him for the experience; a bushman, Dad said, had to be an all-rounder, and bores were as much his business as mustering stock.

It was Judith's and my job to look after the plant while they were gone. We could tie the donkeys up during the day, Dad told us, and use them to tail the plant – give them something useful to do for a change. Patrick came with us, of course, and because we couldn't bear to leave him behind, Larry came too, lolloping about with his nose down on the scent of lizards and euros.

On the second day, chores all done and tiring of inactivity, we decided to haul firewood for the camp.

'We can use Todd, like Dad does,' Judith said.

'Better not.' I was aware how often our schemes went wrong and opted for caution. 'We could use a donkey, though. Jack's the biggest.'

'He couldn't pull a tree!'

'So we'll use two. One behind the other. C'mon!' I could see it in my head, the donkeys, small and manageable, and the great piles of wood.

'The collars won't fit. But we can pad them with something. Dad'll never believe it.'

But it proved more difficult than we'd thought. Jack, collared, chained and attached to a log, just swished a bored tail when given the office to start. We hauled his bony head this way and that, without once budging his front hooves. He was stuck to the ground as if growing from it. He lopped his ears and looked at us from lidded eyes, patient as the hills and just about as immovable.

'We'll have to get Korai, too.' I wiped my hot face on my sleeve. 'Maybe it really is too heavy for one.'

'Seein' he hasn't even tried it, how would he know?' But Judith went to catch Korai, anyway. We chose the smallest collar and stuffed it with bags. Then we put the breaking roller on her and tied the hames back to it to stop the whole thing sliding over her head when she lowered it. Patrick, bored, wandered off to play, taking Larry with him.

The little jenny was just as difficult. It took the two of us to get her going, which meant there was nobody to drive Jack. He'd move if you switched his rump, but never very far, before Korai, yoked behind him, would stop, making him pull her too. I couldn't see how anything so small could weigh so much, or be so stubborn. We made about twenty yards in this fashion, then Judith flopped down in the nearest shade, fanning herself with her hat.

'I've had it! I bet even Dad couldn't move 'em. They're yarramun trees, for true!'

'What do you mean?' I hurled my stick crossly at Jack, striking his rump. His ears twitched, but that was all.

'I dunno – it's what Dad says. "Tisn't gunna work, anyway.'

'Yes, it will. Patrick can help, he's just messing around.'

I waved at him to come and he did, still carrying the tin of little stones he'd been collecting. I think he wanted to replace his marbles, but we never found out because as he ran over to join us, both donkeys pinned their ears back and took off. Judith and I scrambled for their heads, whooping encouragement, and just as suddenly as they'd started, they stopped. Judith saw it first.

'Rattle your tin again, Patrick.'

He did and again both animals were galvanised into action. After that it was easy. With Patrick hooking on for us and shaking the tin when they stopped, we towed in more firewood than Jack Rice could jump over, which was how Dad described big heaps of anything.

'That'll do.' I eyed the pile with pride and rubbed the sweat patch behind Korai's ear. 'We'll never burn that much! Let's give them a drink before we take the gear off.'

So we led them across to the trough, which had a float guard but no cap rail, and that's when Patrick — just to see what he'd do, he said afterwards — leant over and shook the rattle right behind Jack's ear.

The old donkey went straight into the trough. He tried to jump it, but the hanging chains caught the edge, so he somersaulted, landing on his back with his hind feet under the copper float. Korai bolted with Judith clinging to her halter.

I caught a glimpse of her going, and of Patrick's anxious face, then there was a frightful racket of hooves against steel and a *whoosh!* as the valve on the four-inch line connecting tank and trough opened. Jack had smashed the split pin holding the float in place.

There was water everywhere — washing over the old donkey's head as he thrashed about, gushing from the pipe, slopping over the sides and edge of the trough.

Patrick wrung his hands. 'Oh, what'll we do? What'll we do?'

'Hold the plate shut!' I yelled. 'There, stupid, where the water's coming from. Push it hard. Harder! You'll just have to hold it till we find a stick or something to wedge it. Dad'll kill us. It's all your fault.'

His voice went small and wobbly. 'I didn't mean to do it.'

Larry, who'd been woofing up and down the trough with excitement, heard the change. He ran back to jump up on Patrick and lick his face. Jack kicked again, humping and thrashing. He got his forequarters partly over and I hauled on his head, but the trough was coated with slime and his feet kept skidding. I tried again and again to heave his head out of the water and turn him. I could see his frantic eyes and big, yellow teeth where his lips had fallen back. His ears hung limp and waterlogged and the breath roared in his throat.

'Holy Mary, he'll drown.' Panic clawed at me. Panting with effort, I seized him by the headstall and one ear, twisting. 'Get up, Jack! Get up!'

Patrick was crying and clinging to the metal plate, but he wasn't strong enough and the water was still coming out. From the corner of my eye I saw Judith belting back – she must have stopped the jenny – and screamed at her to help me. Then Larry stuck his head into the trough, felt around under water, and grabbed hold of Jack's leg. He didn't nip it – he crunched down hard and hung on, a proper cattle-dog bite.

It did the trick. Jack surged out of his slippery bed like something electrified. His coat was sodden, the black cross over his withers smudged with green slime as he stood, wild-eyed with terror, snorting and stamping his feet, and trying to look everywhere at once. Another dog might have barked, or continued to bite him, but Larry just sat back on his haunches, head on one side in the way he had, moving his stubby tail and looking very pleased with himself.

After that we had only to reattach the float (which was dinted but mercifully not holed) with a bit of wire in place of the broken split pin. As long as it hung true and didn't leak, Dad would notice nothing amiss. We certainly weren't going to tell him what had happened.

Jack's collar was soaked, but we hung it in the sun and hoped it would dry before Dad got back or looked at it closely. And we made a great fuss of Larry. Dad had been right – he was clever. And you couldn't beat having a handy dog about.

NINE

Right from the beginning Dad said we must learn to read tracks.

'Nothing's more important.' He swept an arm out over the backs of the plodding team to take in the sand and scattered mulga trees with their patches of lacy shade. 'City folk might reckon that's empty space, but it's a news sheet. The tracks you see are the stories written on it.'

Judith and I exchanged doubtful glances. It didn't look like a news sheet to us, but the scary emptiness he said it wasn't. The trees were all the same. Their dark trunks and glinting greyish leaves stretched forever, crowding either side of the narrow road. Viewed from the wagonette their foliage formed an undulating grey sea, one that could swallow you up, just like a real ocean would.

But as the weeks went by and we became accustomed to our surroundings, those feelings disappeared. It was only at night, when the ululating dingo chorus troubled the starry stillness, that they returned. Then, fearful in my swag, I'd feel the scrub begin to crowd in on the camp. Grey, endless miles of it, formless and unknowable, filled with nothingness. It wasn't a news sheet then, columned with prints of wildcat and wallaby, headlined with stories of nocturnal doings, but a place of monstrous darkness where no roads ran. A place where the nothingness could crush you to death.

The daylight world was different. And as the weeks and months passed in camping, travelling and riding, my fears gradually faded. It was just country – landscape. Trees and hills and creek-beds. The trees had names and uses, and there were special things to remember about each one of them. Whitewood foliage, for instance, poisoned horses. Supplejack was a drought fodder and must never be cut or burnt. Trees were the traveller's friend, as were the dry, sandy creek-beds. Dad showed us where to dig in them to find water, and how to use the sun and the east–west line of the ranges whose names we often didn't know to guide us back to camp. He was a thorough teacher, and we the perfect age to learn. Sian was fourteen, Patrick eight, Judith twelve and I was thirteen. Kids, like colts, were best trained young, Dad said.

By now he could no longer baffle us with unfamiliar tracks. Before his knuckles had finished making the imprint in the smoothed sand we'd be crying, 'Wallaby! Perentie! Pussycat!' He was pleased, but never satisfied, with our efforts. It wasn't enough just to recognise tracks, he said, because they were no more than the alphabet of sign. To understand the story they told, you had to string them into words.

I saw what he meant the day we rode home from Kirrim Soak and crossed the fresh prints of a ridden horse.

'Sian,' Dad said. He glanced at the sun, which hung low above the scrubline. 'Gone after the horses. He musta left it late, he's cantering.'

'No, he isn't,' I said. 'He's been thrown – look. He had Starlight today. She's dumped him.' I pointed to the smoothed patch to the right of the jumble of overlaid prints. I could see where he'd knelt, his fingers pressed to the ground. 'Wonder what started her off?'

'Work it out,' Dad said. 'She's cantering along, nice as pie. She's passing that anthill and shies – there, see, where her hooves dug in? Then she bucks and takes off. Sian hits the dirt, jumps up and runs after her. What she see on the anthill, eh?' His gaze roved over the ground. 'Here's a clue – it's got long toes for its size, and runs on its hind legs. Take a look an' tell me what happened.'

I took my time. The tracks belonged to some sort of lizard, smaller than a goanna but much larger than the little burrowing dragons. There were no drag marks of a tail – so it had to be a frill-neck, carrying it high as he ran. I nudged Sunny across to stand in Starlight's tracks, imagining her cantering, the red sand firm to her feet, her shadow moving beside her. And all at once I saw what had happened.

'It was a frilly, sunbaking. It must've moved when Starlight's shadow crossed it. That's why she shied. And when she bucked, it jumped off the anthill and ran.' I turned my head and pointed at the closest tree. 'Bet you it's up there now!'

'Not bad,' Dad said, and I felt ten feet tall. He didn't often deal out praise.

Shortly after that we moved camp again, trundling down the track to Kirrim Soak, which was a sort of boxed well sunk in the bed of Ixion Creek, a tributary of the Plenty River. When we learned the name of the latter on first sighting it, we'd wondered derisively what there was supposed to be plenty of. Sian suggested sand, but Dad took him up short.

'Don't think everyone a fool just because you are. There's soakage water under that sand, hundreds o' tons of it.'

Water was Dad's god. He couldn't stand to hear it made light of, even in fun.

There was a mill on the Soak; it pumped into a pair of stock tanks that fed a trough, the water coming sweet and cold from the sand. Huge gums lined the creek-banks, littering the ground with their cast-off bark. We gathered it to start our fire that day, sniffing at the remembered scent as it burned. Dad had pulled the wagonette up in the shade of the gums, back from the trough. To give the stock a chance to drink, he said.

Later, the camp chores done, we ran down to play in the white sand drifts, and to hunt about for tracks. Cattle- and horse-pads snaked down the dusty banks, jolting over the exposed roots of the eucalypts. The soft earth carried a myriad overlaid cloven hooves, smudged by the wandering tracks of a dingo. There were kangaroo prints in the sand, and the markings of birds, beetles and a big perenti. Sian scared Patrick with a story of it sneaking into the camp at night. 'Rot!' I said loudly, just as Judith turned up a crab shell in the sand. Marvelling, we clustered to look at it, and I glanced up in time to see an emu followed by eight striped chicks, stalking, like figures in a frieze, along the top of the bank.

I found them again next day, having ridden out without saying so for just that purpose. If I caught a chick and took it back to camp, I reasoned, Dad would have to let me keep it, because it would die if let go on its own.

I rode Sunny again and stuck out optimistically along the horse-pad, leaving the mill wheel spinning briskly at my back. It towered above the camp, taller than the tallest gum – I would see it from miles away.

It was soft country close to the creek, dusty red soil with thickets of whitewood, neat as orchard trees, and scattered ironwood. Con-kaberry clumped their prickly stems together, and the dry grass rippled in the wind like pale fingers waving. Sunny blew softly and shook her head, jingling the bridle rings. There were brumby tracks on the pad, and high above a hawk rode the blue billows with spread wings.

The emus, when I found them, took me by surprise, lying hidden in the black shadow of a supplejack. I saw a neck like a moving branch as the cock jumped up and took off, with the chicks holding formation around him. Whooping, I cantered after them, waiting my chance. Emus would attack, Dad said, if you threatened their young. I was hoping to panic and separate them before vaulting off to run the closest chick down. I'd marked it out at once – the littlest one, piping in distress as it ran and already falling behind. When it was far enough back I jumped off and chased it on foot.

Everything went as planned, until Sunny pulled her hastily looped reins free. I glimpsed her trotting off behind me just as the chick dived into a thicket of conkaberry, and had no choice but to abandon the hunt in favour of catching her. That took ages, and was only possible in the end because the trailing reins snagged on a fallen bloodwood branch.

The emus had gone by then, of course. I cantered back, searching for the conkaberry bush, but I could see at least six scattered through the light scrub and none looked any more familiar than the others. I rode a slow half-circle, staring at the ground, searching without success for my own tracks, and when I looked up there was the creek timber in front of me.

My fingers felt suddenly stiff on the reins because, without even noticing it, I'd somehow turned completely round. Just so there could be no mistake, I kicked the pony into movement, trotting to the bank to stare down into white sand drifts. It was the creek, no question – a bit wider here, but otherwise the same. Baffled, I sat there trying to work it out. The Soak had to be downstream to my left, except that the sun and the shadows were in the wrong position if that was correct. Something cold moved inside me and I knew, before I looked, that the mill wasn't going to be there.

Panic congealed my blood. I was lost. A pulse beat, heavy and slow, in my temple, but nothing else moved. The leaves hung straight down beside me, and the only sound was my frightened breathing and the distant caw of crows. When I stared around, the trees all looked the same, I couldn't tell one from another. Their branched arms beckoned me in a hundred different directions, but every way led into the emptiness between those sinister trunks.

The only thing I could recognise in the whole landscape was a clump of conkaberry bushes, so I rode towards it. I pulled up beside it and Sunny blew gustily, making my heart jump in my throat. I clutched the reins, looking ahead for another conkaberry, and after that another, concentrating on the dull green tangle of growth to avoid the menace of the trees. I knew as soon as I looked at them they'd begin crowding in on me.

After the fifth clump there weren't any more. I swung down beside it, boots crunching in drifts of old leaves, and crouched there, pressing my back into its prickly shelter. I kept my gaze lowered, which was why I immediately saw the bony hand near my foot, sticking out through the leaf trash as if to grasp mine.

I started violently, then froze, my gaze glued to the skeletal fingers. There was no disturbance or smell of death, just clean, bleached bone, fingers spread wide as if to catch the leaves it lay among. I raked through them with a stick, almost afraid to look, fearing the sudden appearance of a face, but needing to know. Then my shaky hands dislodged a knuckle, and a finger-bone rolled over to point a black clawlike nail at me.

Realisation and relief came together, but to be certain I thrust my arm under the bush, scooping the leaves aside, to disclose the kangaroo's head.

I'd changed my position to reach down, then had to wriggle sideways again, flattening my face to the ground to avoid the prickly branches. And it was from that angle, with one eye screwed shut, that I saw the toe track of my boots, just inches from my nose, with beside them my spread handprints where I'd scrabbled under the bush on hands and knees.

I sat up slowly, never taking my eyes off the faint imprints, hope a painful pressure in my chest. This was where I had left the chick to run back to Sunny! Which meant that the camp must be some-where to the south of where I sat. Holding my breath, I lifted my gaze above the tree line, searching far away, then near and still nearer – and there, scarcely half a mile distant and flashing like a heliograph in the sun, was the mill-wheel at Kirrim Soak.

The tension spilled from my limbs like water, taking the stiffness with it. I'd been wrong about the creek – either it was the Ixion looped back on itself, or the bed of the Plenty before the two junctioned. I stared that way now, but was seated too low to catch even a glimpse of gums. All I could see was grass, the pastel froth of whitewood foliage, and the shining leaves of coolibah and supplejack. Their anonymity and menace had vanished as completely as my fright at finding the bones under the bush.

I sifted the brittle flakes of dead leaves through my fingers, scattering them over my tracks. It didn't obliterate but merely hid them, in the same way that the glitter of the mill blades hid the menace in the landscape. My prints would be lost forever the first time it rained, but the other thing would always be there, waiting for each traveller.

When I rode into camp, Dad was stropping his knife on his boot. He tested it on the hair of his forearm, then snapped it shut saying, 'Well, what'd you see, Kerry?'

I shivered in the hot sun. 'Nothing,' I said, 'and trees.'

TEN

The bay mare we called Satin belonged to Merv Jackson. Jubilee Jones, the blackfella who worked for Jackson, brought her over to Carmencita bore with several other unbroken colts. There were a couple of quiet old mares with them too, just to steady them down. They trotted about the trough on springy fetlocks, snorting, while Jubilee sat his horse in the shade, ready to block them if they bolted.

Dad said, 'Stick the billy on, Kerry,' and jumped onto Sian's mare, Tassle, to show Jubilee where the yard was.

Later, while the two men sat over their tea, we ran up there to get a proper look at them. It wasn't a very big yard – Dad had built it by wiring rails to standing timber – and it was pretty full of colts. There was a buckskin, a blue-grey, a brown and two bays. These last looked like (and were) sisters, one older and plainer than the other. They trotted nervously, snorting at the rails and wheeling short about. The muscles rippled like water under their sleek hides and their eyes were wide and wild. Only the old mares stood aloof. Judith, who could do things like that, coaxed one of them over to her just by talking. She was still scratching the mare's ears and playing with her when Dad turned up.

'Right,' he said. 'We'll catch two today and let the rest go for now.

'They can't get out o' the paddock, so we can yard 'em again whenever we want to. Go and slip a bridle on old Jeanie for me, Judith. And Sian, you bring the ropes.'

I don't know whether Dad planned it like that, but his first loop settled over the head of the older bay, the one we came to call Satin. While she fought, rearing and screaming on the rope's end, he cleared the yard, save for the other filly and the old mare that Judith had petted.

We called the other bay Silk. 'Just a baby,' Dad said, pulling her lip back to show us her teeth. Once the headstall was on, he gave her to Sian to bag down, then got Jean in alongside Satin and began the business of hobbling and collar-roping her from under the big mare's body.

Satin was four, older than the others and a lot tougher. Buckskin and Silk were no trouble; Legs hurt his neck and was let go again to recover, and the brown killed himself in the yard before he was named.

Satin fought every step of the way. Dad worked her without let-up, on the lead rope and in the long reins, then riding her further afield each day as her soreness eased and the scars of the breaking yard healed. She'd lost condition, of course, unlike Silk who still

94

looked the pretty thing she had been that first day. But Satin, with her tail pulled and the gloss off her, was just plain ugly – poddy-gutted, high-rumped, hollow-necked. She had a wild eye, showing lots of white, and wicked feet. She'd kick anything that moved near her.

Dad liked her. She had Welsh pony in her breeding, he told us, and you couldn't beat that for guts. He liked her fiery nature. We kids often rode his horses, but he refused to let even Sian near Satin.

'You wouldn't get a saddle on her, for starters,' he said. And a bit later, when one of Merv Jackson's riders wanted to borrow her to shift some cattle from the bore, we saw what he meant. The stranger was wary of the mare and she knew it. She ran backwards, snorting and rolling her eyes when he approached with the saddle. The moment it touched her back, she plunged away, bucking wildly, aiming a whistling kick that just missed the man. He was young and tall, with stringy blond hair and a red face. He looked both shaken and angry.

'You call this broken in?' he yelled, picking his saddle out of the dirt.

'Put the hobbles on her, boy. And ride her in the yard,' Dad said. 'I never told yer she was quiet.'

We all went up to the yard then. Dad fidgeted around, swearing under his breath while Satin played up, working herself into a fearful lather. The moment the stranger hit the saddle she threw him, then careered around the yard, bucking and squealing with the stirrup irons clanging over the seat. Because we were all watching, he had to get on her again, and this time she threw him into the rails, then tried to jump them herself.

Dad unsaddled her then. He was furious. He threw the bridle at Sian, snapping, 'Catch Buckskin, he oughta be able to manage him,' and put a headstall on Satin and tied her up. She flinched when he touched her, stabbing backwards with her hind feet, her ears laid flat.

'Don't come that bloody nonsense with me, girl,' he growled, and she snorted sharply, showing the white of her eye.

Later, when she'd cooled down, he went back to the yard. We went too – you couldn't have kept us away. We watched silently from the rails as he shin-hobbled the mare and saddled her. Satin stood tense as a coiled spring, snorting in short blasts, but we weren't worried. Dad could ride anything in hide, as the bay mare would soon discover.

As soon as the hobbles were off, he whipped into the saddle, fast and low. And as her head jerked down, his hand, holding a broken surcingle, followed, doubling it under her belly. She roared in fury, exploding across the yard in a twisting blur punctuated by the smack of leather against hide. He hit her until she quit, then waited until she pig-rooted half-heartedly, and hit her again. When she finally stopped, sweat blackened her hide and dripped in sudsy foam from the saddlecloth. Her flanks were heaving, her legs trembled, and blood leaked from one dark nostril.

Dad cooled her down, straightened the saddle and remounted. 'Drop the rails,' he said. Then he cantered away up the fence, the mare moving sweetly under him, and vanished into the scrub.

It was mid-winter by then. The other colts went off to the stock-camp for a bit of light work before they were turned out, but Dad kept Satin. None of the stockmen wanted her. He rode her mustering, teaching her to follow a beast, to jump from walk to gallop in a couple of strides. She had the makings of a camp-horse, he said, and that was his highest praise.

'Why don't you buy her, then?' I asked.

'Can't,' he said briefly. 'Jackson won't sell the station brand. Pity. Some new chum'll ruin her, but that's the way it goes.'

'She's so ugly, with that skinny neck and big belly!' He snorted in amusement. 'She's in foal, that's all.'

∽

A week later, while the mustering camp was still there at Carmencita, the brumbies got into the paddock. Dad could have shot them, and maybe he was going to, but he was riding Satin back to the yard when they bolted out of the scrub in front of him, towing Tassle and Spider in their wake. He took after them, and a moment later it happened.

We'd heard the thundering hooves. We ran to look and saw the horses stream away, heads and tails high, and the flutter of Dad's blue shirt behind them. Then the lead swung, chopping suddenly to the right, rumps where their heads had been but a moment before. Satin dipped her shoulder and swung with them – straight into the leaning ironwood across her path. The world seemed to shudder as they hit, then freeze into immobility.

We ran. The men from the stock-camp were running too, Jubilee and the cook and someone else. Dad was on his back, half under the tree whose roots stuck, rude and exposed, from the red earth. There wasn't any blood but his face was grey, and he cried out when the men pulled the tree off him.

Sian looked white and frightened, and that scared me worse because he was older, he should've known what to do. Patrick was crying. I hung onto him so he couldn't touch Dad.

Judith gulped, 'I'll get Satin.' She'd been plaiting horsehair when she ran out to look and still had a fistful of it.

'No,' Dad croaked. He moved his eyes to find Jubilee. 'You, mate. Don't let ... kids ...'

'I'll fix it,' Jubilee said. He and the other men lifted Dad onto the camp truck, which the cook had brought over, and drove him off to Red Tank. They had a medicine chest and a wireless there, and the storeman's wife had been a nurse.

Satin was crippled – permanently, we hoped. Her chest was bleeding and she couldn't put her near fore on the ground.

'Bitch!' Sian yelled at her. She didn't even jump but just stood there, with her head down. Back at the camp he kicked the tea billy so hard it buckled in half. The freckles were like brown spots on his white face. 'He's gunna die,' he burst out. 'He's gunna die and leave us.'

'He is not!' Terror squeezed my stomach and I flew at him. Then we were rolling and punching on the ground. 'Don't you say that!' I screamed. 'Don't you ever say that again!'

Jubilee fetched his swag and camped by our fire that night, and next day they brought Dad home. He was sitting up in the front of the truck, but he looked awful. We had to help him get out, then almost carry him into the shed to bed. His ribs were broken, and his wrist, and his right leg might as well have been. He had refused to go into hospital, so the storeman's wife had given him some painkillers. He said he would get better, but seeing him lying there, so still and grey, none of us believed him.

Satin's recovery was faster. She stayed around the trough for days, visibly losing condition, but eventually began to limp further afield. Her foreleg slowly healed. From carrying it she began limping on it, then walking evenly. It was only when she trotted that a limpy gait returned. Weight loss had made her pregnancy obvious. Standing at the trough with her scarred shoulder, hollow neck and great belly, she was the ugliest thing in the paddock. We four hated the sight of her.

Dad's temper got shorter as the months passed. He could get around the camp leaning on the shovel by then, but that was all. He couldn't ride or work, and inactivity drove him crazy. We kids, struggling to perform the tasks he'd done so easily, seemed only to exacerbate his helplessness.

We minded the goats and tailed the horses and Sian rode the fences. Summer came with longer days and the tank emptied quicker in the hot weather. So when the wind failed and the mill needed changing onto the pump-jack, Judith and I decided to do the job ourselves, rather than worry Dad with it.

Luckily for us, he lurched around the curve of the tank just in time to prevent Judith, halfway up the mill tower, from knocking the connecter free of the lower rod.

'Jesus, save me!' he yelled. 'Leave it! You'll have the whole lot at the bottom of the hole.' And, horrified, I saw I'd forgotten to clamp the rods to the pump-jack arms.

Sian fared no better. Mending a broken section of fence where bulls had fought through it, he lost the pliers, which must have slipped or bounced from their scabbard on the ride home. Dad was livid. He sent Sian back twice to look for them, but each time he came home sulky and empty-handed.

∽

Satin must have foaled around then because she suddenly stopped coming into the trough. She'd been running on her own ever since the accident. At first she'd been too lame to keep up with the others, then, by the time her leg healed, Silk and the rest had gone with the stock-camp. We had grown accustomed to seeing her plod in each afternoon and immediately noticed her absence.

'She'll have foaled,' Dad said. 'Probably water at night for a bit now, then join up with the mob again.' He was getting round without the shovel by this time. His ribs and wrist no longer pained him, but he still couldn't bend his bad leg. He said he didn't need to on a quiet horse and one morning, a couple of days later, he got Sian to bridle Rose for him.

'You can come too, Kerry,' he said. 'Catch the old man when he falls off, eh?' It was the first joke he'd made for ages, and I ran gladly, jingling the bridle as I went, to get Mort.

We rode at a walk, criss-crossing the paddock, touching the fence here and there, finding little groups of horses and cattle.

'We might see Satin's foal,' I said, and he nodded, sitting square in the saddle, smoke puffing from the bowl of his pipe.

'Might, at that.'

It was strange to feel so happy again. The day seemed to sparkle under the blue, blowy sky. The feed was thin and dry and willy-winds tore through the light scrub in dusty spirals, but it didn't matter. The leaves of the gums twirled in silvery flashes as the breeze turned them, and the sun glinted on the barbs of the new fence when we rode onto it again, near the creek crossing.

'I'll check it,' I said.

Dad nodded and ambled on while Mort, grunting, stiffened his legs and slid down the steep bank.

The first thing I saw, stuck through a loop of wire on the anchor tree, was the missing pliers. Sian was supposed to have lost them on the opposite side of the paddock, but once I'd checked them for the punch mark Dad had on all his tools I knew they were his.

Shrugging, I stuck them in my saddlebag, hurrying in order to catch up with Dad.

'Okay, was it?' he asked, and I nodded.

'Sian's hung another log across under the cables.' I didn't say anything about the pliers because I wanted to produce them as a surprise when we got home.

'He's a good lad,' Dad said. Then he pulled his pipe out and sniffed. I could smell it too, growing stronger as we rode – green bone and dead hide, the stench of death.

'Outside the paddock,' Dad said, 'in the corner there, it'll be a wallaby.'

But it wasn't. It was Satin and her newborn foal, side by side. They had perished. The mare lay, shrunk now to a hide-covered skeleton, with her eyes and soft parts pecked away, and the bones and tiny hooves of the foal beside her. Her head was twisted on her neck so that her empty sockets stared past the tiny corpse at the fence.

I felt sick. 'She could've gone to Moontah bore,' I said. Sian must have intended her to do so – I knew now why the pliers had been there. He'd let her out through the creek crossing and hung the extra log across so she wouldn't get back. But she could still have gone to the next bore for water, maybe pick up with the brumbies. He hadn't meant to kill her. He'd just wanted to get rid of her, so Dad couldn't ride her again.

'Carmencita's the only water she'd know,' Dad said. 'Prob'ly squeezed out through a creek crossing when the foal was coming, then couldn't get back. Poor little bitch. Well, it's usually the good ones yer lose.' He picked up the reins. 'No use glooming over it, Kerry. Yer own horses, yer loose 'em – and this one wasn't even ours.'

I didn't tell Sian where I'd found the pliers. Instead, I dropped them on the horse-pad coming home that day, just out from the trough. Judith picked them up next morning, and we got Dad's usual lecture about looking after gear.

Merv Jackson wasn't too upset by the loss of the bay mare, either. 'Had me doubts about her from the start. Hard to get blokes to work the touchy ones,' he confessed. ''N no point in breeding buck-jumpers from her.'

Only Jubilee seemed to care. He called the spot in the angle of the fence where she'd died Satin's Corner, and the name caught on with the station men.

I never let on to Sian that I knew, but while the corner was there, neither of us could forget. Even when the rain brought fresh grass to hide the bones and Dad started breaking new colts, her name, and our guilt, remained.

ELEVEN

Sputnik had come out of old Humpy's mob. Dad had so named her because she was a high-flyer. Her hide was a harsh red colour, her mane and tail gingery. She had four white stockings and a broad white blaze down her face – only stripes could have made her stand out more.

Sputnik fought like a mad thing in the breaking yard, roaring through distended nostrils, spattering herself with foam and blood. She was a skittish ride too, shying and snorting at shadows – ever ready, in the paddock, to banner her tail and take off. Hard to catch, touchy to handle, for all her schooling, the red mare remained, at heart, a brumby.

Work was the answer, Dad said. He wanted a word with Jack Taylor over at Red Tank, and had a fancy to visit him by way of the New Dam site, which lay east of Carmencita bore, in the unfenced country loosely bounded by the Wallis Creek track to the south, and a nameless spur of range, curved like an outflung arm, to the north and east. It was a lot of country to look in, but space was something Dad understood. He liked to take new country into himself, plot its edges, and make it his own.

He and I would go for a look-see through it, he said. We loved these excursions, which he took us on by turns. Long, often tiring rides, but ones touched with the glamour of the unknown. New country was an adventure. It didn't matter if we never encountered a soul along the way – seeing the land itself was enough.

We started off with the sunrise, when the day stretched ahead like a clean page, gold-edged with light, patterned with bird-calls and the clop of hooves. Sputnik bounded and snorted from bush to bush, shying at shadows, while Mort spanked along and Clancy, the packhorse, blundered behind.

There was no track, but Dad, sitting as if he were glued to the saddle, held to some unseen line. Every so often he'd signal with his hand and I'd look ahead to see what he'd spotted, or veer obediently to the right. Under the tilted hat brim, his eyes, pinched half shut, missed nothing. We went in awe of this ability of his – he could read tracks, find water anywhere, steer by the stars. Plain skills anyone could learn, he said, once they made a habit of noticing things. He used these trips to show us secrets we had not discovered for ourselves.

Carmencita country was sandy red loam timbered with ironwood, dark clumps of supplejack, and the pale green froth of flowering whitewood. We passed the dry clay bank of Spook's Hole and the corner where Satin had perished last summer, then came to the gate in the back of the paddock. Beyond was unfenced bush. Expectation tingled through me at the sight of the range, blue-hazed with distance, and the scent of the gusty wind.

Sputnik pranced through the opening, foam dripping from her bit, and made a flying leap from the gate. Dollops of lather creamed the edge of her saddlecloth. I could smell the rank heat of her, mingled with Dad's tobacco and the baked scent of dry earth.

We rode until the shadows fell small, while the ranges crept closer. They seemed to float in the brilliant light, their ochre and orange outline slashed by shadowy gullies. The trees were low-branching, with twisted and knotty trunks, their feet buried in stone. I saw native bees crawling from a hollow in one, and showed Dad. He was pleased.

'You'd get a feed there,' he said. 'We haven't time now, but how'd you get it out without an axe?' He liked to pose problems for us. One day, he said, our lives might depend on nutting out the answer.

I thought about it seriously. He'd told us of the man who'd tried to reach into a high hollow limb by standing on his saddle. The horse had moved under him, and he'd died there, hanging by his trapped arm which his own weight had prevented him from freeing.

'I'd throw my circingle round the trunk and over the first branch, and hang my stirrups off it,' I decided. 'I could stand in them, then, to reach. Then I'd poke a stick down the hollow and dig the honeycomb out.'

'Pretty good.' He waved at a little clump of mulga on the glazed edge of a claypan. 'What d'you reckon – dinner camp?'

There were euros that afternoon, lifting lazy heads to watch us pass. And a wedgetail, great wings outspread, riding the thermals high above us in the blue. Later a perentie scuttled out of the grass, and Sputnik frizzed like a cat, going straight up, with a snort to flatten timber. She came down on rigid legs, every muscle tensed. Mort lopped an ear at the big lizard, but Clancy took off, tail streaming, the pack gear rocking wildly.

'Gormless great fool,' Dad grunted, and I grinned.

That night we camped on a soak Dad made in a creek-bed. There were old brumby scrapes there, and he pulled the shovel off the pack and dug until the water came welling, cold and sweet, through the sand. He let the horses in to drink one at a time, then sank a second, deeper hole beside it, one into which we could dip a billy.

There were other brumby signs about, dried dung in the gum litter along the bank, and tracks, but none of them fresh. Dad belled Sputnik and hobbled her down on the swivel, and she lunged from the camp in awkward hops. The two geldings shuffled placidly after her, feeding as they went.

After supper I took the billy down to the soak for breakfast water. The channel of the creek was a cool tunnel filled with the scent of damp and gum leaves. I crouched in the sand beside the hole and saw a star trembling in the depths of the soak. It vanished as I scooped the billy full, and I waited, watching for its return. The smell of eucalypt was very strong, clean and sharp in my nostrils. Crickets clicked in the sand but fell silent when the dark was split by the sudden howl of a dingo.

My heart jumped and I felt my nape prickle. It wouldn't come near the camp, I knew, but it was comforting to see the glow of the fire over the bank, with the heated air rising like mist above it, and Dad's shape hunched there with the stars sitting on his hat.

The morning brought a wind to flutter shirtsleeves and blow away the flies. Clancy, trotting with his tail blown sideways, trod in a goanna hole and somersaulted.

I roared with glee, the noise sending Sputnik skittering, showing the whites of her eyes.

We'd hear the scraper working in the dam if it wasn't for the wind, Dad said. We could already see the dust smudge above the scrub line. Then, as the clutter of tents and fuel drums came into view, we saw the great yellow vehicle crawling over the torn earth and heard the shattering roar of its diesel engine.

The contractor's name was Harry. He was big and thickset, with stubble and greasy hair. There were two other men, one little and bald with a dirty bandage on his hand, the other a blackfella with quick, sliding eyes and a soft voice. With my jeans and cropped hair they took me for a boy, paying me no attention beyond handing me a pannikin and a slice of brownie. It was speckled with fruit and I bit into it hungrily. Breakfast had been miles back.

Dad told them we were heading for Red Tank, and Harry gave him a letter to deliver. Then he climbed up onto his huge machine and it roared into life again. When I looked back from the top of the rise it was tearing at the bottom of the hole, and the camp was hidden, once again, in a fog of dust.

We had lunch from the waterbag – half a billy for tea and the rest to get us to the Tank. My lips felt tight and dry from the wind. I smeared the fatty selvages of the meat over them and sat back, replete. Mort and Sputnik, tied nearby, drowsed and rattled their bridles at the flies.

The Taylor place was half a mile beyond Red Tank, a sprawling corrugated-iron building with a lawn and trees and a sagging netting fence. We rode up to the gate to the yapping of dogs. There were four of them of the breed Dad called Allsorts – and two sheep, a pet kangaroo, and a boy a bit older than Patrick, but rough and unkempt-looking.

The hinge was broken, so the gate wouldn't open. We climbed over the fence instead, where the boy indicated. There was a sheep yard, with low rails and a race, built up against the far side of the garden. A dozen sheep were camped in it under a big mimosa tree starred with yellow flowers. The boy, whose name was Trevor, stuck his face next to mine.

'We're gunna kill one of 'em, tonight. Me and the old man. Yer grab 'em and stick the knife in and the blood squirts everywhere, buckets of it! Bet yer don't like blood, do yer?'

'Better than stupid kids,' I said and trod heavily on his bare toes with my boot.

Jack Taylor came out with his wife. Dad handed over Harry's letter and she rushed off again calling, 'Melly, there's a letter come, Melly.'

Dad and Jack Taylor were talking. They wandered over to the sheep yard, leaving me behind. The boy was showing off, jabbing his fists at the kangaroo. It didn't like it. It was a big male and made a noise like a curse, rearing upright with its strong forearms hanging over the soft fur of its chest.

Mrs Taylor bustled back then, and clouted him. 'He'll get yer one day, Trevor, an' serve yer right. It's Kerry, ain't it? I seen yer round with yer dad. How old are yer, Kerry?'

I said I was thirteen and she beamed, looking me up and down.

'I tole me gels you was. Just getting yer figure, an' all.' I squirmed and went red. She laughed, a loud, fat woman in a dirty pinny. ''S'orl right, dearie. Gels blossom at your age, boys turn inter louts – I should know, had four of 'em meself. Come an' siddown. Me gels'll bring the tea, soon as Mell's read her letter. She's marryin' him, y'know – Harry Wharton, the dam-sinker. When she turns seventeen, 'er dad said, 'n' not a day sooner. Ain't hardly a month orf, now.'

We had tea in the garden under an old pepper tree. There was a rickety table, its fourth leg propped on a brick, and an assortment of chairs. A shaft of sunlight speckled with dust motes shone on a pink seersucker cloth and crockery. There were scones and a date cake on a flowered plate with a gold rim, just like the one I used to wash at Gran's place.

'Pretty, ain't it?' Mrs Taylor turned it admiringly. ''S'orl what's left o' the set. They was a wedding present.'

The roo crawled to the table and swiped a scone, and I watched, astonished, as Jack Taylor poured tea into his saucer, then lifted it to his mouth and sucked it out again.

Sarah told me that the two pet sheep were called True Love and All Shook Up.

'Why?' I said and she stared.

'You don't know about Elvis?' She was dumbfounded. 'You're kidding!'

'No.'

Her arms were plump and white against her blue dress. I stuck my grubby hands out of sight under the table. Melly's nails were painted pink and her breasts were round as oranges. I could see the top of them in the neck of her dress. Even Sarah, who wasn't quite fifteen, had a chest that stuck out like a pouter pigeon's. I hid my boots under my chair and rubbed at the grass stain Mort had slobbered on my shirt. Melly told me about her wedding dress and then there was nothing left to say. They knew nothing about horses and they weren't interested in sheep.

'Smelly, stupid things!' Sarah wrinkled her nose. 'Mum reckons your dad's gunna buy 'em, anyway. Be good, that. They wouldn't be hanging round the place at the wedding, then.'

Melly was pretty in a fat sort of way. I thought of Harry's baggy eyes and big yellow teeth and wondered why she wanted to marry him. He must have been nearly as old as Jack Taylor himself.

I helped carry the tea things inside and asked Mrs Taylor for the toilet. It was in the bathroom and there, on the wall alongside the shower cubicle, was a spotty full length mirror. I stood before it, staring, seeing myself for the first time in ages – we had no mirror in the camp. A thin, brown girl with knobbly legs and arms stared back at me. Even when I breathed in as hard as I could, it made no difference to my chest. Dad had cut my hair too short on top and it stuck out. My legs were like sticks. I looked ridiculous. I thought of Sarah's full bodice – no one would ever mistake her for a boy.

Dad was packing some paper-wrapped chops into his saddle pouch when I returned. I thanked Mrs Taylor, then we left. Everyone came to the gate to see us off, waving and calling like old friends.

We'd head for Chalmers Soak, Dad said, which would leave us only fifteen miles to do tomorrow.

It wasn't far to the Soak. We washed the horses' backs down

and hobbled them, and later I had a bath under the overflow. When I got back from it, the cockies were winging down creek to roost, rising and falling like tossed paper against the darkening sky. Dad had grilled the chops on the shovel blade.

'Enjoy them,' he said. 'Jack might eat his flock, but we won't be. The only mutton you'll see after this feed will come from goat.'

'Are we going to buy the sheep, then?'

'Yep – what's left, any road. We'll shepherd 'em, cut scrub. Get a mob of nanny-goats. That'll give us meat and milk. We'll have to move outa the station country, o' course.'

'Who's Elvis?' I asked, but he'd dropped the shovel on the fire to burn the grease off and wasn't listening.

～

Mort was cranky next morning. He didn't want to be caught and laid his ears back when I girthed him up. Sputnik stood like a lamb to be saddled and didn't even jump when Dad let the stirrup drop against the flap.

'That's the way,' he patted her neck. 'Your salad days are over, girl.'

We followed the track for the first part of the journey. I had to pick a stick for Mort to keep him up to the red mare's pace, because Dad had pulled his colt-slapper on her. This was a length of supple, folded leather. It stung like a horsefly and she felt it down her shoulder any time she broke stride. I soon had a stitch in my side but never thought of complaining, for this, I knew, was how horses were made.

The morning stretched on, hot and still, before us, then Dad veered off the track and headed bush. We'd cut across the corner of the paddock, save the dog-leg around it.

'How many goats?' I asked, continuing last night's conversation, and he turned up a palm.

'Hundred – two if we can get 'em. I'll see old Wally again. Maybe Box Hill too. They've got a big mob of nannies.'

We already had a dozen goats because Dad had swapped the donkeys for them with Wally Pearson, a pumper at Mt Mary bore. He'd got Trooper, a broken-in grey gelding, in the deal as well. That was six months ago, but they lacked a billy-goat, so no young had been born. I wondered how we'd look after two hundred.

By the time we reached the fence, the shadows had shrunk to midday. There was no gate but Dad undid the ties at several posts, then dropped a log across the wires and we jumped the horses over. My stomach creaked emptily but there were only a few miles to go, so we swung up again and pushed on.

Then at last the mill-wheel came into view, spinning briskly above the tree line. Clancy, his load creaking, trotted ahead, whinnying. And then I could see the end of the bough shed with the wagonette pole sticking out, and the chains hung over it.

Patrick was playing at the tank, making roads with a homemade toy. He saw us and jumped up, but Sputnik didn't even twitch. She made straight for the trough like any other working horse and buried her muzzle in it. I slid down Mort's shoulder, getting a sight across his neck of Judith setting the billy on the fire. Then Sian came to catch Clancy and lead him off, and there was nothing for us to do but unsaddle, wash the horses' backs down, and let them go.

They fed away side by side, then got down to roll in the red sand, kicking vigorously to tip their bodies right over. They clambered up, front end first, and shook themselves, then dropped their heads again to graze.

And standing watching them, my saddle at my feet, I could see no difference now between the red mare and quiet old Mort. Dad had been a fair prophet – her youth had passed. It made her more valuable, but I couldn't help feeling sad.

TWELVE

It rained a little bit the day we took delivery of the sheep. About ten spots, if you caught them all, but a good sign, according to Dad. When I asked him why, he winked in high good humour.

'Might be rehearsing for the real thing.'

I didn't think so. I had never felt drier or hotter. We'd been all day collecting and counting the sheep and getting them down to Red Tank where we were to camp that night. There were five hundred and twenty, including a handful of half-grown lambs, all in a weakened condition. We'd have to battle for them till it rained, Dad said. There should have been a thousand in the flock, but Taylor had let half of them die from neglect when a bit of effort could have pulled them through. Drought and dogs had done for the grown sheep, while the wedgetails had got the bulk of the lamb drop.

Weak or not, they were aggravatingly stupid animals. It took hours just to get them clear of Taylor's tumbledown fences and through the mulga to Red Tank. We were grazing them across the flats between the Store and the riverbank when an old ewe tripped over a root of a huge dead gum and tumbled into the hole the tree had once filled. I waited for her to get up but she just lay there, kicking feebly on a bed of drifted leaves.

Dropping Drummer's rein, I slid down into the hole, expecting her to bolt, but she didn't move. Her dirty brown wool was surprisingly deep. I got a two-handed grip and heaved, but it was like pulling on the fallen gum. Her legs hung limp and she made no effort to help herself.

Sian came then, still carrying the twig of whitewood he'd been using to switch at the flies. He was feeling good, and just to be funny grabbed the sheep's head and stuck the twig in her mouth.

'Hang on to that, for a tic,' he said, and made a grab at her shoulders, but the ewe jumped up and took off, shaking her head violently until the whitewood fell out.

'Mono-minded, see?' Sian was grinning.

'What?'

'It means single – like a mono-winged plane.' Sian had been into making model planes at Renmark. 'Sheep can't think of two things at once, so, when they sulk, stick something in their mouths. Smart, eh?'

'No.' I was cross. I was hot and tired and thirsty, and I wished I was back under the trees in the Taylor's ramshackle garden, with as little to do as Sarah. She'd been painting her nails when we were there, plump and cool in a gingham dress, worlds away from dust and heat.

At lunchtime, when Dad sent me in to help Mrs Taylor, she was sitting down in the walkway between the bathroom and the kitchen, languidly fanning herself.

'Ta, dearie,' she said when I offered to slice up the bowl of cold potatoes she had waiting on the sink. 'I'd be that glad of a hand. Melly's in gloves till the wedding, and Sarey's got her flow today, ain't yer, pet?'

'Pardon?' I hadn't understood.

'Her monthlies, dearie. Why, ain't yer started yet? I would've thought –'

'Oh, yes. Of course.' I grabbed hurriedly at a potato. 'D'you want them chopped, or just halved?'

'Halved'll do. When did yer start, then? Both my gels were early, but it doesn't always foller.'

'Last year.' I wished women weren't so alarmingly inquisitive.

'And did yer dad talk to yer, dearie? Not that a man could know much about it, I reckon.'

'I read a book,' I said hastily. 'When I was eleven. We had this friend – Mrs Fields. She got me a book and some . . . things. Judith read it too. Shall I put the spuds on the plate with the meat?'

'Yeah, do. I'll chop a few h'onions in vinegar – don't you go eating none, Sarey. Did yer book tell yer that? Yer shouldn't take nothin' sharp like vinegar or lemon with yer flow. Nor hot baths – only makes the cramps worse.'

'I'll remember.'

I didn't have to worry about hot baths, I thought, climbing back on Drummer to follow the sheep. We showered straight out of the stock tanks, either standing under the overflow or using a siphon hose hooked over the tank rim, with a flat stone or bit of tin to stand on. Dad had made up a canvas screen fixed to trimmed saplings which we just rolled up when we shifted camp.

∾

It was dark by the time we got the unfamiliar sheep-break sorted out. This was a yard made entirely out of knotted ropes and pulled taut around steel pegs. When the gate section was closed and tied off, we led our horses back to the lean-to, where the packs were, and unsaddled. The wagonette and the rest of the plant were back at Carmencita. Dad was going to fetch them when we got the flock to Chalmers Soak – we'd have to rough it till then, he said.

Sian was hobbling up, Patrick was already flaked out on the pile of swags. I felt cross and dirty and disenchanted with everything. A fat spot of rain struck my cheek and I wanted to scream at the sullen sky. I wished I was Sarah Taylor in a lamplit room, with a mother to fuss over me and worry about whether I took hot baths. It was nearly two years since we'd left Sydney and in all that time I hadn't once sat in a real bathtub in a proper bathroom.

It didn't rain that night, but it was early morning before the cloud cleared and the air cooled. Patrick, who often talked and sometimes walked in his sleep, spent a restless night hoying at sheep and getting up to find his bridle. He was overtired, Dad said. He himself was up, with the fire lit, before Sian went after the horses, and the sheep were out of the break and on their way by dawn.

It was a long slow day's work getting to the Soak. The first of many. We eventually settled into a camp in sand-ridge country, a mile or two beyond Chalmers Soak. We tailed the sheep there, collecting them up every afternoon for the wearying trek into the trough. They were very weak, and if you bustled them, half a dozen would fall and lie kicking feebly, held down by the weight of their wool.

Dad and Sian cut scrub and we let them range as far as they could walk. Dad got a couple of bags of grain for the horses, packing them on Polly. We fed only those we were working, but the condition on all of them was slipping away.

'What'll we do if it doesn't rain?' I worried one day, plodding in behind the flock. We'd begun to carry the lambs across our pommels to save them the energy-sapping drag to the water.

'It will,' Dad said.

Another 200-odd wethers turned up on the property next to the Taylors', and the owner delivered them to us in his stock truck. Then the goats Dad had been dickering for arrived, a sea of shaggy-coloured coats, black and blue and tawny and white, with wedge-shaped faces and knowing, yellow eyes. Judith and Patrick and I named all two hundred of them, from Jimmy-Jack, the biggest wether, down to Fairy and Sprite, the smallest twins.

The sheep-break wouldn't hold them. They climbed through and under it with ease, but we belled the wethers and after that, when Sian got up grumbling with the morning star to find his horses, Judith and I rose to go after the goats.

Eventually it rained. Just drizzle at first out of banked grey skies, then heavy set-in rain that beat on the canvas all night and soaked into the dry timbers of the old Queen. An hour before dawn, with the roar of it undiminished, Dad opened the break and chased the sheep out, slapping them along with his hands.

'What y'doing?' Sian asked blearily.

'Getting them out. They can pile up and smother each other if it's wet enough.'

'They'll clear out.'

'Nah. Isn't a sheep born with that much brain. Brrr!' Dad rubbed himself in the dark, and I heard his boots squelch as he pulled them off. 'We can give over cutting scrub, any road.'

Dawn broke wet and cold over a sodden world. The trees dripped steadily, and the spinifex rings looked greener already. When the horses came in, we rode out to find the sheep and spent the day tailing as usual, dripped on alternatively by clouds and trees.

The skies cleared that night, and next day we pulled the fly back and let the camp steam dry in the sun. Everywhere you looked the ground was furred with green where the nine-day grass was coming through. Give it a week, Dad said, and we'd be in clover.

'We going to stop here now?' Sian asked.

Dad shook his head. 'Couple of weeks till they strengthen, that's all. Old Merv's given us a fair crack o' the whip. We'll repay the favour by moving on. We'll have to be looking at shearing soon, too. Well, it'd be a dull world with nothing to do.'

∽

There was gidyea at Karuba bore. We made camp in the middle of it, and Dad built a three-sided goat yard out of fallen tree trunks.

Jean snigged them in, broad haunches flattering to the pull, then we all helped crowbar and lift them into place.

Gidyea was an awkward bitch with all those lateral branches, Dad said. He was right. I hated the stink of its blossom – like a bad smell at the back of your nose – and the hairy grey spiders that lurked on its bark. It was difficult firewood too. Slow to catch, heavy to lift, tough to chop. Axe-blades lost their edges just standing next to it.

Grass never grew under gidyea, but in a bit of a clearing just beyond the camp, dozens of dead sticks thrust out of the gravelly ground. We were yanking them up when Dad, coming past with another log, made us put them back. They were blackfella grave markers, he said, and ought to be treated with the same respect as Christian crosses – or would we chop them up for firewood too?

It was May. Shearing time. The nights were growing chilly, and the yellow bobbles of gidyea blossom carpeted the camp. You could only get free of the smell of it out on the windy ridges with the flock, where the green feed now sprang fetlock-deep. Dad and Sian had cut scrub until the rain came, the sheep following the sound of the axes thunking standing timber. The goats, with their greater agility, had climbed any tree with a lean on it, but now with the new grass there was plenty for all.

Karuba bore was only recently equipped. Dad carted a load of rails and built some catching pens next to the trough, and a frame for a sorting table and shearing floor. It was red sand at the bore-head, so each day he flooded it to hold the dust down. Next he lifted the boards off the bed of the wagonette to make his floor. Then he stretched wire netting over the table frame, set up the old lever press we'd acquired, and got the portable shearing stand into position. We were ready to start.

The weather got colder as the sheep-pads leading out through the gidyea deepened. At night the goats stayed longer in the shelter of their pen, and the horses' coats were furry as bears'.

'Hard winter coming,' Dad said.

My teeth twinged on cold mornings, little shooting pains that felt like I was biting on the points of the frosty stars hanging over the gidyea. It seemed a crazy time to be depriving the sheep of their wool.

The first fleece we took came off old Camelneck, an ancient ewe that fell one day while negotiating a gully. She kicked a few times, then just lay there, apathetic as a stuffed animal. She was wood-poor under the wool. Dad spread his saddlecloth, took the hand-shears from their scabbard under his quart pot, then set her up on her rump against his knees and began.

Afterwards I carried the bulging load of greasy wool back to the bore on Jody. There Dad showed me how to throw and skirt the fleece. He put the topknot in one bag and the skirtings in another. He dropped the fleece in the press and said, 'Know who's got a fair-sized flock? It's the bloke can press a bale of topknots. Don't think we'll be doing that, somehow.'

I laughed until my jaw stabbed with sudden pain. We had seven hundred and thirty-three sheep and twenty lambs. The tufts of wool from a sheep's head would fill half a sugar bag, if they were loosely packed.

We started properly the next day. There was no gate on the main pen so Judith and I blocked the entrance while Dad and Sian caught half a dozen sheep and hauled them over the rails into the smaller pen. They were wethers – big, full-wool merinos, very heavy and very strong. Patrick grabbed a double handful of sheep too. Sian, red-faced from exertion, yelled at him.

'Get out of it! You can't do that.'

'Can so!'

The wether raced across the pen. When it hit the rails, Patrick let go of the wool and went for its horns. The sheep rammed through his legs and took off again with Patrick's head bobbing above his tail. It ran straight into Dad.

'Good one, son,' he said, and dumped it over the rails. 'Righto.' He waved at Judith and me. 'Take 'em away. That'll keep us busy enough.'

From then on, every day was the same. Catching sheep for the pens at sunrise, then the engine would start and, as the flock fed away, Dad would pull the first one onto the board and dig the handpiece into the wool. Sian learned to do one side – but always the same one, because Dad's back would knot up just at that point.

After the first week Sian said he didn't care about not learning how to do the rest of the sheep. He wasn't planning on being a shearer anyhow.

Patrick was rouseabout and skirter – which meant he had to pull off the dirty, pill-stained wool – but he couldn't reach high enough to bale the fleece. Sian did that. And when the bale was full, we all helped swing on the lever to press it. Our hands grew soft, and Judith's hair, which was brown with red points in it, started to curl. It was the lanolin in the wool, Dad told us, that did it. The stuff beat ointment and curlers by a country mile.

One day, Quentin Meadows, the dogger, turned up at Karuba with his wife and rattly old Bedford truck. He'd come to give us a hand, he said. He made camp at the bore, on the edge of the damp ground that Dad was still flooding every morning.

We kids liked Quent, even though he was simple. His truck was full of traps, half-cured dingo scalps, and pongy bottles containing his secret lure mixture. He wouldn't tell anyone what was in it, but it worked like a charm. Dogs used to queue up for his traps – dying for a sniff of it, Dad said. We tried to explain the joke to Quent but he couldn't get it.

Mrs Meadows' name was Etty. She was lined and brown, with frizzy grey hair, and looked as tired and used up as the dog scalps. She never talked much but she kept a neat camp. She always had a thatched firescreen and a twig broom for sweeping the ground clean around their tent. And her sugar and salt tins were polished enough to blind you.

Next day, while Dad was trying to teach Quent how to engage the clutch on the handpiece without stalling the engine, Mrs Meadows made us toffee. She set it in a big enamel pie plate, then broke it up with a hammer. It was waiting for us at dinner camp – bubbly, amber chunks sweeter than nectar.

That's how I got the toothache. I bit down on the sharp edge of a chunk of toffee and my head exploded with a pain I couldn't get rid of. It was inside my face like a hammer on a drum, throbbing in time to my pulse. Dad said it was a decayed molar and I'd broken through to the nerve. He twisted a bit of wool around a match and dabbed some oil of cloves on it. My gum burned afterwards because I'd jerked when he touched the tooth, but it helped dull the pain.

The rest of the shearing was terrible. All I could think about was the flaring agony in my jaw. Sometimes it stopped for a time, as if it had got tired and gone to sleep. When this happened I'd try not to wake it, not to get cold air in my mouth, or drink anything hot. Not to chew, or jolt my head.

When it got unbearable, Dad put more oil of cloves on it. And on the worst days Sian took my place with Judith, while Dad tried to keep his temper with Quent. He'd rather have a toothache himself, he said, than put up with much more of his help.

Half the flock was shorn by this time and the sheep presented a strange appearance spread across the green sand ridges. Even the frosty dawns, when their breath smoked in the cold air, didn't worry the fleeceless animals. Cold ached in our chilblained fingers and stung our noses and ears, but they still rushed, leaping in follow-the-leader patterns, when Dad counted them out of their rope enclosure. He counted by fours and threes and sixes as fast as they came, while Sian or I tallied the hundreds as he called them. We kept track with a handful of pebbles, dropping one into our shirt pocket each time he yelled, 'Hundred!' Real sheepmen, Dad said, could count three separate runs of sheep simultaneously and yell at the dog as well.

At sunset each day we drove the flock past the bore to collect those sheep shorn that afternoon and return them to camp with the rest. Then there were still the horses to hobble in the chilly dusk, and goats to milk. The carbide light flared a halo of radiance over the table as we ate and washed up, then we tumbled thankfully into our swags which were spread on bag stretchers. Since Quent had arrived, the nights had been silent. He had trapped or scared off every dingo within cooee, so that now only the wind sounded under the gidyea, or an owl's wings above it.

Except for the night I heard the singing.

My tooth had been very bad all day. Fiery lances of pain pulsed through it until the whole side of my face was hot and puffy. Sian went out with the sheep, and when Dad came home that night he heated a shovelful of coarse salt in the camp oven, then rolled it in a towel for me to hold against my cheek. It helped a bit. I was shivery one minute under the blankets and hot the next. My eyes burned and the blood thudded, slow and heavy, in my ears.

I dozed and woke and dozed again as the hours passed. Finally I was fully awake, cold all over and with a horrid taste in my mouth. The pain had subsided to a dull throb and the heated towel was chilly and lumpy beneath my jaw. I pulled the blankets tight around me, tucking my chin down into them, and that was when the spider ran over my face.

I hit out blindly and jumped from the bed. The ground was like ice under my feet and I trembled – from fright as much as the freezing air. I hated spiders. As stiff as a hackled dog, I backed out of the fly. It might be anywhere, on the blankets, or running into my boots. I grabbed the army greatcoat Sian wore horse-tailing and went over to squat by the fire.

There were only embers left but it didn't matter. Gidyea coals gave off a radiant heat that lasted for hours. Hunched into the coat, I spread my hands above them and felt warmth gradually suffuse me.

I think the singing started then – or perhaps it was just no longer masked by the sound of my teeth chattering.

It was faint at first, and only after I lifted my head to look, and saw the flame of the other fire, did it become clearer. It wasn't a big fire, but it wasn't that far off either – somewhere over the other side of the clearing. It flickered and vanished, then flickered again, a small flame that swelled and died as the voices did. Then, under the pale starlight, I saw the shape of moving figures and realised that the dancers were blocking the light.

As my eyes grew accustomed to the darkness, details became clearer, like a picture emerging from shadow. I saw limbs and naked breasts and hands clapping thighs to the beat of the wailing song. An old man led the singing. Clad in skins, he sat just apart from the rest, plying clapping sticks before some upright object stuck into the ground. In front of him the dancers moved, torsos and shoulders outlined in white. Feather crests grew out of their hair and leafy bracelets encircled each limb.

They were as real as the throb in my jaw, the heat of the embers against my skin. Smoke curled into the starlight and dust lifted under moving feet. I saw the slinking form of a dog nosing a sleeping child, and all the time the rise and fall of the song, with its incomprehensible words and melody, plucked at me. They danced the rushing wind fetching the clouds from afar. And the thunder spirit storming through them. They danced the hush of the waiting bush and the terror of the blazing light splitting the pregnant belly of the sky. I saw the rain pelting down and the draggled ears and hunched shape of wallabies in the wet. A goanna in the flooded gully and emu tracks on the wet claypan. I was wide awake, and I knew they couldn't be real. The old man hawked and spat, shifting his grip on the clapping sticks, then the whole scene vanished. The singing stopped, the fire died. Behind me, Dad's voice was as loud as a shout.

'What are you doing there in the cold, Kerry?'

'Just watching. They were singing. Old blackfellas. Did you hear them?'

'Hear what?' He peered at me. 'You've been dreaming. How's your face?'

'It's all right, now. I wasn't asleep.' I yawned. 'The dancers looked like wind and clouds – you wouldn't think they could, but they did. And the old man must've been a hundred. There was –'

'You can tell me in the morning,' he said. 'Back to bed now.' And because the dancers had made me forget the spider, I went.

～

In the morning Dad insisted I'd dreamed it all. While the sheep were being let out, I rode over to the far side of the clearing, trying to find where the fire had been. But there was no ash, and only goat tracks showed around and between the grave markers.

My tooth stopped aching altogether soon after. There was a hole in the gum below it. Dad said an abscess must have burst there and told me to wash my mouth every day with salty water, until it healed.

When we had only fifty sheep left to shear, Quent took a message to Red Tank for the carrier to come for the wool. Mrs Meadows boiled up some wattle bark and boot polish to make a dye, and Dad cut a stencil out of a golden syrup carton lid, and we branded the bales. Shearing was over.

We pulled down the pens at the bore and refloored the old Queen, but we left the goat yard standing among the gidyea when we moved on.

THIRTEEN

We were breakfasting in the half-light of dawn, eating chops as usual, when Dad suddenly chucked the rest of his to Larry.

'I'm sick o' goat,' he said, swallowing down his tea. 'A man'll be bleating himself next. I'm gunna get us some beef.'

'How?' Sian asked, not as though he really wanted to know, more as if he were reminding Dad that the closest station boundary was at least a hundred miles away.

Dad just gave him a look. 'You'll see.'

We were camped just north of Bonya bore, tucked discreetly out of sight of the road behind a couple of low hills. No sense advertising our presence, Dad said. Travelling stock were supposed to travel, although this was vacant crown land with no leaseholder to worry us. We hadn't seen a soul for months, but that didn't mean the next caller wouldn't be a stock-route inspector intent upon moving us on.

The sheep flock on the trough at Paradise Bore, 1958.

The two youngest. Patrick with Skimpy's four-week foal, 1959.

Wagonette and team at the Serpentine Crossing of the Georgina River, 1960; me on the driver's seat.

My father ('Dad'), Pat McGinnis, known to all as Mac, 1960.

Coming out of the Georgina. Me on the seat, Sian's face visible past my legs, 1960.

Judith at Grassy Bore, Ardmore Station, with Confetti and Keepsake, two young fillies, 1961.

Part of the plant at the Rockhole, Splitrock Station, 1962.

Patrick on Yerra, 1962.

Rockhole, Splitrock Station, with truck in background, 1962.
Left to right *Judith, Patrick, Dad.*

Packhorses ready for the road, Redwater Yards, 1963.

Packmare Ninka carrying tucker boxes and beefbucket,
Redwater Yards, 1963.

Plant horses – Darkie, Prudence, Wombol, Token, Belle and
Shuffler – in the Gregory River, Gulf Country, 1965.

Patrick on Peso, during droving trip, 1964.

Judith with Carol. Patrick, half-visible, is packing the mare, 1966.

Me with Carmen, 1966.

Patrick packing a horse (Juggler), Old Station Yards, Gregory, 1966.

Beyond the camp the country ran back in a broad valley to the base of the Dulcie Ranges. Bonya Creek came down on the eastern side, shallow, like all the desert creeks, but widening out where it crossed the valley. The mill and tank stood beside it, the great wheel turning above the gums. The steel trough, a hundred feet long, thrust out onto the red flat where roly-poly tumbled and at night the brumbies came to drink. Often we'd hear them snorting and trotting in the dark and next day see their tracks on the pads their feet had cut. Sometimes they got among the plant and then Dad would ride out with the rifle. After that they'd vanish for a week or so and we'd know they had moved away to another water.

There was no need to rig the break. Dad had found a huge dump of empty 44-gallon bitumen drums which he carted, a dozen at a time, back to the camp. There, by standing them in a large circle with a foot of dirt thrown into the bottom of each to add weight, he made a roomy yard in which we enclosed the sheep at night. The goats we milked and let go. They always came back, and they could give Ed Hilary points in climbing, Dad told us, so a few forty-fours wouldn't hold them.

Goats were the battler's friend, we knew. They gave us meat and milk and made surrogate mothers for orphaned lambs – but we did get sick of endless goatmeat. On the stations, beef could be got for the asking, but this wasn't cattle country.

'There's cattle here, all the same,' Dad said. 'As you'd know if you used your eyes. There's a mob of scrubbers watering at the bore.'

A thrill of excitement shot through us. We'd long been familiar with the tales of his scrubber-running days in the Dawson Valley, so we knew man-shy cattle were no pushover. They had the ears of a fox, the nose of a bloodhound, and heels of the wind. You didn't just ride out and muster them, and we waited expectantly to hear what Dad had in mind.

It turned out to be ambush. After breakfast, he saddled Rose and rode out to locate the scrubbers. He was gone until nightfall. The moon, which was full that night, had just cleared the creek timber when we heard Rose crossing the gravel towards camp. She was a six-mile-an-hour walker, a pace she could maintain all day, so they'd covered some ground since morning.

Dad was hungry but pleased with himself. He'd found the scrubbers' other watering place, a spring in the ranges at the head of a gully, which grew into a tributary of Bonya Creek. Plenty of cover for the horses and ample room in the rocks to lay up with a rifle and wait for them. There were fresh tracks on the well-used pads leading into the spring and signs that the cattle often camped there in the edge of the scrub.

He finished the cold meat and rice pudding we'd saved for him and sent us back to our swags. We'd need an early start tomorrow, he said, but he could as good as taste the beef.

Next day he and I rode out with a packhorse. Sian had been going to come too, but there were horses missing which he had to stay behind and find. I led Dumpy the packhorse, Dad rode Simon, his big skewbald, and I had Mort. I'd started with Spider but he sent me back to change her.

'Where's your sense?' he said. 'You couldn't sneak up on a statue with that noisy bitch.' She did whinny a lot because she had a yearling colt in the plant.

We crossed the valley and headed into the hills, with the shadows falling to our left. Gravel ridges followed the grassland, then broken gullies and outcropping rocks.

As the sun rose and we twisted deeper into the range, following some map in Dad's head, the air smelled of spinifex and the woody aniseed stems the horses' hooves crushed in passing. We saw birds and a lizard or two, passed euros feeding on the slopes or at rest under the prickly conkaberry bushes, but that was all. Once we came upon a cattle-pad, looped like a thin ribbon across a gully, but Dad motioned me urgently to one side. He had pocketed his pipe when we entered the range and stopped talking. Riding behind him, dragging Dumpy when she balked at the rough bits, I could tell what to do by his hand signs.

The spring was deep in the hills, a sort of basin sheeted with black stone through which the water welled into shallow pools. The scrub grew to the edge of it and the black rock reared up on three sides like a smooth curved wall. There was a shelf about eight feet up, itself overhung by another leap of black stone, the front of it screened by the twisted arms of a gum growing at its foot behind the spring. We climbed onto the shelf. Dad boosted me up, handed me the rifle, our lunches and water bottles, then shinnied up himself, straddling the tree limb to do so. We made ourselves comfortable in the shade of the overhanging rock and there we stayed until late afternoon.

I was weary of it long before then. Unable either to talk or move about, I found the day endless. I watched the birds – finches, wagtails, budgerigars – come to drink. Then a wildcat with sunken head and body slunk to the water's edge. Later, euros appeared and a dingo. Dad levelled the rifle at him but didn't shoot. That was when

I noticed that the rocks at the side where the cat had first appeared were covered with drawings. Pictures of hands, mostly, and kangaroos with patterned innards.

I wanted a closer look at them, but when Dad finally quit he was too grumpy to wait.

'You've seen that stuff before,' he said, yanking Simon's girth tight. 'And we've wasted enough time already. Somethin' must've put the wind up 'em or they'd have come in.'

He was right – something had. It was late when we got back. The sheep were yarded and Sian had just finished hobbling up. He pulled the pack off Dumpy while Dad and I unsaddled and said offhandedly, 'Well, I found 'em.'

'I hope so,' Dad carried his saddle over to the rail.

'Not the horses.' Sian was scornful. 'I mean, I found the cattle. Followed them for ages, right until they split up. They never even knew I was there.'

'Jesus, Mary and Joseph!' Dad roared, strangling his pipe. 'What'd I ever do to deserve you? So they never saw you or smelt you blundering around behind 'em? But they split up, yer said, which means they did. And I spend six hours squatting like a shag on a bloody rock while they're making holes in the horizon! Who d'you think yer are, Davy Crockett?'

Sian was abashed. Dad stumped away swearing, and the evening meal was a silent one. Nobody complained about goat or mentioned beef. And there were no squabbles about the washing up.

Dad had a quick temper but he got over it quickly, too. You just had to give him space.

For a couple of days after that nothing happened. Sian's horse came back without him one day, but it turned out he wasn't hurt or lost. He hadn't even been thrown – the mare, a chestnut called Tassle, had simply broken the reins and cleared out when he tied her up for a moment. It was the second time she'd done it. Dad said it was a habit that could have fatal consequences for her rider, and one that needed curing.

He put hobbles and a greenhide headstall on her, leading the rope down through the middle ring of the hobble-chain. Then he slipped a bridle over her ears, tied the rope around the trunk of a sturdy mulga, and hooked the reins up to a slender branch. Tassle stood docilely. She was quiet enough, a pretty, light-boned creature with a golden mane and tail. Pulling away was her only vice. She blew softly through her nostrils, lopping one ear our way, as if wondering what it was all about.

'What if she breaks her neck?' Sian fretted.

'Then she won't leave you some day in hundred-degree heat, thirty miles from water,' Dad said. 'Better her death than yours.'

Sian scowled, unconvinced, just as Tassle made a bid to escape. She plunged away, the reins whipped free, and her hobbled legs shot up the rope and smacked her under the chin. She toppled onto her side, thrashed around, then scrambled snorting and trembling to her feet.

Dad hooked the reins up again. 'She'll get the message,' he said. And she did.

A week later the scrubbers returned to the bore. Dad found their tracks at dawn, a row of twin crescents in the soft dust of the creek-bank, when he rode out to check his traps. His enthusiasm for beef instantly rekindled.

'No messing about this time,' he declared. 'We'll cart our swags down to the bore tonight and camp. Take turns at watching, and I'll shoot one on the trough. 'S lucky there's still a fair bit o' moon.'

Towards sunset we put the packs on Clancy and Dumpy, trussed the five swags across them, and led the horses the half-mile down to the bore. Once round the hill, we could no longer see the camp and sheep yard. The ground was churned with tracks and the feed eaten down, but the cattle must gradually have grown accustomed to it and to the rattle of horsebells over the weeks we had camped there.

It was dark by the time we were settled in a patch of scrub on the creek-bank, downwind of the trough. Dad arranged a pack-tree to serve as a rest for the .303. He placed knives, axe and beef bags beside it, then flipped the backsight up on the rifle, squinting down it to work out the distance.

The moon would be up around midnight, he said. Judith, being youngest, could take the first watch. I was to be next, then Sian. We were to keep our eyes on the trough and wake Dad quietly if the cattle came.

With that all settled, Patrick then demanded to be allowed to watch too.

'Okay,' Dad said. 'You can watch with me, then Judith. We'll call her when you get sleepy. Crawl over here.'

We lay down then, listening to the creak and clank of the mill pumping and the sough of the wind in the gums. Patrick was soon asleep. I heard Dad pulling a blanket over him and rousing Judith before I drifted off myself.

It was still dark when Judith woke me. The evening star had

gone, but the pointers to the Southern Cross blazed like diamonds. I felt wide awake and peered intently at the trough, hoping I'd be the first one to spot the scrubbers. Far up the valley the horsebells tonged softly. A curlew cried from the creek, and I heard the *thump! thump!* of a euro's feet. They stopped suddenly and I pictured him erect in the sand, ears turning, nose lifted to our scent.

Time passed slowly, broken only by the small night sounds – the thin squeaking of bats, the *whoosh* of a night bird's wing. I stared so hard at the trough I began to imagine shapes beside it. But if I glanced away for a moment, they'd vanish, so I knew they weren't real. The others breathed softly around me, and Patrick chuckled in his sleep. When the moon's lambent glow silvered the tips of the creek gums, I poked Sian.

'Anything?' he whispered.

'Not yet.' I lay down and fell instantly into sleep.

The shot sounded like cannon fire. Sian woke with a yell, and the rest of us shot upright, heads ringing. The moon was far over towards morning, the trough and flat clearly visible in its cold light. We could hear Dad swearing as he lowered the rifle.

'Didja hit it?' Sian, on his knees, peered around for the fallen beast.

'Go back to sleep,' Dad said, disgusted. 'I shot the bloody thing in a dream. Must've dropped off for a minute. Saw it clear as print – a young, broken bally cow. Just there, on the creek-bank. But if they ever were within five miles o' the joint, they won't be back now.'

He struck a match, looking for his pipe, and Sian said, 'Uh – whereabouts on the bank?'

'What's it matter?' Dad snapped. Then we all heard the chugging gurgle of falling water. 'Jesus, God!' he moaned. 'A man can't do anything right!'

At daybreak we rolled our swags and walked back to camp. Sian got the horses in while I cooked the chops. Then Judith and Patrick and I went out with the sheep while Dad and Sian spent the morning cutting a patch from a forty-four lid and bolting it over the hole he'd shot in the tank.

Next evening we killed another goat. Beef, for the time being anyway, was off the menu at Bonya bore.

FOURTEEN

Paradise was seventy-odd miles south-east of Karens Creek station, a government bore set down in a shallow basin of some nameless range. Blackfella country, Dad said, as we rode through the stirrup-high growth between spreading shade trees and clumps of whitewood.

'How can you tell?' I asked, and he pointed to old axe scars in a bloodwood's bark, and the hole high in its trunk.

'Cut with a tommy'awk, see? Last year, maybe. Blackfellas been climbing that tree for honey. There's bark strips gone off the bean tree there, too. That'd be the women, looking for grubs, or maybe they just wanted something to twist into string.'

'P'raps they'll come back,' I said.

Then we reached the trough, and Dad stared about while the horses drank, giving the place the once-over and picking a campsite.

It was November. Hot and dry, with the yellowed feed crunching like sand underfoot and the horizon given over to aqueous mirages. The sun burned down from a dusty sky, and by midday everything, from Dad and the stock to Normie my tabby kitten, sought the shade.

Only not the same piece of shade. Dad didn't believe in cats. Natural killers, he called them, and Normie had only lasted because I had the wit to keep him hidden for the three days after old Grader Jack gave him to me 'way back at Red Tank until my birthday arrived. Dad had muttered a bit when he found out, but the cat was still with us, along with the goats, the sheep, the horses and the dogs.

We backed the wagonette in under the bean trees in the curve of the creek, and, there being no other stock to worry about, set up the sheep-break behind the double tanks at the bore. The camp was moated about like an island. The creek, no more than a steep, dry gully, choked with old debris, looped about three sides of it, enclosing a girth-high expanse of swamp growth as lush as anything we'd seen since the last rain. There were stands of wild hibiscus, a forest of bean trees coming into bud, and feed so thick it took the horses days to flatten walking paths through it to the trough.

After the weeks of dust and heat, it was like tumbling suddenly into fairyland. The black shade of the bloodwoods rested the eyes, and plovers piped in the sedge of the overflow, where scarlet dragonflies darted on gauzy wings. The stock settled happily into a routine of long dinner-camps and we combined our shepherding duties with a thorough exploration of the country surrounding the bore.

It was Judith who found the blackfella cache in the hollow blood-wood. She'd climbed up into the fork of the tree to see how far the flock had got, and immediately spotted the bundle wedged into the white-ant-eaten hollow. It was wrapped in wallaby hide that was thin and supple from use, and when we opened it there were two flat bits of carved wood with pointed ends, each one tied to the other with twisted strands of human hair.

The bundle had a strange, musky smell – of smoke and animal fats and darkness. It made me uneasy and I glanced around quickly, as if its owner might suddenly appear. I wished we hadn't touched it.

'Put it back,' I urged.

'Why? Finders keepers. Anyway, they chucked it away.'

'They didn't. They hid it. Dad says this is blackfella country. So they'll come back for it. Maybe it's a special tree you're not supposed to climb, like a spirit place or something. It's giving me the creeps, Judith. Put it back.'

Reluctantly she did as I asked. 'We coulda kept it,' she grumbled.

But Dad, when we told him, said we'd done the right thing. I was glad, and even more so a few days later when a band of fifteen blackfellas, on walkabout from Karens Creek, turned up at the bore. They drifted in, silent as shadows, a little before sundown – men, women and children. The men carried spears and throwing sticks, the women coolamon and dillybags. The young children were naked; the rest, barefoot and shock-headed, wore dirty cotton clothes. Half a dozen mangy dogs followed them.

They camped opposite us, where the thickets of whitewood provided easy chopping for their gunyahs. They were very shy. The kids ducked out of sight when they saw us at the bore, and the women turned their faces away.

The first morning, two of the men sidled over to wait near the horse camp for Dad to notice them, then asked for meat. He said they could have a goat, if their women brought him some bush tucker.

'Youia, old man,' they said.

They had come 'longa holiday', they said, and night after night as the moon waxed fuller, they sat about their smoky fires, clicking their clapping sticks and singing their wild melodies. Their dogs howled in sympathy, but when Larry forgot himself and tried to join in, Dad threw his boots at him.

'Jesus, Mary and Joseph! That bloke at Karens Creek had his wits about him when he sent 'em away. How much longer's this gunna last?'

None of us knew.

Beanwood was pithy, easy to carve, so Patrick shaped himself a boomerang and made friends with two of the black boys about his size. They played at hunting, sneaking through the scrub looking for wallabies, but it was hard to track anything with the flock coming and going all the time. Then one day they knocked a goanna out of a tree and stunned it enough for one of the men to grab. That was okay, but Patrick's next act was to kill a pair of finches, swiping them off the trough's edge with the flat of his throwing stick. It was pretty skilful aiming, but Dad came down on him like a scrub bull. You killed to eat, he said, not to pass the time.

That was when Dad decided Patrick needed more schooling, because, unlike the rest of us, he'd never been a good reader. Dad dug out and discarded *Growing Roses* and started him off on *Jock of the Bushveld*, our only other book. Patrick hated it, but he plodded through it because he had to. He did his times tables too, for these basics of reading and figuring, Dad said, were the key to anything else he might ever need to learn.

~

In the first week of December, the Aboriginal ceremonies abruptly ceased and something much more dramatic happened.

It was noon when the light first dimmed. I was watering the flock, sitting on Drummer at the trough, when I noticed the blurred edges of the shadows. Puzzled, I stared up at the darkening sky, just as the first wail sounded behind me.

Patrick's friends darted past the tanks then, eyes rolling whitely, and a hullabaloo broke out among the gunyahs. Because something black was eating the sun.

I squinted – then, remembering, relaxed. We'd learned about eclipses in school. The blackfellas hadn't, though, and by the time the shadow had passed over the sun's face, they'd vanished. There were no fires that night, or singing, and at daylight, when the flock went out, only the wind moved in their camp, stirring the cold ash and walking through the empty shelters. Nothing but a torn dillybag was left, and a trail of unpeeled yalka bulbs, spilt from some running woman's coolamon.

After that the weeks oozed stickily by, with only Jock's progress through the Bushveld to mark one day from the next. Dad, who always seemed to know the date, was making plans to shoot a turkey for Christmas dinner when he had an even better idea.

'Ginger beer,' he said, snatching the pipe from his mouth, one dinner-camp. 'We could brew it – here, give us a look at that tuckerbox.' He pawed through it, pulling tins out and muttering the while. 'Sugar, dried fruit, yeast, ginger – bottles! We'll have to get bottles. Righto, kids! We've got the makin's – all I need to finish the job is for you to turn me up a dozen empty bottles. School's out till after Christmas, Patrick. Catch yerself a horse and go looking too.'

'Where?' Judith asked blankly, and Dad gestured largely with his right arm from east to west.

'Old camps. Somebody cut the track in here. Somebody carted the tank 'n' mill and put 'em together. They'd have had sauce, pickles, rum. Find where they camped, then look in their rubbish dump.'

'But even if we do – find some, that is – the caps'll have rotted away,' Sian objected.

'Look, d'you want this beer or not?' Dad stuck his hands on his hips. 'You find the bottles and I'll take care o' the rest.'

Ingenuity being his middle name, we believed him. We scoured the country, recalling the location of every cut stump, every glitter of glass, or axe-marked pole we'd ever noticed. It was funny how you did that, Judith said, filing such stuff away without even realising you were doing it.

'What's ginger beer taste like, anyway?' Patrick asked.

'Oh, sort of prickly and cold. You wouldn't remember, but we used to have it at Gran's. She kept it in the icebox, and you could see all the little sparks rushing up the neck when you opened it.

We always had it at Christmas.' I sighed, remembering the first one after my mother's death, the heaped plates and presents, and grief like a grey pall over the grown-ups. Judith and I had got dolls' prams, over which Gran had wept in a noisy, abandoned way.

'Your dear mother planned to get them ...'

Her bleary eyes begged acknowledgment of her loss, but I'd turned away, hating her tears and hating the smart, fawn pram with its collapsible hood – hating even the monster pudding with its treasure of hidden sixpences.

I didn't like Christmas much, but it was better out here, where there couldn't be a lot of fuss with presents and paper angels and things.

'One of us oughta ride back to Valentine Creek,' Sian said. 'Where the road camp was, remember? Bet there's fifty bottles there in that big dump!'

In the end we got fifteen, all shapes and sizes, with one beauty about seventeen inches tall. Some fancy liqueur bottle, Dad said. He'd spent an afternoon chopping out a sugarbag's nest that the blackfellas had missed. Honey made a better brew than sugar, he said, but it was the wax from the comb he really wanted. Melted over his homemade corks it would produce a perfect, airtight seal.

The beer took a few days to make. Dad brewed it in a bucket, strained it through the back of an old cotton shirt, and sealed the bottles. He laid them tenderly in a box beneath the wagonette, then got Sian to fill it with creek sand. At dusk on Christmas Eve, he said, we'd chuck a bucket of water into it and next day it would be as cold as any fridge could make it.

Christmas morning started like any other, with chores to do — goats to milk, breakfast to cook, horses to tail. Dad went after the plant, heading out before daybreak with his bridle on his arm. He returned in the grey light, bareback on Trooper, driving the other horses, and hooked the grey's reins to a bean tree on the edge of the camp while we hobbled up. The chops were cooked and we were just sitting down to them when the first of the beer bottles exploded.

It wouldn't have mattered if my kitten hadn't been fooling about in the tree Trooper was tied to. But he was. And when the bottle went off like a bomb, Normie leapt in the air, missed his footing, and plummeted down, claws extended, onto Trooper's back.

The grey didn't muck around. He went straight up in a flying buck, that dislodged the cat and tore loose the reins. Then Trooper bolted, kicking and snorting through the camp, bug-eyed with terror. I caught a glimpse of a bristled-up tabby shape flying for the safety of a dead gum in the creek just as Trooper cannoned into the water bucket. Then he barged through the fire, which had sunk to coals, spreading our breakfast to the four winds. Everyone ran to help block him up, and behind us the scattered coals burst into flames in the debris-choked creek-bed.

It was Sian who yelled, pointing to the camp, and we turned to see the creek behind it roaring with fire. It was as red as the bean tree blossoms but a different shade. The boughs nearest to the creek danced with a life of their own, not shared by the further branches, then their leaves crisped and fell.

'Jesus, Mary and Joseph!' Dad bellowed. 'Move, the lot o' yer! Grab the polers. Chuck those swags onto the wagonette!' He scooped up the winkers Sian threw at him and slapped them on Todd. 'Get along the bank there, try and hold it. Jesus! What a turn-up.' He jammed the bay into position and flung the harness onto him. Judith was already bringing Jean, struggling to hang onto her as the plant, frightened by the fire, lunged away with clanging bells.

Sian had yanked a green bough from a whitewood, I grabbed another from the bushes in the firebreak, and we slashed and flogged frantically at the flames threatening to escape out of the creek's channel into the swamp. Nobody had thought of the flock, but they were safe as long as the fire stayed in the creek. Behind us we heard Dad roar, 'Hupp! Jeanie, Todd!' and the crack of the whip mingled with Larry's barking.

There was a second loud report as the turn-out swayed past and a shower of sand stung my neck. Another ginger-beer bottle had burst. The flames seemed to leap at us, long tongues shooting out to lick at the flattened grass stems where the Queen's wheels had rested. Sian dropped his tattered branch and rushed at the sand-filled box lying between the tracks. He grappled one end.

'Give us a hand!' he yelled, face scarlet with heat.

'What?' I gaped at him.

'Help me – you damn-blasted idiot! Throw it on the fire! It's wet, isn't it?'

He was bent over, heaving at it. 'Don't argue! Just damn-do-it!'

Sian only swore in Dad's absence. It was a sign he was in deadly earnest. Obediently I grabbed my end of the box and our Christmas treat sailed into the flames. At once another bottle blew apart in mid-air, with a gratifyingly dampening effect enhanced by the wet sand. The fire must have almost exhausted its fuel, for suddenly, all along the channel, the flames were sinking. The emergency was over.

It had made a mess of the day, though, putting us behind with everything. The tea billy had vanished into the burning creek, so we had to make another before we could start recooking breakfast. The goats, being free agents, had cleared off while the sheep were still in the break, and the camp was all at sixes and sevens.

Christmas dinner, when it came, was very ordinary too – late, undercooked and short on cutlery, for Dad's mad dash with the wagonette had shed half the tuckerbox overboard and we hadn't yet found it all.

'It could've been worse,' he told Sian, who was inclined to grumble. 'We might've lost everything – home, transport, livelihood – and instead, what was the damage? A couple of spoons and forks gone missing, and a mangy cat.'

I'd completely forgotten Normie. Dad's words brought back the picture of him streaking up the dead tree and my heart turned over. The gum stump smouldered blackly – I could see it from where I sat – and what was left of its branches stuck out of the drifts of hot ash in the creek bottom.

I started up, dinner scattering from my overturned plate. 'Normie's dead!' I shrieked.

He wasn't, but we'd put in half a day's grieving before we found him that evening crying under the wagonette. He was furless, raw-footed, his eyes sealed shut and bits of his lips, ears and tail burnt off. We stared, horrified, trying to see how to comfort him without hurting him more.

'Oh, look at his poor little feet!' Judith cried.

'And his eyes.' I felt sick. 'Oh, I wish he wouldn't cry so much!'

'Poor little bugger's a proper mess. I'll knock him on the head.' Dad reached to take him, and though, deep down, we must all have known it was the only merciful thing to do, the thought of anyone handling that tortured flesh was too much. All four of us rounded on him.

'You shan't!'

'He'll get better.'

'I won't let you!'

We cried out furiously, glaring at him.

'It's Christmas!' Patrick said tragically. 'You can't kill things on Christmas Day.' His lip was wobbling – he was very tender-hearted.

Dad tried to argue but he never liked tears and retired, defeated.

We made a nest of soft rags in the hide slung from the back axle and laid Normie in it. It was dark there and as cool as anywhere was. He cried most of that first night. The noise tore at us, but we still wouldn't admit that we should have let Dad put him out of his misery. We fed him milk, and bathed his eyes until the fused lids separated. And on the third day, as I squatted in the cramped space under the wagonette, stroking his head, he purred. Joy blazed through me, not just because he was going to live, but because our instinctive decision to save him had been right. Peering at him in the dim light I saw the faint shadow of new fur on his skin, like a promise of life. He'd look a bit funny with his missing parts, but he'd survive.

I was so happy that for the first time in years I remembered what Christmas was supposed to be like.

FIFTEEN

There was winter rain that year of 1959. It fell ahead of us so that we came onto it after weeks of scrub-cutting and hauling weakened sheep back onto their feet. It made you believe in Heaven, Dad said. But I thought it was more like an emerald sea than harps and clouds.

We could only stare at the greenness of it. We had never seen a colour so intense. It flowed to the limit of vision, lapping at the dark trunks of the trees, shooting vivid tongues into the mouths of gullies at the foot of the Dulcie Range.

Almost overnight the stock picked up. The horses raced onto camp each morning, bucking and farting. Dragon's breath steamed from their nostrils and their bodies smelt sweet from the green feed. Their coats thickened as winter deepened and, horse-tailing of a morning, when the frost crackled underfoot, we'd push our frozen fingers under their manes to ease the pain of chilblains.

Nights were like echo chambers beneath the white brilliance of the stars. The bitter cold seemed to magnify sound. Lying snug under the Wagga blankets Dad stitched for us, we'd listen to the *whoosh!* of mopokes' wings and the distant quavering howls of the dingoes. Sheep would cough and stir in the break, and sometimes the fire would flutter as it hit a pocket of sap. And always, like a song on the wind, came the background ripple of the bells. I loved winter nights – it was getting up with the morning star that was hard.

It was coming up to lambing time and Dad was looking for a place to stop. Somewhere out of the public eye, he said, which made us grin because we'd scarcely seen a soul since the wool went with the carrier, months ago, at Karuba bore. The goats were producing the occasional kid, often giving birth overnight or on the dinner-camp. We'd carry them in the wool press, which made an excellent cage, handing them over to their mothers when the flock caught up to the wagonette. The nannies happily accepted them back – but it would be a different story with the ewes, Dad said.

So we passed by the rotting posts and weed-grown mullock heap of Bellbird Mine, and the timbered flats of Two Bird Creek. Then the camp by the roadside where the dingoes got into the goats, savaging Cedric, one of the big stags, so badly that Dad had to shoot him. And we came at length, at dusk, to Unca bore, under the shadow of the Dulcie Range.

A tawny-coloured nanny we called Shirley had kidded on the track that afternoon. It was a premature birth of triplets, delivered on the move. The tiny bodies slid onto the grass and lay still, mewling weakly as Shirley licked them clean to the accompaniment of throaty love sounds.

I pulled up to wait when she delivered them, squatting at a little distance, holding Tony's reins, one eye on the sun. It was getting late, and though Shirley crooned her nanny song and nudged the kids, they lay as her busy tongue pushed them, limp but not lifeless in the grass. I could see their tiny ribcages move and the bloody slack of their chewed-through birth strings. Two were white, the third black. None was larger than my hand.

In the end I took off my woollen scarf, wrapped them warmly and stowed them in my saddlebag. Then, remembering that Tony, being stone-blind in one eye, was given to shying, I carried the bag and walked. Shirley bleated along behind, still shedding the after-birth. We were on our own by then, the flock, having travelled on, was now cantering up to the trough to drink before being penned for the night. Dad took one look at the kids and made to take them.

'Born too early. I'll knock 'em on the head.'

'No!' I cradled them to me. 'I'll poddy them. I'll milk Shirley and feed them with the eyedropper we had for Normie. They'll be all right.'

Scratching his beard, he sighed. 'They won't, Kerry. They're weeks too early. They'll die of cold tonight. You can poddy another kid – God knows, there'll be plenty of 'em born. Just pick a healthy one. These are too small to live.'

'I'll make them,' I cried fiercely. From nowhere the tears sprang. 'They won't die because I won't let them! Nothing does, if you care enough! Just because they're little –'

'All right,' Dad said. 'All right. But don't say I didn't warn you.'

He plucked the oven hooks from the firebreak bushes and swung the camp oven out of its bed of coals. While I stood sniffing, holding the kids, he spaded dirt over the glowing embers and tested the heat with his hand. 'Get a bag over that and cosy 'em in there,' he said. 'They'll be warm at least. And get a bit o' milk from the old goat. They'll need a feed every coupla hours.'

Bedding the triplets down into the warmth of the oven-hole, my spirits rose. He would help – so he couldn't truly think it hopeless. Unwrapping the kids, I looked at them. Two were males, the third – the tiniest – a little white nanny, perfect in every detail. You could see the pink of her skin through her silky hair. Her ears were like folded ribbons, her tiny nostrils as pretty as any flower. I could feel her heart pumping against my palm as I held her. It triggered a fierce protectiveness, out of which their names seemed to grow. Steffie for the nanny, Boots for the black one, Jerry for the other.

The routine of chores and the evening meal passed in a dream. Only the kids were real. Their mouths were scarcely large enough to accommodate the eyedropper, but Dad had said they had to suck it. Just squirting the stuff in was no good because it would wind up in their lungs. Cross-legged by the fire I held them in my lap, patiently dipping the eyedropper and squeezing it onto their tongues, feeling a great surge of triumph if their mouths moved in response.

Night came, but I didn't notice. A teaspoon of liquid an hour. And all three still lived, though the cold cut like a knife at the edges of the blanket I'd pulled around me. Sian and the other two were asleep under the wagonette, out of the dew that would be frost by morning. And in the break behind the camp the sheep drowsed and coughed and chewed their cuds. When the fire burned low Dad, who slept beside it, got up to lift another log on.

'Go to bed, Kerry,' he said each time, but I wouldn't.

Boots, the black one, died first. He was cold when I picked him up, the shine already faded from his hair and velvety nose. I fed the other two and renewed the coals beneath them before bedding them down again. The bells were silent by then, only the creak of the slowly turning mill and the splash of water could be heard. The stars were like frozen icicles hanging in blackness. The moon was down. Somewhere off in the night there came a sharp, blasting snort then the thud of trotting hooves – brumbies wanting to water and alarmed by the alien smell of the flock. Half dozing I heard them sneak in, the false starts and gusty sighs, the squeal and thud as the stallion kicked one of them, then their departure.

The early stars had set and the night crackled with cold. Next time I felt for the kids, Jerry was dead.

Dad woke me, padding over to call Sian to get after the horses. I was lying in the foliage of the firebreak with the blanket around me. High in the east the morning star glowed like a silver lamp. The fire had sunk to coals. Dad put a log on, raking at the ash with the oven hooks, and looked across the new flames at the stiff little bodies in the camp-oven hole.

'They weren't ready, Kerry.' He shook his head. 'I tried to tell you. Caring isn't always enough. Your mother would still be alive if it was. When the goats come in pick yourself another little 'un for a pet.'

'I've already got one.' Triumphantly I lifted the corner of the blanket to show him Steffie sleeping curled, like a fluffy tennis ball, on my stomach. Her ribs went in and out and every now and then her tiny mouth worked as if sucking. 'She had three whole tea-spoonfuls last feed.'

'I'll be damned!' His jaw dropped, then he laughed. 'Well, I wouldn't o' given threepence for any o' their chances. Just shows.' He didn't say what, but lifted the billy onto the fire. 'Better get your head down again, I'll see to breakfast this morning.'

~

We stayed a week at Unca – Dad said it would be a sin to waste such feed by rushing on. But it wasn't the lambing camp he was looking for. The dingoes were too bad, for one thing. The foothills of the range rose a bare half a mile behind the bore, providing easy cover for the wild dogs. They were hunting in packs, and twice they got into the goats in daylight. The first time Dad, hearing the wild clamour of the bells, left the trap he was setting to investigate. He rode over a swell of land to find a family of dogs – two adults and three half-grown pups – charging a defensive circle of goats. The older ones, those with horns and fighting experience, were standing them off. Sheep, Dad said, didn't have that much nous. It'd be the equivalent of dingo Christmas if they got among the sheep.

Steffie still slept in the heated camp-oven hole but no longer needed hourly feeds. Every day I lifted her onto her feet and watched her legs collapse under her. And then at week's end, as I spread them again for another try, she stiffened her muscles and stood wobblingly erect. My yell of triumph brought everyone, even Dad, running to watch.

Last thing before the wagonette moved out I rode Darky up to the bore and dropped the reins over the float guard at the trough. Sian had already left with the horses. Patrick and Judith were pushing the flock together, so there was nobody to overlook me, which was how I wanted it.

With the lump of charcoal I'd brought from the camp I wrote their names in big letters on the tank: 'Boots and Jerry, June 1959. RIP.' Sian said animals didn't have souls. They were meat that died and rotted, he said, but what did he know?

Stock tanks always had messages on them from other travellers. We read our way around each one we came to, and others would do the same. They wouldn't know who the names had belonged to, but they'd know that whoever wrote them there had cared.

I washed charcoal smudges off my hands in the trough and swung onto Darky. We were going onto the Thring bore for the rest of the winter. Unca had only ever been a stopover along the way.

SIXTEEN

The Thring Bore was stuck down on the bank of Marshall Creek, right on the edge of the desert. A drover had told Dad about it, back at Red Tank, and especially about its name.

'It ain't that I'm tryin' to say, "string" or "thing" and can't,' he explained earnestly. 'It's really Thring. Silly damn name. Good water – old Tom Hanlon used to camp there. Had a bit of a hut, few horses. They reckon his ghost haunts the place. Never seen it meself.'

It was the dead of winter when we got there, but the land was a vivid carpet of colour. The winter rains had brought the desert wildflowers out, and for two days we'd travelled across their brilliant spread. We stared until our eyes ached, at the beauty and quantity of the blossom. The wagonette tracks wound ahead of us, crushing a path through mile upon mile of yellow and white and pink and purple growth. If green was there, the eye couldn't notice it amid the violent riot of colour.

For the first mile or so we had picked them, darting from clump to clump behind the flock, dragging our mounts by the reins. Judith and I made daisy chains to wear. We stuck them in our hats, plaited them through the horses' manes. At dinner camp we rolled, like colts, on the flowery banks, and tore up handfuls to pelt at each other. But there were just too many of them. It was like being in a chocolate factory with no desire left to eat. So we rode and stared and after the second day only noticed individual blooms – the un-squashed daisy the wheels had missed, or the fringed, golden head brushing our hand as we unhobbled a horse.

Dad was as pleased as if he'd arranged it all himself. 'Might wait twenty years to see a sight like that,' he said. He shot a kangaroo for a change of diet, and we had roast roo meat and baked pumpkin for dinner that day. The pumpkin came from Unca bore, where a previous traveller had left the seeds to the whims of the seasons. It was the proper thing to do, Dad said, to make provision for those who came after you.

We were carrying thirty-odd lambs and kids by the time we reached our destination. Our flock, Dad said, was about to double. So the first job would have to be a nursery for the orphans, or they'd wind up dead from cold.

The Thring was standard government issue – mill, tank and forty-foot trough, watering nothing but the wild things. There were brumby tracks around it, also camel, marsupial, perentie, cat and dingo. Tom Hanlon's old hut stood to one side with a railed grave behind it. There was no headstone, just a bit of tin nailed up, on which somebody had scratched with mordant wit: 'Tom Hanlon. His Claim'.

The old shack was falling to bits. Built of corrugated iron and bush timber, it sagged on termite-riddled beams, its leather-hinged door creaking in the wind. There was a galley on the lee side of it – half a tank hooped over a rusted fire-stand, with bits of charcoal still visible through the tangle of weeds around it. The rubbish dump was a midden of glittery sauce and pickle bottles, mixed with the rotted frame and wheels of a sulky that poked broken shafts at the sky. Grass had grown through the rubbish, roly-poly crowded the galley, and the old man's horses had presumably died or gone bush with the brumbies long since.

Sian, casting a speculative look around, said we might dig up the hut floor – to see if a cache of gold was buried there.

'No fear!' Judith said. 'His ghost might get us.' Then Dad mentioned in passing that old Hanlon had been hunting copper, so there wasn't any point. Nobody would want to bury that. We talked about the ghost, whether the stories were true and if we really might see it. Dad, overhearing, told us to have a bit of sense. People created ghosts out of their own fears or longings, he said. He'd personally never seen one and didn't expect to. I couldn't decide one way or another. There was the strange corroboree I'd witnessed at Karuba, which Dad still maintained was a product of fever and imagination. I didn't think so, but sometimes I wondered.

Once I had wished passionately to see my mother's ghost, hoping that I might suddenly happen upon her essence in some quiet room of the house. If she loved me enough, it would happen, I thought. But it never did, no matter how still I kept or how long I waited.

Now, I couldn't see why (if there really were ghosts) Tom Hanlon's would hang around – maybe for years – on the chance of finding somebody to haunt.

We were too busy to worry about it anyway. The ewes were lambing in droves and the wild dogs had followed us from Unca – and sent all their mates an invitation as well, Dad thought. He hated dingoes. When they yelled at night, you could hear the bells go silent for a bit, and the sheep shrink to stillness in the break against the background rumble of Dad's swearing.

Lambing ewes sneak off to give birth, so Dad rode out daily, scouting for the tracks of missing animals. Sometimes he'd find mother and young safe, at others he'd return with only the lamb across the pommel of his saddle, or the wet skin of the ewe which he'd fling over a rail to dry.

'I wish old Quent was here,' he'd say. We did too. It was months since we'd seen him, but we hadn't forgotten the scrumptious toffee his wife had made us. Other people might call Quent 'Short-change' (because he was five bob short of the full quid), but he was still the best dogger alive. He'd put a bend in them for us! Dad set traps too, but we only had five of them, and he wouldn't use strychnine in case our own dogs took a bait.

He rode back from checking the trap line one morning and found us all in the camp drinking tea. Rambler snorted and sidled, and we saw he had two scalps threaded through the monkey grip of his saddle.

Dad slung them over a branch, stepping down just as the brown horse shied from the green skin in front of his nose.

'Stand up, yer old fool,' he growled without heat. 'Who's watching the sheep?'

'Me and Kerry.' Judith waved her pannikin at them. 'They've hardly moved since they were let out. You got two dogs?'

'Seven.' Dad helped himself to tea.

'You mean two traps had two dogs in them – together?' Sian was incredulous.

'Nope. One had six in it. Hear anything?' He cocked his head as a thin crying sounded. Patrick got it first.

'Pups! She had pups in the trap! Didja bring 'em back?'

'In me saddle pouch. Watch the brown don't boot you. He's a bit fresh this morning.'

They were like tiny pigs – blind little sausages with wet birth strings and pug faces. They mewled and strove against each other, burrowing for teats no longer there, helpless as only the newborn are.

We looked at them, unmoved – even me. None of us wanted to save them. By now we had seen too many wanton killings of other baby things for that. Foals with their hamstrings chewed through, kids buried alive, lambs torn apart – dingoes killed for sport as often as for meat. Dad swung the tiny heads against the nearest tree, then dropped them into a sugar bag which he handed to Patrick.

'Hang 'em up somewhere out of the camp. They'll make bait for the traps when they're ripe.'

Patrick had scarcely done so when he came scampering back. 'There's a horse coming!'

'What d'you mean, a horse?' Dad swung around as the heads of our saddlers went up. Gunner whinnied and was answered by a trumpeting challenge. Then, across a field of yellow daisies, we saw the brumby stallion coming, crest up and tail high. He skidded to a halt fifty paces out, dipped his head and uttered a piercing snort. His nostrils flared as he scented us, then he squealed and trotted straight at the tied horses.

'Let's run him!' Sian reached for his mount's reins, but Dad didn't move.

'Keep still. He's green, this one. Proper myall, and not a bad sort, either. Never seen a man before. Been kicked out o' the mob by the boss horse an' looking for company. We'll get him in the yard without galloping. You slip down there and pull the rails wide.' Sian nodded intently. 'Plant yourself somewhere close but out o' sight. I'll ride Gunner and lead Kerry's mare. He'll foller. You get the rails up soon as he's in.'

It worked just as Dad said it would. The yard was small but solid, and it seemed to puzzle rather than frighten the horse. When he found Gunner and Jody being led away, he trumpeted and tried to push through the rails, then snaked his neck down and took a chomp out of the bark. We were entranced.

'He's not even afraid of us,' Patrick crowed. Before anyone could stop him, he ducked into the yard. Instead of wheeling away, the horse, a deep-barrelled liver chestnut with a heavy neck and neat head, lowered his nose to smell Patrick. And a moment later the big, yellow teeth clamped down on hat and hair and swung him off his feet.

Patrick screeched. Then Dad was through the rails, roaring,

'Jesus, Mary and Joseph! What'd ya do for brains?' He whacked the horse in the face with his own hat. It dropped Patrick and reared, and Dad, for once, wasn't quick enough. The rising knee caught his cheek and sent him sprawling.

Patrick's hat was bitten clean through so that his hair stuck out the top, and Dad got a black eye the size and colour of a ripe plum. He began breaking in the horse that same afternoon, saying that a good lungeing on the rope would teach him a bit of respect for people.

Early next morning Judith saw the ghost. Korai, the dawn star, hung shivering high in the east, and it was dark and freezing cold. Sian was away after the horses. The goats, as sometimes happened, had split up – half were still camped outside the sheep-break, the rest were across the creek. We could hear the bells quite clearly. Judith went after them, scuffing down the track in the dark, and was passing Tom Hanlon's grave when the white shape rose out of the ground and wailed at her.

She was back at the fire in a flash, eyes big as saucers. Dad, who was forking the chops over and dabbing hot water on his shiner, told her irritably to act her age. He sent her off again, but this time she took Larry and made a big loop around the bore to avoid passing anywhere near the grave. The goats came back in a jangle of bells with the dog lolloping behind, but we milked and fed the poddies with one eye turned on the surrounding blackness. When it came to haunting, none of us knew exactly how far spooks might range.

As the stars faded and the first grey light spread along the horizon, the horses came trotting onto camp, Sian bareback and miserable with cold, behind them. He slid off near the fire, dropping the reins, and bent to warm his frozen hands.

'Couldn't catch the new colt again,' he said. 'So he's come in, in hobbles. And there's a goat had twins down on the grave. She was cleaning them up as I came by.'

'That'll be old Hanlon,' Dad said. 'Versatile fella – ghost one minute, nanny-goat the next.'

Even Judith laughed, but that night, when we took the lantern out to search for the lost lambs, his words were comforting to remember.

The moon was growing. It threw stark shadows across the night-scape, which in some ways was scarier than solid darkness. Muffled in our ankle-length army greatcoats we trod carefully, stopping often to turn our ears from the wind and listen. Sometimes a thin bleating guided us, sometimes the yellow lamp glow fell on the cold little bodies already too weak to stand.

Once, as we were prospecting a hollow, a pair of yellow eyes shone back at us out of the grass. We froze, expecting a dingo, but instead heard a goat's familiar warning snort. She'd cleaned up after the birth and lay watchfully, still as a white stone in the moonlight, horns like black swords above her triangular face. Her babies were tucked against her flank, inside her hind leg. The wind eddied in the hollow; it would carry no scent beyond it, nor could immobility betray her. We left her, knowing she would be safe.

Back at camp the rescued babies had to be fed by coaxing them to suck a finger stuck in a bowl of warm milk. Larry licked their faces clean, then we tucked them into the nursery – 44 gallon drums lying on their sides, floored with dirt, each with an end removed. At nightfall Dad shovelled coals around them, banking their glowing heat with ash. While the frosts crackled on our swag wraps, the babies slept warm and dry, woolly heads and silky ones side by side in their heated cave.

Next day the nanny we had seen rejoined the flock, but another hadn't been as lucky. We had heard dogs hunting in the night and knew, by the choked-off cry, that something had died.

Riding through the wet grass, with the morning shadows long on the ground and the spiderwebs etched in crystal against the light, Dad and I found them. I saw the dead kid first, sprawling like a rag puppet in the grass. There was dirt on the fine, white eyelashes, blood on the soft hooves. Scarcely a foot away, its living twin pressed flat against the earth as though frozen there. When I lifted it, I had to pull its legs straight and hide the awful terror of its stare under my coat. The nanny was further on, her throat torn out.

'Bastards!' Dad muttered savagely. 'Two of 'em, see? One come at her from the side – see where she charged? It got the kid anyway, then she ran and his mate was waiting. The little bloke lay doggo – maybe they never saw him, or forgot him when they had the nanny. Jesus, Mary and Joseph! What I wouldn't give for a sight of old Quent.'

That same day Dad started work again on the new horse. He'd gelded him – to get a bit of peace, he said – because the plant was in an uproar with a stallion among them. Medal, as we called him for the bronze sheen on his coat, savaged the geldings mercilessly. Though hobbled, he drove the mares about, head weaving, trumpeting his stallion call. Old Tony fled before him until his hobbles broke, then sneaked back to stage a raid on the mares. We laughed until our ribs hurt to see him cut out Dumpy, Yerra and Queeia, and head bush with them as though the devil were on his tail.

Medal was a bit too smart for his own good, Dad said, but cutting settled him. He'd had his first ride out of the yard the day Sian spotted the dust puffing into the blue above the mulga.

'Somebody coming,' Dad said. He swung the billy onto the coals and stood waiting by the fire. The dogs ran forward, barking, and we all stopped what we were doing to stand and look. We hadn't seen anyone for months. When the nose of the old green Bedford ploughed into view, we yelled and waved at its occupants – Quent, grinning from ear to ear, with Mrs Meadows, tiny under a big felt hat, beside him.

Quent was excited by the flowers, which we'd grown used to, and the quantity of dog tracks. We shared our news over the tea, telling him of the dead sheep, and Medal, and how Judith had mistaken the goat on the grave for Hanlon's ghost. His guileless eyes widened and he stared, hands on spread knees.

'That true?'

'Yeah, but it wasn't a ghost,' Patrick assured him. 'Come and see the nursery, Quent. See how we keep 'em warm.'

The short afternoon passed quickly. The Meadows pitched their white calico tent just below our camp, and built the fussy fireplace that Quent insisted upon. The milking was done, the feeding over. Almost at once the sun dropped from sight, a full moon rose over the dunes, and the night had come.

Beyond the range of firelight, Sian was hobbling up. The last horse done, he stepped clear of the bunched animals just as a wave of terror swept through them. They bolted in a single surge of violence, the sound of their hooves tearing the night apart. We gaped, deafened and amazed amid the dust, too stunned to think, battered by the hideous clamour of their bells.

Sian was shaking, the freckles blotching his white face.

'What happened?' I yelled, but Dad was already swinging his arm, pointing at the dunes.

'Camels.'

We stared at the shape of them, black against the great copper disk of the moon. 'Horses hate the smell of 'em.' His voice dropped to normal as the noise faded. 'Where's me colt?'

Sian flapped his hand, laconic for once. 'Coming.'

He was too – in great surging lunges in the hobbles, ears laid flat and the whites of his eyes showing. He should have known camels, but Dad always said horses weren't programmed to think, they just reacted.

I doubt Medal even saw the camp he was charging through. Mrs Meadows shrieked and gamely flapped her pinny in his face as he tore into the little white tent, bursting the ropes like cotton, and galloping on, shrouded in flapping calico. He overtook the oblivious Quentin, himself yelping questions as he bustled towards us, like a hawk overhauling a sparrow.

'Be'ind yer, man!' Dad roared in a voice to split stone.

Quent looked back and momentarily froze, mouth and eyes staring. 'It's Hanlon's ghost!' he screamed, then his legs started pedalling, and he made a flying leap for the wagonette. He was clinging to the side-rail, trying to ram his head under the seat and shaking all over, when Medal went past.

'Chase it away! 'Oh, chase it away!' he sobbed, and the front of his pants were all puddled wet.

It had been funny at first, but now we didn't know where to look.

Mrs Meadows was shrieking like a train whistle and laughing hysterically.

Tears smeared Quent's face, and his mouth trembled like a little kid's. 'Etty,' he cried. 'I wet myself, Etty.'

Dad said, 'Jesus!' and chucked a pannikin of water over Mrs Meadows. The shock of it stopped her in mid-laugh.

'Oh, dear,' she gasped. 'Oh, deary me!' She pulled water from her face with her two palms. 'The tent's gone.'

'So's my plant,' Dad said. 'Quent's in a bit o' strife too. We've gotta get those horses back. Your tent won't be far – I'll find it.'

He did, but it was torn almost in two. A branch had snagged it, pulling it free of the horse so that it floated in spectral folds amid the mulga – more like a ghost than Medal had ever been. But nobody said so. The guilty shame we felt at having witnessed Quent's collapse had put us off ghosts for good.

Dad repaired the tent next day, lock-stitching it with waxed thread. So it would last, he told Mrs Meadows. He spliced the broken ropes and cut two new pegs to replace the smashed ones. He was sorry for her. I was too, but she didn't seem to need it.

'He's a good man, Kerry,' she told me. We were in the mended tent and she was tipping the milk I'd brought her into her own billy. Outside, Quent was fiddling happily with his traps, as if last night had never happened. I'd been studying him, wishing it hadn't, when she spoke.

Embarrassed, I looked away, mumbling, 'I know, Mrs Meadows. I like him too.'

She smiled. 'Call me Etty. What with the upset last night I nearly forgot, but there's a parcel for you. Something your dad asked me to get next time I was in town.' She put the billy aside and rummaged in the depths of a calico bag slung from the tent pole. 'I got some for your sister too – you're only a year apart, ain't you?' Mystified, I nodded, and she beamed, handing me a tissue parcel. 'Some's got pink roses on 'em. I reckoned you'd like that.'

Under the paper were half a dozen teenage bras. I fingered the fine soft cotton uncertainly. I was both pleased and alarmed by the growth of my breasts, which had suddenly sprouted like fat, spring buds from my chest.

'They're pretty.' I smoothed my fingers over their white slinkiness, and Mrs Meadows – no, Etty, I remembered – patted my hand.

'Tell you what, I've gotta step out for a moment. Why'n't you try it on?'

When she returned I showed her, shyly, holding my shoulders back instead of slumping, the way I had been, in a bid to disguise my troublesome new shape.

'You look grand. Lotsa girls your age are plump, but you're that ... willowy.'

We both giggled then at the unusual word, and I saw that she was younger than I had always thought. Screwing her hair back, she said, 'It'll be nice to have you girls for comp'ny. Both of you come whenever you want. We'll have some real good talks, and I'll show you how to make toffee.'

We took her at her word, visiting often at the little white tent. There was plenty of time, for it wasn't Quent's way to rush things. For days he slopped about in his unlaced boots, humming over his preparations and talking to himself as he prepared to make war on the dogs. Sian shadowed him about, hoping to discover the secret of his lure, but Judith and I weren't interested. Confident in our new bras, we scanned old dress catalogues with Etty, and read the bits of serials in her collection of tatty magazines, and talked about growing up.

Over the next few weeks the carnage in the flock ceased. The births tailed off, then stopped altogether, and the flowers faded to papery husks. When the nights were silent again, Quentin came to our fire, his face radiating uncomplicated pleasure.

'I killed dem dogs, Mac. All finished. Pack up'n go back now.'

'You've done a good job, mate.' Dad shook hands with him. 'We'll see you round, sometime.' But I knew we wouldn't. Our road lay eastward.

Judith and I hugged Etty, knowing we'd not see her again, or funny old Quent, or even camels walking like black paper cut-outs against the rising moon.

SEVENTEEN

It was late afternoon of a quite ordinary day when Snowy turned up. We were at Jervois then, running the sheep up the big valley wedged between the Jervois Ranges, and living in one of the huts along the creek-bank.

It was once going to be a town, Jervois. A huge crushing plant had been built to handle the copper from the mines. Well, half built – then copper crashed, Dad said, and the money ran out. So there was an acre of steel and tin, overtopped by mantislike gantries – and underneath them concrete washing vats now tumbled full of roly-poly and lizards baking in the sun. Butcher-birds warbled high on the cross-members of the buildings, and you could kick pipe fittings and tools (worth hundreds of quid, according to Dad) out of the sand. Everything had been left to rot.

The hills around gaped from the miners' diggings. Their slopes were scarred with scrap metal – flaky ore buckets, truck bodies, a busted set of camel canteens too big for any horse to carry. Patrick even found a handful of detonators one day. Since then we'd been forbidden to go near the workings, but there were plenty of other things to occupy us.

We had a lot of trouble with the water, for one thing. It was just a soak in the creek-bed with a mill and a shonky engine on it. It took hours to fill the tank each day. Dad, who spent half his time fiddling with the engine or pulling the mill rods, said he'd have put a dam in before he moved a spade of dirt for any other purpose.

Anyway, there we were, just us and the abandoned field, with its empty huts and derelict machinery in the early October heat. And that day, lazing in behind the flock, with the dipping sun throwing shadows before us, suddenly there was Snowy.

The road ran east and west but he came up on us out of the north-west, which meant he must have crossed the range through the Gap. He was riding a chestnut, leading a brown and had a bay packhorse following.

We pulled up and waited, intensely curious. He came slowly, accommodating his pace to the lame horse. He rode like a stockman. Clean-shaven, tall and lean, with a red-checked shirt and a scarlet bobble of whip-crackers stuck through his hatband. His fancy oxbow irons glinted in the sun.

'The brown's lame in the off fore,' Patrick said, trying to sound like Dad.

'Is not,' Judith said. 'The poor thing looks like it's walking on hot coals. Its feet hurt, not its legs.' Judith was mostly right about such matters.

Patrick changed the subject. 'Bet he's wondering who we are.' But he lost out there too, because the stranger already knew.

Up close he was youngish, teeth white in his tanned face. He lifted his hat, which made Judith giggle. 'G'day,' he said. 'I'm Snowy.' He had twinkly blue eyes when he smiled. 'You must be the young McGinnises.'

'Some of them,' I said gruffly, then went hot at the sound of my voice.

Patrick, who was never shy or embarrassed, got three questions in before my face cooled.

'What d'you call your brown? She's pretty, isn't she? Why's she lame?'

'Stone bruising.' There was regret in his face as he passed a hand down her neck. 'She's pretty, orright. There's studbook blood in her, young fella. I call her Shadow.'

'Mine's Yerra. Didjer know that means "Fly" in blackfella language? Are you going to camp tonight? We're taking the sheep in to yard 'em now – you can come with us if you want.'

'Right you are,' Snowy said gravely, man to man.

I was just going to tell Patrick to put a sock in it when Snowy looked over, a laugh on his face, and winked at us. It won us both.

Dad was waiting as usual to see the flock yarded. He came across to meet Snowy but his glance kept sliding away to the lame mare. She really was a beauty, even though she moved as if walking on bloody stumps. Dad slid a hand down her near fore and picked it up.

'Jesus, Mary and Joseph!' he said. He touched the sole and the mare jumped as if he'd stuck a knife in her. Gently he lowered the foot and stood, hands on hips, looking at her. 'Miracle she made it here.'

'I know.' Snowy was brief. He sighed and scrubbed his hand over the back of his neck. 'She's always been soft-footed. Shouldn't have brought her. Have to leave her now – she won't travel for weeks. Maybe we could do a deal? I'll need another saddler, and she's a good mare. Won me a few races in the past.'

'With feet like that she might starve before she mends. Wouldn't be much good to me then,' Dad said. 'But I'll think about it. There's a bit of a fenced yard at the back o' the hut we're in. You can stick 'er in there for the night. There's feed 'n' the ground's soft. You're welcome to camp with us. Where're yer heading?'

'East,' Snowy answered shortly. Maybe he hadn't liked Dad's implied criticism. He said no more about his destination, and Dad didn't ask again.

He was good company. He stayed that night and the next, resting the horses and trying to get another one out of Dad as a swap for the brown mare. Dad was being deliberately indecisive, of course. He wanted Shadow from the moment he set eyes on her, we all knew it. But even Patrick knew better than to say so. You leave the dickering to me, he used to say. Keep your mouths shut and your ears open, and you might even learn something. And we had, because we knew it to be a tactical error on Snowy's part to be so eager to complete the deal. None of us would tell him so, though. We wanted the brown mare too.

When he wasn't looking over the plant or squatting on his heels in the shade yarning with Dad, Snowy was ours to enjoy. Compared to our humdrum existence, his life was one of high adventure. He did station work, but he'd also been in a circus performing roping and whip-cracking tricks. He'd raced Shadow at bush meetings and entertained the racegoers afterwards with recitations, yodelling and his harmonica.

Patrick immediately wanted him to yodel for us, and he did. His whip was a fancy one – black and white roohide with a white-hide fall and a scarlet whip-cracker. Made from silk, he said, and he showed us the two spares tucked under his hatband. The cane handle had a plaited grip and a fancy knob at the end. He could crack it with both hands. He did the Sydney Flash for us, cracking it both sides, overhead, behind and before in one long, thundering volley that made our ears ring.

'Dad can do that,' Patrick said.

'Can he?' Snowy tossed the whip and caught it with his other hand. Then he snaked it sideways round a tuft of dried daisies, flicked his wrist and deposited them at my feet. He grinned, laughter lines spoking the corners of his eyes.

'How about that, though?'

Just on sunset, with the sheep yarded and the milking done, we took him up Billy-goat Hill. He wanted to get a look at the country before pushing on. Dad, who'd finally agreed to swap Spider for the lame mare, had drawn him a mud map to steer by. But paper was only paper, he told us, and he didn't want another cripple on his conscience.

It was a steep scramble to the top of the hill. It rose behind the creek, pocked with adits and heaped about with tailings, but its top stood clear of the timber with a view to Wednesday week. The ranges ran in a line from east to west, long ridges of rock smeared ochre and purple, with the great slash of the Gap cut through their front to the north-west.

Southwards lay the desert, fenced about with mulga and drifting dunes, perilous country for travellers. East, the track was plainly visible for some distance, two winding wheel-ruts dodging lone hills and rocky outcrops before vanishing under the green froth of white-wood and bean-tree foliage.

Below us dusk was dimming the outlines of buildings and the wide sweep of the valley, criss-crossed now with sheep-pads. The wagonette was an oblong smudge alongside the tin hut. The fire beside it gleamed brighter as the light departed, and the sound of the bells floated up to us as the horses fed away. Shadow whinnied after them, out of the yard where she spent most of her time lying down. It was the only good thing about Snowy's going – that we would be keeping his beautiful mare.

'Maybe we'll meet up again, down the track?' Sian said.

'Bound to.' Snowy nodded. 'Mac's a travellin' man, like me. Bit slower of course, with the sheep.'

'Oh, we won't have them forever,' Judith said. 'We're going droving when we get to Queensland. In a year or two.'

'When you're all grown up?' He was teasing. I felt the betraying blood rush to my face and was glad of the darkness. I hated it when he laughed at us.

'We nearly are now.' Judith was indignant. 'Kerry's already fourteen –'

I kicked her shin, hard. What was the use of trying to act sixteen if she kept blurting out the truth?

Snowy made no answer. He was peering at his feet, placing his high-heeled boots carefully. 'Last thing I need's a busted ankle,' he said. 'Let's get down before it's pitch-dark.'

He left next day, before sunrise. It was the best travelling time. He shook hands with Dad, said, 'See ya, kids,' and, riding Spider, dropped over the creek-bank and out of sight.

The chestnut and the bay, on lead-ropes, jogged behind. We all stood staring after him until Redback, Spider's yearling colt, began to whinny and tug at the rope he was tied on.

'Righto,' Dad said then, 'get that flock out. Takes tucker and space, not yard time, to grow wool, y'know.' Dragging our feet, we obeyed. All the shine had gone from the day and nothing but sheep and tedium were left.

∽

A week after Snowy's departure, our second visitor arrived unannounced, as the shadows shortened towards noon.

'We've got popular of a sudden,' Dad muttered, lifting his head to listen. Then he left the saddle he was counter-lining to stare at the approaching landrover. There were just the two of us – the others were up the valley with the flock. We couldn't see the occupants as the vehicle bumped towards us, but the moment they stepped out Dad stiffened. I recognised him too. The copper from Hartz Range – the one Dad had had the row with over Tony, the branded horse we'd taken from old Humpy's mob of brumbies and kept.

They were looking for Snowy. Well, Noel Harcourt was the name they used, but I knew immediately who they meant.

'Never heard of 'im,' Dad said, cold-eyed. He stood there, not inviting them into the shade of the fly rig, slowly filling his pipe. 'What's he s'pposed to've done? Pinched a horse?'

Constable Smedley reddened. 'Duffing,' he said shortly.

'Oh,' Dad nodded. 'Pinched some cattle. Didja check they weren't already his?'

The other man had a sergeant's chevrons on his sleeve. He said reasonably, 'Look, there's no mistake about this. One of the station blokes blundered onto 'em – Harcourt and his mate, I mean – actually branding. They cleared out in a panic. We've got the cattle, the brands, and we've picked up the other bloke. Harcourt himself can't have got far yet. There's only so many tracks and waters in this country.'

'He shouldn't be too hard to nab, then,' Dad said. 'Told yer, never heard o' the man. Hasn't been a soul come along that road for months, till you turned up today.'

When they'd gone I said, 'They meant Snowy, didn't they?' My mouth was dry. 'He's a crook! D'you think they'll catch him?'

Dad shrugged. 'Sooner or later. Thought there had to be something like this be'ind him, to explain the mare's condition.' He stabbed the awl into the counter-lining and began to roll and wax a new thread. 'None o' our business, Kerry. Just forget he was ever here.'

Desolation swamped me, submerging my bright dream. 'He was . . . nice.'

'Most con artists are. Stands to reason.' Dad licked the thread end. 'Good blokes – on the outside. Only they'd nick their grandmothers' teeth for gain. The mare prob'ly weren't his to swap either.'

I stared at him, then over my shoulder where Shadow's bell tinkled along the creek. She still couldn't move off the sand country. 'What if the police had seen her?'

'I've got a receipt,' Dad said, very dry. 'The signature isn't exactly clear. But it ain't Harcourt. And you can take your pick o' the date. Nobody's gunna prove when he was where, from that.'

Snowy must have planned it all when the mare started to go lame. Maybe even making us like him was a ploy – so we wouldn't betray him when the police came. The hurt ached in my chest and stung my eyes. I wished Dad had told them.

Later, when he'd gone off to check the water level in the tank, I pulled out the silken whip-cracker Snowy had dropped that last morning and looked at it. I'd carried it buttoned in my shirt pocket and had been going to keep it forever – but not any more.

Snowy was like Maori, I thought, the buckjumping brown we'd had that Dad had swapped away. He'd been sly too; a handsome horse, sound in wind and limb but rotten inside. You could grow a crop of spuds, Dad said, in the streak of dirt he had in him.

A tear spilled onto the cracker. I knuckled my cheek, watching the wet spot darken the silk, then I dropped it onto the fire, which had sunk to pale coals. It made a tiny hiss as of a thing in pain, then smoke curled up from it and a flare of ruby flame. When that had gone, only the shape of it was left – a shadow in the ash.

EIGHTEEN

Telegraph Jack died, and was buried at the old Jervois mine workings, where the red sand country rolled up into the copper-rich
Jervois Ranges. He died from a crook belly, a local cattleman told
Dad. It might have meant anything from food poisoning to appen-
dicitis, but he was a bush black so nobody really knew. Or cared.
It was blackfella business, as was his burial – the corpse going into
the hole in a sitting position with the lower legs lashed together
to prevent his spirit walking.

They put sticks around the grave and never again referred to
him by his skin name, or looked openly at the spot where he
lay – or rather sat. It took quite a bit of muttering and foot-shuffling
during circumlocutory natter from Dad to elicit that much, and
we wondered why he bothered. It was blackfella business, after all.

Jack's only property seemed to have been his woman, subsequently allotted, through kinship or custom, to the old man known as Pretty Peter. And a jute-wrapped bundle poked into a deep crack in the rock where a wallaby-pad dropped down off an outcrop near the grave.

Dad spotted it when he was out on a colt one day and, knowing it could only belong to the dead man (or it wouldn't have been left there), fished it up with a long stick and cut the spinifex gum sealing it shut. It must have been corroboree stuff – a mixing stone stained with ochre, human hair woven into strings, strips of wallaby hide, and two flat bits of glass-smooth mulga, painted and carved.

Back at camp we fingered them curiously, tracing the concentric patterns scored in the wood, sliding our palms over the silky chiselled surface.

'He can do good work when he wants to, the old Abo,' Dad said. He wrapped the pieces in a torn shirt and dropped them in his trunk, where they stayed for years, arcane souvenirs of the region.

Because men had abandoned what they had built there, the Jervois country always seemed emptier to me than anywhere else. Distance and low prices had beaten the mine, as any but an optimist (which Dad said was another name for a fool) should have seen they must. There wasn't a white man within a week's ride of the place, just the bore and the narrow track, and in the valley the clutter and flapping tin of the derelict workings.

Here the desert, with patient stealth, was already reclaiming its own – weathering, drifting over and breaking down. As straight lines blurred and squared edges crumbled under its assault, the sheds, gantries and conveyer system sunk into the landscape, things my gaze slid easily over, no longer really seeing. It was only when a bird's carolling echoed within the high roof of a shed, or my horse's hooves clanged on half-buried steel that I became aware, not of the desolation around me, but of those who had once lived here and were now gone.

The workings were more real at night, under the moon shadows, when feeding wallabies thumped between the ruins, and curlews wailed like crying women around the hut on the creek. The hut had been the mine manager's and stood solitary, a solid block of shadow under crowding gums. Judith and I found a cracked sugar bowl in the yard there once, and the broken face of a china doll, its painted blue eyes faded to white smears.

After the first time we never went back. The air was cool, almost cold, under the gums, and the silent rooms creaked and sighed at us. Leaves pattered, like scratching fingers on the roof, and there were bats, little ones, squeaking and swooping in dark corners. We knew that it was here, if anywhere, that Jack's hobbled ghost would appear – white teeth horribly visible in its dark face; bare, bony feet silent on the sanded floor.

Pretty Peter's mob came regularly to the soak in the valley, and sometimes we'd glimpse them further afield, stick figures swimming through heated air. They seemed to materialise and vanish, like smoke, melting into the landscape in languid strides. The women came to the tin-built store for their government rations of flour, tea and sugar, and occasionally Peter himself, eyes rolling nervously at the chained dog, to ask Dad for curra – meat.

Peter was called Pretty for the same reason a big man comes to be known as Tiny. He had the small stature of desert men, with skinny wrists and bird-claw hands. There was a scar like an axe chop across his left temple, which pulled that side of his face awry. His tattered clothes flapped on him, and he smelled of dirt and grease – the musty, smoky odour of dog and unwashed flesh that hung about blackfellas' camps. He had little English. Dad got along with sign language and pidgin, but we all came to recognise the words he used most: meat, water, horse, tucker. 'Weeia' meant little boy, 'quadja' was water, and there was a different name for every tree.

Dad had a soft spot for old Peter. He asked him about the bush tucker the women collected, and even hooked the team up once to cart water out into the dry country beyond the mine, where Peter had a fancy to camp. When they came back, they had a billyful of gritty bulbs the size of peas for us. Dad said they were considered number-one tucker and were known as yalka. There was also, he said, a corroboree coming up, which Peter had intimated we could attend.

This happened after the Lucy Creek mob arrived. It was high summer by then, days of brazen heat when earth and sky melted together in shimmering mirages, and rocks burnt the hand that touched them. In the blacks' camp they were singing for rain, filling the smoky nights with loud, monotonous noise, interrupted by the howling of the camp dogs. The clouds built over the ranges and blew away, and built again above the blistering heat of the valley, and night after night the singing went on. The beat of it seemed to sink deep into the earth and pulse there, like a hidden heart crying out for relief. Even in the daytime I could hear it behind the slow buzz of flies, a vibration in the silence like a distant, muffled drum.

The Lucy Creek mob numbered twenty or more men, women and children. They came with their dogs and bundles and throwing sticks and built scanty sapling shelters for their stay. A holiday air prevailed. Dad gave them a big wether for meat and that night the singing was stronger, with added voices. Next day they painted for the corroboree.

We went across at dark, stumbling through the huddle of gunyahs and yapping curs to the fire. Dark hands beckoned and pulled Judith and me down among the seated women, away from Dad and the boys. A dog growled and I shrank back, squirming away from the odour of stale flesh. The singing rose and fell, dying to a long, drawn-out mutter, then rising again with a wild yell that made me jump. I searched for familiar faces in the dimness, but even Peter, sitting apart from the rest, looked different, his body free of its white man's rags. There was a bundle of kindling within arm's reach of him. It must have been placed over coals because it flared into sudden light, and by it I saw the slender wand of wood, crowned with white feathers, standing upright in the ground before him, and the tribal scars patterning his body. He gave a yell, which both astonished me and brought the dancers in at a stamping run from the outer darkness.

It can't have lasted very long – only the time it took the armful of tinder to burn and die – yet the hypnotic prancing seemed endless. I remember the drifting smoke, and leaping shadows behind the paint-streaked bodies dancing with lowered eyes before the totem stick. I remember the driving beat of the women's palms slapping their naked thighs, and the sudden glimpse of the quarter-moon overhead, netted in bloodwood leaves. The men had bunches of whitewood tied round their calves and white corella feathers glued to their bodies. Lines of red and yellow ochre streaked their faces, emphasising the broad black noses and jutting brows.

Peter's yell ended it as the firewood collapsed into coals. The unburnt ends flared briefly, the dancers vanished, and I saw him lean to the totem stick and pluck it swiftly from sight. And, for an instant only, I saw his eyes – not the shifty, opaque gaze he wore when he came begging for meat – but one blazing with purpose and power. I stared at him, at his bare, sunken chest and scrawny, old man's arms. If I had picked up a stick and felt it wriggle in my hand I could not have been more amazed.

The singing continued all night. They only used five notes, Dad said, and he was sick of them all before they stopped. The dawn came in muggy with promised heat, the clouds building like wet, grey bags over the ranges, and in the late afternoon the storm burst. It rained all night, hammering on the tin roof of our shelter, a relentless downpour that deluged the land. The ranges and flats ran with the flood tumbling all before it into the creek. We woke to the drip and gurgle of water and utter silence from across the valley. The deserted, flattened gunyahs were empty, the blacks gone.

'Four inches!' Dad tipped it from the tin he'd used to measure it. 'Old Peter can give his tonsils a rest now, eh?'

'He didn't truly make it happen, did he?' In the cool morning air it was easy to doubt I had ever heard the throb of his song in the earth.

'Maybe not.' Dad spun the tin onto a post. 'Maybe he just knew it was coming and organised a bit o' noise and fancy dress. Magic or knowledge, there's not much difference.'

But the greatest magic wrought was the change the rain made to the land. I thought I knew the desert, but nothing, it seemed, was what it appeared to be – the country's barren skin a cloak no more real than old Peter's pose of submissive beggar. The frogs came first, burrowing free of underground sleeping sacks, riddling the night with their joyous songs. Ducks arrived, planing down into temporary waterholes where plovers already clinked and ran. And everywhere desert red was overlaid with a green so vivid it hurt your eyes. Even the derelict mine workings were briefly affected, their rust glistening with dew, their tattered walls knee-deep in sappy coils of roly-poly bush.

Feed grew right to the foot of the neglected trough, while the stock gorged on the moisture-rich parakeelya, or drank at the creek. The camp across the valley stayed empty, and there was no call for Dad to unlock the store. Just as well, he said. It meant he and Sian could get on with freeing up the brake shoe on the front wheel of the wagonette because, with the new grass, we'd be moving on again soon. Old Peter's mob wouldn't be back, though, until the water on the desert was gone. Maybe weeks. They'd be visiting those parts of the country shut off to them save immediately after rain.

Sian squinted into the distance. 'Reckon they'll still be belting out little ditties?'

'Man-making, more like. Coupla those Lucy Creek lads were old enough for initiation.' Dad picked up the screwdriver and hammer again and bent over the wheel. 'Blackfella business, any road. Let's get on with our own.'

~

That summer Dad and I took the goats across a 35-mile dry stage to Cockroach Hole. It was an ugly name in a land where water meant life, where without it you died in twelve hours. I never wondered who had named it, or why, but three years in the land bordering the Simpson Desert had made us all wonderfully single-minded.

Bushmen, both black and white, had died in that country. Hardy, experienced men who had perished through a single mistake. Dad made us learn their names, their histories – and that it could also happen to us. 'There's no second chance.' He dinned that into us, and we believed him.

At Tarlton Downs, with its boxlike homestead built on a stony ridge within a semicircular sweep of ranges, we came to the end of the government bores. For hundreds of miles they had dotted our route east, marching across the land at twelve-mile intervals, the staging distance for cattle. Our goats handled it quite well also, but thirty-five completely dry miles was something else. Thirty-five miles in November with temperatures over the century was dangerous.

We waited ten days at Tarlton for an eastbound traveller, and could as easily have waited a month on that seldom-used track. When he eventually appeared he agreed to offload two 44-gallon drums of water at the fence which crossed the road twenty-seven miles ahead.

Sian, who was a perennial doomsayer, said, 'What if some drongo comes along and tips it out?' Sian always expected a horse to buck or a bore to pump dry.

Dad stared at him. 'Bushmen respect water. But if it happens – if the water isn't there – send Judith back to stop me. You keep going. That's all you've got to do. Just keep going and get those horses through.'

They left next morning, Sian high on the driving seat of the wagonette while Patrick and Judith followed with the plant. We had kept five horses back, three for the saddle and two for the packs, and my poddy foal which still needed milk. All swung on their halters whinnying after the plant, particularly Starlight the buckjumping brown mare, whose flanks shook with the intensity of her calls. Larry, and Julie the little black Kelpie bitch Dad had swapped a saddle for, soon after we got the sheep, capered at Dad's heels – but he ignored them, standing with his hands on his hips, staring after the turn-out. Like he was trying to will Sian through the dry miles ahead.

There were four 44-gallon water drums aboard. Two would give the team horses a drink that night, the rest comprised the travelling rations and safety margin for the camp.

They would cover fifteen miles a day, a good slog for the team pulling the heavy vehicle. For water that night Sian had to take the plant onto a bore located somewhere ten miles to the south of the road, then return them to camp. He had to hobble them on feed, find them again in the early hours of the morning, and be yoked up and travelling by sunrise on the final twenty-mile stage. It was a straightforward operation, unless he bogged the turn-out or failed to find the pads that would lead him to the bore, or the brumbies got among the horses.

'Well,' Dad said. 'No use worrying now, I s'pose.'

He and I passed a slow day packing up and shepherding the

flock. We were to start in the late afternoon, but Starlight altered that by going bush with the pack. She bucked over the horse-paddock fence, shed her load across half a mile of stony ridge, and was yarded with the saddle under her belly and one shoulder ripped open.

Dad effected running repairs to the gear, switched her original load for the heavier canteens, and tied her head to her girth to hamper further activity. Then with the dogs 'getting away back' with gusto, and with just enough visibility to see the range against the sky, we started out.

It was a moonless night, black as a coal pit under the white blaze of stars. You can't see anything by starlight, which casts no shadow, but the lighted brilliance above us lifted the smothering blackness and provided guides to steer by.

The goats travelled with a murmurous bleating overlaid by the steady rattle of bells. *Bong, bong*, went the large Condamine on Jimmy-Jack the big wether leader. I could picture him striding it out with his silky beard and the sweeping horns that could stand off any dog. Old Stripey's bell tonked dully, and little Fairy's had a tinkling note. Further back in the flock, Hilary's and Charger's jangled together, and from somewhere about the middle came the jingle of the packhorse gear.

The night felt cool but sharp-edged, as if it were an echo chamber magnifying all sense impressions. The sand granules crunched under Darky's hooves, and liquid rumblings came from inside her. The flock's feet pattered like rain on the fallen mulga leaves, and the night smelled of horse and dry grass, of Dad's tobacco and the warm, musky reek of goat.

I wondered if Sian had found the bore yet and whether Judith, alone in the camp with Patrick, would be scared if the dingoes howled. It was empty, desolate country. Only the wild things, a few blackfellas, and, once in a long while, a wandering white man to talk to. I was glad I was making the dry stage with Dad. He was the rock, the touchstone of my existence. A quick, impatient man, tough as the springy mulgawood and twice as enduring. It felt good to be grown up and responsible enough to share in a task he himself did not consider easy.

Before the first of our guiding stars sank from sight, Gunner, the spare saddle-horse, got sick. He had dropped gradually back from the lead and now began to stagger and groan and lie down.

'Colic,' Dad said, and I heard him swear. 'Pull the gear off him and leave him.'

He reined Trooper away, leaving me to take the hobbles and tongued bell off the blue gelding's neck. He had only one eye and belonged to Patrick and would be lost to us forever once he was left behind. He would pick up with the brumbies if he lived, or go back to the station, and riding on I mourned for him, as for one already dead.

In the hush of midnight we stopped to eat, and rest the flock. I slept until the billy boiled, then Dad woke me and we ate damper and salted goatmeat from the packs by the light of a frugal fire. Trooper and Darky grazed nearby while the foal slept and the packhorses, which could feed as they travelled, stood tied up. There was blood on Starlight's leg and it glistened black in the fire-shine, and all around us the goats lay, jaws wagging as they chewed the cud.

The meal over, Dad scraped sand over the fire, then we stood the flock up and went on into the black stillness under the blazing stars, heading for Cockroach. On and on, sleepy in the saddle and already thirsty again from the salty meat, listening to the sloshing of the canteens and the dogs' yipping, thinking of Gunner somewhere far behind us.

Endless rocking miles later the stars darkened, then began to pale towards daylight. I had never before ridden east into a new day's birth – it was like watching a picture emerge from blank canvas, seeing the light spread fanwise to touch the rock outcrops with ochre and orange and lay a patina of silver over the dull grey mulga leaves.

Dawn is the best time in the desert. The air is cool and fresh then, and perceived distances are real, if only temporarily.

We stopped for breakfast, to water the dogs and milk the goats for the foal.

Resaddling afterwards, Dad said, 'Well, that's the easy bit behind us. It'll be uphill work from now on.'

Riding on I found it hard to stay awake. Twice I nearly tumbled down Darky's shoulder as she plodded behind the flock, which was travelling in earnest now, driven by a growing thirst.

The goats fairly romped along, bells ringing busily, ignoring both the feed and the attempts of their young to nurse. In the cool beginnings of the day it seemed they would make nothing of the distance still stretching before them, and my heart lifted.

By mid-morning, with sand and air heating like a stoked oven, it was a different story. Ground and sky glittered hurtfully, the sweat dried in a stiff white rime on our clothes, and the heat shimmered in waves above phantom lakes ever receding before us. Distant anthills bobbed like running emus in the mirages, while the trees wavered and vanished as you watched. It was shaping up to be a stinker of a day, filled with the buzz of flies and the dogs' desperate panting. Birds and goats alike were silenced by the heat.

The packhorses maintained a steady pace but the flock had lost cohesion, straggling from tree to tree and dodging about them. The dogs no longer worked, and twice I saw Larry stop and look back. I called sharply to him each time because there was no returning now. If the greatest heat still lay ahead, so too, by Dad's reckoning, did the shortest distance to water.

When the shadows were smallest, we reached the water drum. The horses were desperately thirsty by then, and I held them back while Dad opened the drums. They buried their muzzles in the hot liquid while the dogs whined and jumped at the bucket, then fought for space in the spillage, snapping at the crowding goats that pressed to the smell of water. Before the last bucketful vanished, Legs lifted his head, ears pricking, and I looked and saw Gunner wavering through the mirage towards us.

He whinnied weakly, drank his scant ration, then folded his knees and sank to the hot sand. His arrival was a miracle of timing, because if he had reached the fence after we had passed through it, he would have died there. Only Larry had known he was following, and a fence was no obstacle to him.

We rigged a fly for the noon camp and sweltered beneath it until it was time to move again. Then Julie, whining at the edges of the shade, refused to follow. She crept piteously on the heels of her paws out onto the hot sand, yelped and ran back. Dad took the hobbles off Trooper's neck and coupled her collar to Larry's, forcing the stronger dog to drag her.

The afternoon was worse than the morning. The heat pressed like a physical weight on the land and rose in solid waves from it. The ground burned through the leather soles of our boots, and the flock tongued and ran back to the sparsest scrap of shade. Gunner wavered doggedly along in our rear, and the older goats – those carrying young, or burdened with dragging udders – were lying down and had to be repeatedly dragged to their feet.

Painfully, mile by slow mile, we battled them on towards the dancing, glittering horizon. The flies buzzed and the sand burned and every stubborn nanny seemed endowed with the strength and obstinacy of a wild mule. I carried a half-grown kid across my saddle pommel until my arm felt like it was breaking from the weight and awkwardness of holding him there. Later I carried Julie, who yelped and wriggled when her raw pads touched the metal dee rings. Later again, I noticed that Larry was missing.

'Back with Gunner,' Dad said. And twisting about I saw him padding slowly with hanging tongue in the blue horse's shade.

Ever so slowly the day passed. As the shadows before us lengthened, the heat lessened, and a dry little wind rose out of the east. There was grit in its folds, but Dad grunted with satisfaction.

'Good. They'll smell the water further. Tired, Kerry?'

He said it kindly, eyes screwed half shut from habit though the glare had gone. He had never encouraged us to admit to weariness or thirst, so I denied it, adding inconsequentially, 'I'm glad we never ate Jimmy-Jack, aren't you?'

'Worth his weight in mutton chops,' he agreed, and behind his beard I saw he was smiling.

Later, when Olga lay down, I cried. Mostly from rage and frustration because she had come so close to making it. Older goats were still walking, even lame ones and kids, but Olga had given up.

'She'll follow,' Dad said, but I knew she wouldn't. He did too. When he stopped to adjust his saddle it was only an excuse. Riding slowly on while the futile tears dried, I knew he would use his stock-knife to pith her before the crows came.

He said nothing when he caught up and I didn't ask. She was only a goat, after all. A half-wild nanny Judith and I had saddled with a silly name. One out of three hundred, and a quitter to boot.

The sun was slipping from sight and the daylight fading when Darky lifted her head at the sudden galvanic movement through the flock. *Bongle, bongle, bong!* went Jimmy-Jack's bell. And with horns undulating over hairy backs, the whole flock took off at the big wether's heels.

The packhorses cantered after them, whinnying. An answering call came out of the mulga, where firelight winked red in the distance. Our tired mounts lengthened their stride along the sandy wheel ruts, and Dad said, 'Smell it?'

There was goat on the wind, hot horseflesh and smoke. Then I breathed in again and caught it, faint and indescribable – water, the most wonderful smell on earth.

We had come to Cockroach Hole.

NINETEEN

Felicity Well was an abandoned Territory station on the edge of the Simpson Desert, a cross on a mud map roughed out in charcoal on a square of cardboard, drawn for Dad by a passing prospector.

'Good water,' the stranger said, swigging his tea. 'Just a bit of a leak in the rusting trough, and the pump lever might need some work.' It was only two years since he'd last been there – nothing much would have changed in that time.

Chewing on damper and salted goatmeat, Sian and I listened, knowing from the detail Dad was collecting he was weighing it up. New routes could be risky. Especially in summer. And prospectors weren't stockmen. They didn't necessarily bother with the surface qualities of land.

In the end it came down to a choice of evils. It mostly did. We were heading for Queensland, and to get there we had to cross the

Walkamen Range, which straddled our route. The goats would make nothing of it, but it meant steep pinches and narrow gullies for the wagonette, and at least three days over stone for our unshod horses. But by travelling south-east to Felicity Well, then describing a dog-leg via Walkamen bore on the edge of Culdee Downs, we could miss the stone country completely. The grazing should be better on the softer going, and it would take no longer. If the old track was still there. And if the Well could water forty horses and three hundred goats.

When the prospector had left us, we waited. Dad rolled himself another smoke, then picked up his bridle.

'You've gotta chance your arm some time,' he said. 'The stone country'll cripple them. We'll try it.'

He rode from camp on Medal and we saw no more of him that day, but it was no cause for worry. We knew he'd be finding the old track, and checking the water level of the Well. Summer in the desert, as he was fond of telling us, was a game that soon weeded out the careless players.

∽

Two days later we reached the Well. The track, unused for years, was covered in places by drifts of sand. It muffled the noise of moving hooves so that a stillness lay over the land, like a spell had been put on it. Sian said it was only the heat, but even the horsebells seemed to clang more raucously than usual.

The goats moved in purposeful rushes, feeding from bush to bush, heads wagging, yellow eyes knowing. Their muted bleatings sank like murmurs into the landscape. But a horse's sudden whinny startled, reverberating like a gong in the heated air.

The walls of the Well had been timbered and there was a raised stone rim and a sort of tin lid to it. The pump was a primitive affair, eaten with rust. Dad, arriving before us, had lashed a new timber lever to the wreck of the old and plugged the leaky trough with a fat-coated rag. He pumped, and we wandered about inspecting the place.

The old shack, set back behind the Well, its verandah collapsing on it, was a thing of crumbling posts and flapping tin. The short feed, so dry it crunched underfoot, grew right to the walls over the bits of twisted metal and blue glass that lay about. A dried tangle of desert-pea stems anchored the fallen chimney to the ground. None of us went inside. All the silence of the day seemed to come from the rusting iron of its empty rooms.

It took hours to water the stock, and there was only an axe-handle of daylight left when we moved on. We'd do a few miles, Dad said, break the back of the morrow's longer stage. I was glad we weren't camping at the Well. There hadn't even been a lizard there, just crows flapping about. They could fly miles for water.

We camped amid spinifex rings that night, with a full moon showing us the hump of the Walkamen Range away to the north-east. The goats settled down, and we could hear the horsebells knocking through the scattered mulga. Feed was short but plentiful. The detour seemed to be working out just fine.

We were moving again by sunrise, bending slightly south into a day of increasing heat and sand. The wagonette wavered on ahead of us through seas of blue mirage, the plodding horses black with sweat. Then a red tinge grew in the sky, spreading higher and wider as the wind got up. We were on lunch-camp by then, but Dad cut it short, heaving the tea from the billy.

'Push 'em,' he said. 'That's a bad one coming. We've gotta make the bore before we lose the track.'

We did, but only just. We rode in a cacophony of screaming wind, hot as a furnace breath, which seemed to have whipped the whole country into motion. The sun had vanished behind the wall of moving sand. Time had no measure. We knew we had reached the bore only by the tortured scream of the mill we couldn't see, and by blundering into the hobbled horses which shuffled past us, heads down, rumps to the stinging sand.

We dragged our mounts to the trough to drink, unsaddled and crawled thankfully into shelter under the wagonette. Dad had parked side on to the storm and dropped the heavy tarpaulin down to act as windbreak and ground sheet. It was smotheringly hot, and wind gusts occasionally shook the sturdy vehicle. The storm roared on and on, spraying sand over us, and eventually the noise and fury of it battered me to sleep.

I woke shivering in the silent chill of dawn. There wasn't a goat or a horse in sight. No sign of Dad or his bridle either, but his tracks showed he'd headed back west. Sian and the others woke then, and we stared in wonder at the change the storm had wrought.

Sand was heaped in drifts against the side of the trough, the tank and the wagonette wheels. Yesterday's feed had vanished under a smooth red carpet that stretched to the horizon. There was no sound of bird or bell. The mill-wheel, gappy with missing sails, hung as still as if painted on the sky. Even the flies had vanished.

'The road's gone,' Sian said blankly. 'Horses too, I shouldn't wonder.'

'They haven't.' I pointed triumphantly. Dad, bareback on old Rambler, the waterbag slung over his shoulder, was leading Wadgeri into camp on a halter fashioned from hobbles and his own belt.

'Don't stand about,' he said in greeting. 'Get the billy on. Then Kerry can come with me. You,' he told Sian, 'keep your eye on the trough. Hang onto any stock that comes back but don't go looking for 'em. There's no tracks, no pads, everything's buried out there.'

It was a strange world we rode into, the sand as bare and featureless as the blue curve of the sky. Mulga thrust startled trunks out of drifts, and shadows seemed preternaturally sharp. The heat increased steadily, and out of nowhere the flies returned. Then, with the shade lying between mid-morning and noon, we found the first of the horses.

'Trooper.' Dad jerked his chin, but I'd seen him too. Out of hobbles, travelling at a steady pace. He shot off at sight of us, tail plumed out like a brumby's, and Dad jammed his hat down and took after him.

'Bloody old fool!' he roared, once he'd blocked him up. 'What's got into yer?' The grey snorted and made another dash. He was keyed up, thirsty, not about to follow or be driven anywhere. Dad saw it too. 'Put your bridle on him,' he said to me. 'I'll have to ride him.'

Trooper snorted at my approach, wanting to chase after the now freed Wadgeri. He was a hard horse to catch, the grey. Bent double, I crept slowly to his feet, caught the hairy tuft of his fetlock, moved his legs together, then cautiously ran my hand upwards. When I had the neck-strap I raised the bridle – and he jerked free and galloped off, Wadgeri cantering behind.

Dad blocked him again. Trailing behind on foot, I saw him snatch the hobbles off Rambler's neck and catch, then saddle, the grey. Rambler trotted after my bay, and as Dad stooped to Trooper's hobbles the horse ripped by him in a great plunging buck. Dad hung on. Then the headband of the bridle snapped and the grey tore free. And kept going, galloping in the hobbles, carrying saddle and waterbag with him.

All three horses were just specks in the distance by the time I'd caught up.

'What will we do?' I asked.

He reached for my bridle, handing me the broken one in exchange. 'You stop here. Get in the shade and don't move. I'll go after them.' He took a slow look around at the immensity of sand and sky, and panic touched me.

'How long will you be?'

'Until I get back.' He tugged his hat down. 'Stay put,' he said and trudged away.

It was very lonely without him. I retrieved my saddle, hung it by one stirrup in the fork of the shadiest tree and sat beneath it. Both Dad and the horses had vanished into the shimmering mirage of midday. The heat played tricks with your eyes, so I knew it was no good straining to make shapes out of wavering blobs in the middle distance. I drew a line in the sand where the shade ended. It would serve as a clock, measuring the passage of time until he got back.

I found a flat pebble, shiny and hard, to suck. It kept the saliva in your mouth when you were dry. I had a pint bottle of water in my saddle pouch, but I wouldn't drink it yet. You had to wait when you were short, until you couldn't wait any longer.

The heat was intense. Sweat sprang out on my skin, which, for a brief delicious moment, turned icy cold as the breeze touched it. I practised juggling, tossing pebbles from right hand to left. I copied into the sand neat prints of animal tracks – dingo, cat, emu, wallaby, goat. I watched the shade shrink, then inexorably lengthen. And still Dad didn't come.

There was bread and cold meat in my saddle pouch. I ate a little and drank a few mouthfuls of water. When it got cooler, I could follow Dad's tracks. Only I'd never catch him up if he was no longer on foot. But what if the horses beat him to the Well, found the dry trough and kept going back to their previous watering spot? What if he never came back? He was breaking the rules he'd taught us, walking in the heat without water. Taking the sort of risks that killed.

Aeons of time passed. I watched the shade move, counted off the mouthfuls of water I swallowed, and clutched my knees – it stopped my legs getting up and carrying me off into the heated emptiness to look for him. If he hadn't returned by dark, I would head back to camp. There'd be a moon – maybe I could find it. But in any case the water bottle was now empty, so I couldn't stay here.

Dad said your head went first when you perished. You did stupid things, like chucking away your clothes. People had died criss-crossing roads that could have led them to safety, they'd given up within a few paces of water they could no longer see. I'd seen the bodies of perished stock but never a dead person. I felt clammy and cold in the middle. Half of me wanted to jump up then and go, but the other half was afraid of the bigness waiting there.

Towards sunset a breeze sprang up. It riffled the sand and sighed against the bridle I'd hooked over a branch. When the bit bars rattled, I stared stupidly at its still shape, then slowly turned my head. And there were the horses jogging towards me out of the sunset, heads and manes limned with light, the sand muffling their tread.

Dad came cantering to block them up. A sudsy lather covered Trooper's flanks and chest, blackened now with sweat. Dad's shirt was rimed with dried salt, his beard spiked with it. He carried a bottle of water, its neck plugged with greenwood, and there was another sticking out of his saddle pouch. The neck-bag slung against Trooper's chest was full – I could smell it as I stumbled towards him.

'All right?' he asked.

I nodded, gulping the sweet well water. It spilled down my chin, wetting my shirt. 'I thought you weren't coming back.' My voice quivered. I couldn't say more, tell what I knew. Tears splashed like rain on my cheeks, the bitter, salty taste of them mixing with the pain inside me. The sun had set. I smelled, without pity, the rank smell of Trooper's steaming body and waited, still gulping at the bottle's ridged neck, for Dad to speak.

I wanted him to laugh at me, to call me foolish. But he just sat silent, slumped in the saddle. His flesh seemed to have shrunk, deepening his eyes, turning his nose beaky in the nascent light of the moon. He had never looked so tired, so – old.

When I had cried long enough, he turned his head and said wearily, 'Catch your horse, Kerry.'

Moonlight blurred his features. Under the hat brim, his shadowed eye sockets stared out of a skull.

TWENTY

We'd just got the team unharnessed after the second puncture when the police vehicle caught up with us.

'You wouldn't read about it in *Ripley's*!' Dad said. We'd had more than three years without a flat. Now our patches were useless, the whole tin perished from the heat of past summers. We'd have to camp, he said, and either stuff the tyre with spinifex, or ride ahead to the next station and get the tubes mended.

That's when the vehicle came bumping towards us. A young copper got out and walked over.

'Glad I caught you,' he told Dad, shaking hands and introducing himself. 'Mike Jameson, from the 'Dangie. Bloke called Robertson wants to see you. He manages Walgra Station. He's looking for contractors to start mustering. Heard you'd gone through with your plant and asked me to bring the message, seeing I had business out this way.'

'Did he then?' Dad scratched his beard and kicked the tyre. 'Well, thanks. I'll check it out when I get this sorted – you wouldn't have a spare patch on yer?'

The copper gave Dad a hand to mend the punctures while we boiled the billy. It was near enough to noon to make no difference. We sprawled on the grass, one eye on the horses, listening to the men talk. Larry, from his possie under the pole, followed the constable's every move. He didn't like strangers in the camp. Julie, the little kelpie, had been sold with the goats back the other side of the border. She'd been Dad's dog so we didn't mind. There'd be no place for sheep dogs, he told us, when we started work in cattle country.

It felt strange to be in Queensland at last, with only the plant to worry about. No flock, no cat even, for Normie had left us at Cockroach Hole – gone bush without a backward look, to seek a mate. Now there was just Larry and the horses, and, by the sound of things, the prospect of our first job.

It took us two days to backtrack to the Walgra turn-off, and until mid-morning to make it into the station. Dad pulled up and chained the wheel a hundred yards shy of the buildings.

'Whatever the boss here is like,' he said, 'he's not planning on hiring a camp o' kids. So stay outa sight. Time enough to show yerselves once I've landed the job.'

Neither Judith nor I wanted to argue with this, but Sian did. After fussing around for ten minutes, he started after Dad.

'Hey! You've gotta wait here,' Judith told him, but Sian kept walking.

'Yeah,' I agreed. 'Dad said for us to keep out of sight.'

'He said for you kids to – I'm not a kid.'

Sian had worked for a few weeks in the stock-camp at the place where we'd sold the goats and, ever since, he'd been acting like he'd been far away and found it better there. He was scornful and bossy with the rest of us and even argued with Dad. And he wanted to get rid of the Queen and get a truck. Neither Judith nor Patrick could understand this, and nor could I.

Dad was rubbing his hands when he and Sian came back.

'We're on the books,' he said. 'No point in losing the job before we start, so you lot take the plant on while I get some tucker from the store. Bit o' luck, the boss won't set eyes on yer for a week.'

''Tisn't gunna work,' Sian said impatiently. 'How can we muster when they dunno the first thing about cattle?'

'Because I know,' Dad said. He hung his pipe from his mouth and spoke around the stem. 'There's a few hundred things man don't know, including what's got into you lately, but you can lay money on me knowledge o' cattle. Listen to me and you'll learn all you need.'

And that was how it worked out. We stayed all season, mustering the gidyea scrubs and holey blacksoil plains where the Bullsheads ran. Walgra was a bullock depot for the Victoria River Downs cattle, which were branded with the horned outline of a bull's head. VRD, as it was known, was the largest holding in Australia. The bullocks came down every year in mobs of fifteen hundred, from the flood plains and scrubs of the north to the grey channels of the Georgina country.

They were lean and wild, the Bullsheads; high-shouldered, with raking horns. Tinners, Dad said. Destined, every one of them, for bully beef, and they must have been aware of their fate, for you never saw anything gallop so hard to avoid it.

There were a lot of camps on Walgra, some among coolibah by milky-grey river holes where the horses splashed and jostled to drink, some in the huge back paddocks where the grass met the sky with only a fence to break the emptiness between. We camped at the Blue Gate and the Serpentine Crossing with other contractors, coming together to draft the road mobs the drovers were waiting to lift.

In the paddock you could track the galloping bullocks by their dust. Dad bought a pair of binoculars from a hawker who drove around the camps, cursing the flies and the country and the stupidity of the men working there. It was the first time, Dad said, anyone had insulted him while actually taking his money. The binoculars helped, though – you could see the bullocks and get between them and the scrub before they knew you were there.

We had never worked so hard, or such long hours. The boss, who went by results, was reconciled both to us and the pace of the Queen. The other contractors had trucks, and Dad was now talking of getting one too.

Ken Bulgar the drover, known to everyone as Brolga, was interested in buying the wagonette. He'd cut it down, take off the front end with the turntable, and make it into a two-wheeled trailer he could tow behind his fifteen-hundredweight Ford.

The Brolga had a wife and two young boys with him. Mrs Brolga, whose name was Thelma, did the cooking. She was a thin, haggard woman who hated the camp life. She wanted to live in town where the boys could go to school. 'But it's no good for Ken,' she sighed. 'At least when he's out bush he's away from the pub.'

There were five men in their camp, four stockmen and a new chum called Bluey – a gangly, freckle-faced redhead who couldn't do anything right. Every horse he got on threw him, again and again. They'd pig-root around, playing up because he was green, while the Brolga shook his head in disgust. He'd yell, 'Get yer feet forward, Bluey, an' yer arse inter the saddle, fer Cri'ssake!' then swear at him for coming off. He had a rough time of it with the other men too, but Dad jumped on Sian when he slung off at him. Bluey was a tryer, he said, he'd turn into a useful hand – if they'd quit riding him long enough to let him learn.

The day came when we drafted the first road bullocks out, and that night we camped the nine hundred head on the wide grey plain before the river crossing. The Brolga would take delivery in the morning, but for tonight both camps would share the watching.

It was cold, and despite the sheet of iron used as a break, the flames flared red in the wind. We huddled by the fire drinking coffee while the moon rose like a great orange ball over the vast blackness of the mob. One of the Brolga's men was on watch and I heard him singing, the sound thin and lonely in the night. It made me shiver, seeing and hearing a proper cattle camp like that for the first time – the white blaze of the stars, the clop of the night horse's hooves, and the men's dark, hunched shapes. They sat nursing pannikins, or with hard palms held to the flames that high-lighted bony or bearded faces under wide hat brims.

Judith and I had begged Dad to be allowed to ride watch too. It wasn't necessary, he said, and we'd get a sickener of it before we were through, but he let us, anyway. I went on with Bluey who seemed amazed to see me.

'Why are you out here, Kerry? Joe's round the other side – it doesn't need three, surely?'

'I wanted to, and Dad said I could.'

I pulled my coat tight around me and burrowed my free hand deep into a pocket. Most of the bullocks were lying down, but a handful had stayed on their feet, huge horns glinting in the half-light. The air was so cold it seared, and I ducked my chin into the loop of my scarf. 'Isn't it great?'

'You think so?' Bluey sat awkwardly, legs straight down and his body tilted forward. His face and hands were raw from weather, giving him a chapped, youthful look none of the others had.

We rode side by side and I began, self-consciously, to whistle. He was riding too close to the mob. I edged Shuffler away and Bluey's horse followed, but all he said was, 'How come you aren't in school?'

'I'm fifteen!' I said, before I remembered. 'Only don't let on, will you?' I added. 'The boss thinks we're all a year older than we are. And anyway, Dad was teaching Patrick – and Judith, sometimes – until we started this job.'

Dad had only quit teaching a fortnight before. His lessons had been verbal ones – questions and answers from the saddle. And coming home from the Magellan paddock one evening, with nine miles still to ride, he'd picked the wrong moment to ask what turned out to be the last one.

'How many inches in a mile, champ?' he said. Patrick didn't answer. He was kicking doggedly at the ribs of a weary Yerra to keep up. 'Well, guess,' Dad encouraged. 'How many?'

'A mob.'

He said it with finality, as if remembering all the miles he'd ridden that day, and the previous one, and the other days stretching back before that. He said it the way somebody might bang down a tool, then dust off his hands and walk away – done with it, forever.

There'd been a bit of a silence while we listened to the wind getting up and burrowed fingers not holding reins into shelter. It was a shock to realise that Patrick didn't care what Dad was going to say, but in the end it wasn't much. He'd always understood Patrick.

'Righto, champ. We'll leave it at that.'

'Anyway,' I told Bluey now, 'we're going droving. School doesn't teach you much about that.'

'Might give you a choice, though,' he muttered, then Joe, riding past growled at us both to make a bit of noise.

I started to whistle, and before I knew it the watch was over.

Next morning the bullocks left with the drovers. It was ten days to the railhead with cattle, and another three back with the plant. We moved out to camp at Moontah bore – all except Sian. Dad sent him down to Mick Patton's camp at the other end of the station to choose the ten stockhorses we were buying from him. We needed extra mounts, but there was no time now to break in our own.

Judith took a bad fall at Moontah, Todd rolling over the top of her when he came down in the holey black soil. Both he and Jean had been pressed into service under the saddle, and the bay was born clumsy. Falls happened at Walgra. Sian, back cock-a-hoop from Patton's camp with the new horses, had Amunga somersault with him. Then, a few days later, at the end of a run, while we held the ringing bullocks, Dad realised Patrick was missing.

He waved us off the cattle and we spread out, heading back the way we'd come, cooeeing through the gidyea. There was no sign of him. Dad sent Sian back to the bore then, to get a smoke going with the old tyres the boreman used to unload the diesel fuel.

'He coulda dropped behind, got slewed in the scrub.'

We could sense his worry while he measured the daylight left. None of us said what we thought – that Patrick could be hurt. We kept riding until Sian's smoke rose in black billows over the distant scrub, then headed in wide zigzags for it. And found Patrick plodding along through the tussocky grass, making straight for camp, towing a crippled Gunner behind him. He hadn't even seen the smoke and bristled when we pointed it out to him.

'I know where I'm goin'.' Then his face shut into his obstinate look and he said no more. His eyes were red and I guessed he'd been crying about Gunner. Dad said you owned horses, you didn't marry 'em – but it was hard not to care.

The drovers came and went throughout the season, taking the bullocks off. Jimmy Chalmers took the second mob, then we mustered for the Brolga again. Bluey was gone from his camp and one of the kids had picked up a gangly pup from somewhere. The Brolga himself, it was said, had been on a ten-day bender after the last trip. And it might have run to three weeks, only his wife had smashed up the rest of the rum with an axe.

Judith and I visited her when the two camps came together again. She made tea for us and talked about the pup, and the house she and Kenny, as she called the Brolga, were going to buy one day, when he gave up droving. She had her wedding photo stuck in a tatty writing case, and pulled it out to show us.

'Bit different now.' She laughed self-consciously and pushed at her straggly hair. From brow to jaw her face was mottled with old bruising, like Judith's leg had been after Todd fell on her.

'Yes,' I said, unthinking. She made a sad little sound that was half a laugh, and I went scarlet with mortification.

'Oh, it's true, Kerry. Looks don't last. You want to make the most of yours – both of you – while you've got them.'

Judith and I exchanged startled glances at this. It was news to us that we had any. Later, walking back to camp, I said, 'D'you think she meant it? That we're ... you know, pretty?'

'Course not,' Judith said cheerfully. 'Pretty means curls and dresses, like the Taylor girls. But you're skinnier than them, and there's my nose – she was just pretending, saying it to be nice.'

Remembering Mrs Brolga's face I said, 'D'you think we'll marry someone who turns out like him? How can you tell anyway? I mean, she wouldn't have got married if she'd known he was going to belt her up, would she?'

Judith shrugged. 'I'm not marrying anyone, ever. You just get the cooking job. And look after kids. I'd sooner be riding.'

～

Dad was pleased with the ten saddlers Sian had picked. They had sound backs, strong legs and good teeth. You couldn't catch them outside a yard, but Larry was a fair horse dog and soon fixed that. There had been a stockman back on a border station who thought it the funniest thing he'd ever seen, the day Dad lost patience with Redback and sooled Larry onto him. He soon quit laughing, though. The dog followed wherever the horse went, biting him at every stride, until the demoralised animal ran back into the plant and stood, just begging to be bridled. The stockman thought it was wonderful – which proved he was a fool, Dad said. Any man who knew stock knew you couldn't drive one horse away from its mates. They always came back, and as long as they did the dog had to win.

We'd named the new horses by then, taking our time because some names we thought of just didn't fit, and the right one always came if we waited. There was Tinsel and Spotlight to go with the rest of our circus names. Dad gave the bay pony we called Rayon (in memory of Silk and Satin) to Patrick, in place of Gunner. There was Brandy, Whisky, Boko – who had a nose on him, Dad said, like a Roman senator – and there was Buster.

She got her name from the gear she smashed. She was part of Sian's string and would rear away the moment he got a foot in the iron, then take off before he could swing aboard. Work would fix her, Dad said. But that was before she wrecked two bridles and got away in the scrub with a new saddle. It had a knee-pad ripped off and a broken tree when we got it back, and Dad went wild. Work could wait, he said. She needed civilising right now.

He put a headstall on her with a thirty-foot greenhide rope bent onto the chin-strap. Buster snorted suspiciously, cocking an ear as Dad dropped the loose coils but hung onto the end. Sian looped the reins up and made a grab at the iron as directed, and when Buster went into her act Dad flipped the rope up over her neck and pulled.

She hit the ground on the broad of her back, and we winced for the old pad doing duty as a saddle. Dad let her up and let her think about it, then got Sian to lead her round before pretending to mount again. This time she landed on her ribs and lay winded, with rolling eyes and gaping mouth, fighting for air. Dad pulled the rope off then, and when Sian finally got on her she stood like a lamb.

The rest of us watched with satisfaction as he kicked her into hesitant movement. She'd cost ten quid; the saddle she'd wrecked forty-five. Once I'd have thought it didn't matter, but I knew better now. And what Dad maintained was true, there were only three sorts of horses – good ones, ordinary ones and the liabilities that could kill you.

It marked a change, that day with Buster – the end of something. We finished early, and when we got back Mr Robertson was waiting in the camp to pick up Dad and Sian. They drove off in a cloud of mystery. And returned near dark, at the wheel of a three-ton truck Dad had bought from the station next door. Our wagonette days were over.

We kept the table from the back of the Queen, but that was all. It was cut from pine that had been scrubbed white over the years, except where the brown scar of our brand was burnt into the middle of it. The Brolga came up with the three horses he'd promised, took an axe to the pole, then hooked the tow-bar onto his truck and towed the old Queen away. There ought to have been a fanfare as it lurched out of sight through the lignum in the grey river channel, but there wasn't. Just the wind and the cockies shrieking.

'Well,' Dad said, as if somebody had to say something, and that was all.

I think even Sian was a little bit sad.

TWENTY-ONE

We were on the road with the plant in the summer of '61, escaping out of the south-west from along the Wills River country down Boulia way. We'd been mustering agisted sheep for shearing, after another cattle job, and without really noticing it, got ourselves boxed in by drought.

There was feed enough on the agistment property. And aggravation too, because Ernie Canton, who owned the land, hated his neighbour Jim Mitchell, who owned the shearing shed. And neither of them could stand George Motts, whose sheep we were mustering.

Mad as cut snakes, the lot of them, was how Dad put it. Ernie and Jim took care never to meet. The last time they'd done so, five years before, one had tried to shoot the other. They'd been neighbours for forty-two years and had grown old hating each other's guts. There were two boundary fences between their properties, separated by twenty yards of no-man's land and enough loosely coiled barbed wire to make a panzer division think twice, according to Dad.

We kids never saw Ernie, who was a bit of a recluse. Dad did, and reckoned he was a head case. Then Ernie found out about Dad being a returned soldier too, and began liking his visits. Old Jim we saw most days at the shearing shed. He'd been a giant of a man but was now crumbling into old age in the company of an ancient sister called Florrie, and about fifteen dogs. There were dogs of all descriptions, everywhere. Old ones, bitches with hanging dugs and puppies tumbling about them, sheep dogs, cattle dogs, kangaroo dogs. You could hear their clamour from the bottom gate as you rode in, and see Florrie waving at you from among the forest of staked tomatoes in the garden.

That was something else they had at Jim's place. The house was bush-built, unsealed, with flagstone floors and open spaces cut in the walls for windows, and it was entirely surrounded by tomato plants. The fruit was everywhere, heaped in buckets and bowls, squashed into the flagstones, and lined up along the timbered edges of the windows.

We had never eaten so many tomatoes in our lives. At every visit, Florrie had another box of them for us. Hers was the dirtiest kitchen we'd ever seen, and though manners wouldn't allow us to refuse the tea she was always brewing, we didn't, Dad said, have to eat. So she gave us tomatoes instead.

The whole place was a mess – the fences were falling down, the roofs sliding off the sheds. Hens scratched among the tomatoes and under the kitchen chairs, and the dogs wandered in and out at will.

The sheds were really interesting, full of old furniture and machinery – there was even a sulky with all the harness thrown in the back.

Patrick was looking at it one day and found a nest of hen's eggs under the seat. He carried them back to the kitchen for Florrie, and she seized his startled ears and kissed him. After that he refused to go near the place.

'You'll hurt her feelings,' I said.

'Hers? What about mine?' He was indignant. 'Yerk! I'll prob'ly die of hydrophoby!'

When the shed cut out and we were packing to leave, Dad sent us all down to the station to say goodbye. Patrick went but he only waved from the gate. Then he hopped back onto Blade and waited, digging the toes of his boots into the horse's girth to make him prance and jerk about, so Florrie would keep her distance.

'Serve yer right if he threw you,' Judith said when we were riding away. 'You might wave to her, at least.'

'I already did.' But he lifted his hand again, and the last glimpse we had of Florrie was her skinny arm semaphoring vigorously above the tomatoes and a shifting sea of dogs.

We hadn't realised just how far the dry had spread in the weeks since we'd moved into the Wills River Country. The agisted land was like a grassed island of plenty, but beyond it the ground lay fissured and parched, like a corpse with the bones poking through. The red plumes of willy-winds roared across it. Crows croaked about the bores, where skeletal cows came to drink, and above the bare earth the edible scrub was stripped as high as a beast could reach.

It was past time we were out of it, Dad said. He'd been through the Big Dry in '44 down in the Corner Country, and seen what drought could do. Creeping death, he called it. We'd head north for the Gulf lands and the monsoon, he told us. It was far safer than waiting and hoping the rain would come to us.

The plant wasn't in bad condition for the time of year and the work it had done, but that changed once we began to move. The horses couldn't graze while they were being driven and there was little feed to hobble them on at night. Their flanks grew hollow and their necks thin, and each night the bells clanged continuously as they walked, looking for grass.

We had our first losses when three young colts gorged themselves on whitewood and died the next day from the poisonous leaves. That night we met the railway line to Dajarra and Dad opened the fence and let the horses in to graze beside the tracks. Next evening we were lucky again, camping beside the wired enclosure of a tiny cemetery – all that remained of an abandoned station. There were three graves but only one headstone, and half its inscription was lost.

Sian hopped over the rusty wire and read what he could of it. 'It says, "Mary Lois" – or maybe "Louise" – then a date. Can't make out the year. Then it's got "beholden" –'

'Beloved,' Dad suggested.

'Yeah, so it is. Then, "Weep not strange" – and the rest's missing.'

'It's stranger, not strange.' Judith peered in turn. '"Weep not stranger". What a funny thing to write! Wonder who she was?'

'Let's just be glad she was,' Dad said. 'There's a night's tucker there for a coupla saddlers. Catch whatever you're riding tomorrow and put 'em in.'

'Can we?' Sian was doubtful. 'Isn't it desecration or something?'

Dad, however, was positive. 'If she don't want tears shed, she's not gunna object to a coupla horses filling their bellies, is she?'

In the ridges north of Dajarra we came upon Alec Dietz camped with his plant on a bit of dry country where a light scattering of feed remained. He'd chosen to gamble and sit out the dry, carting water from the closest bore, and hand-feeding his plant.

He'd been there some time already. You could tell by the track he'd made running back and forth in the truck, and the piles of old black dung on the horse camp. There was a truckload of fenced-off hay stacked behind his fly-rig and a dozen bony horses standing around it. They looked worse than ours, particularly the mares and foals, always the first to weaken.

We drank tea with him, squatting on our heels in the hot shade of his fly. He spoke confidently of the rain coming before Christmas. Or by mid-January at the latest. Practically guarantee it, he said, but he sounded like Patrick mixing wishes into facts. Under the edge of the fly, the heat shimmered on the pile of hay. It didn't look much. Not to save a plant.

When our horses appeared, driven by Sian and Judith, Alec's head turned to watch them pass. They walked steadily, hobbles chinking against the tongued bells, snatching at dried stalks and old leaves. We had a hundred and twenty two, without the three poisoned colts, some of them unbroken.

'They look okay. You'll get 'em out, no trouble,' he observed gruffly. His gaze lingered on the tailers. I wondered if he was sorry he hadn't got out himself when he could. It was too late now — the hay was keeping his plant alive, but those horses we could see looked too weak to work.

'Good luck,' Dad said as he shook hands when we left, which was funny because he didn't believe in luck, but maybe he wanted to cheer Alec up. He looked pretty lonely as we drove off, standing there framed by the fly, with the barren hills and listless horses behind him.

We lost old Tony in the river channels at Walgra, in the Serpentine paddock. He bogged there when his hind foot, sliding between his braced front ones, hooked over the hobble-chain, bringing him down to smother in the soupy mud.

Dad looped a cable about his hind legs and towed him out with the truck. He retrieved the hobbles, sloshing them clean in a bucket. When he tossed the water out, it sank down a crack in the black soil without even wetting the surface dust.

There was no feed at all in Serpentine. The horses lipped at fallen leaves and twigs, and that day we lay up through the heat of noon, then drove on far into the night, making distance in the cool.

Crossing Walgra was like riding back through time. We passed the paddock where Gunner was crippled, the camp where Amunga fell on Sian, the gate where Mr Robertson told me, 'I've seen better hands than you'll ever be put up trees by these bullocks.' (At the time I was out on foot, where the cattle could see me.) We laughed, remembering how green we'd been, and kept riding.

Far ahead of us clouds began to build, and at night heat lightning played along the horizon. We were getting there, Dad said. Then one evening, when the horsebells rang heavy and dull under a blanket of grey cloud, it rained a little. Fat, warm drops which, ceasing even as they began, left the ground swarming with centipedes, risen from cracks in the soil at the first touch of moisture.

By daylight the clouds had gone, cleared by a desert wind and a rising tide of dust. We plodded north that day, with eyes half shut, the heat like a physical weight on our shoulders. Gradually the air grew moist and dense again. Clouds reappeared and lightning ripped once more at the sultry skies. And then one day there were pools on the road – real ones, owing nothing to mirage. Shallow brown puddles with bird tracks on the muddy edges and a green smudge of new grass coming through.

'Jesus, Mary and Joseph be praised!' Dad said, as if it were two inches of rain and the feed fetlock-deep already. It soon was, however, for all around us the showers and storms continued. We'd see them building, the dark cumulus clouds piled half a mile high, with the solid curtains of rain sheeting down beneath. Showers came out of nowhere. They fell while the sun still shone, before or behind us, dewing the horses' hides with silver droplets, while rainbows arced through the drizzle above them.

The plant's condition improved rapidly on the green feed, and their spirits too. The day the truck bogged crossing a running creek, Tumbler threw me and shortly afterwards got rid of Judith too. Sian got on him then, to teach him a lesson, and we shrieked to see him hit the dust in turn.

It was wonderful what a bit of green feed could do. The horses bucked and farted coming onto camp, pluming their tails like brumbies. We'd find a place to sit out the Wet, Dad said, and break the colts next March before we started looking for work. We could travel a bit longer yet – the rain we were getting now was just early storms.

'Why not stop here, then?' Judith said, and Dad snorted.

'We're not in the desert now, my girl. Here is somebody's bullock paddock. And the station's not gunna stand for that. Nope, we'll have to rent a paddock. 'S that, or chase horses all Wet.'

We pushed on, and as Dad had predicted the storms tapered off and the sweltering heat returned. We bypassed a dam to camp instead on Two Moon Creek – really no more than a narrow gutter cutting across the open plain – and that night were invaded by birds.

They came on a rush of wings, drawn like moths to the yellow fire-shine, and fell on us out of the startled air – a flock of budgies, dazed and exhausted, clinging to hats and clothing, teetering on bucket rims. We heard their bodies smacking into the windscreen, dying as they hit, and it was only when I swept the carbide light over, killing the reflected glow in the glass, that the carnage stopped.

We tried to count, and then to estimate their numbers, but the night defeated us. There must have been hundreds of them. One fell into the fire and died with gaping beak in a scorch of feathers. We moved all the live ones we could back into the darkness, guiding their clutching claws onto any support. Sundown must have caught them on the open plains with nowhere to perch, Dad said. Then, instead of a tree, they'd found us.

Next morning at grey light, they were gone. Swerving and twittering, they swept up in a green spiral to flash away across the plain. Judith and I collected the dead birds and laid them together in the grass, all their magic stilled. I wondered if it had rained yet, back at Dajarra.

While the dry spell held, we moved on to Camooweal, camping on the Common there. It was a summer hang-out for drovers, Dad said, and some of them came to visit. They talked horses and routes with Dad – and Sian, who would no longer just sit and listen, as the rest of us did, when company came.

Dad swapped Bimby Collins a nice bay colt in exchange for a packsaddle. Bimby was an old cattleman with a property outside town. He agreed to rent us a spelling paddock, and provide a killer as well. It was about four days' travel for the plant, Bimby said, and there was a hut, a horse paddock and a set of yards. The paddock was in good shape, about six miles from the hut, with nothing but a few bullocks running in it. Bimby was on his way out there himself, to load a truck of butcher's cattle for the Isa. If Mac liked, Bimby said, he and one of the lads could go along. Give him a hand to load up, and take a look over the place too.

It was Patrick who went. He and Dad threw their swags onto Bimby's truck while the rest of us put the plant together and hit the road again – well, two wheel tracks really, winding on through ridgy lancewood country as red as desert sand.

Judith and I drove the horses, our attention divided between them and the promise of the killer. It was ages since we'd had fresh meat. We'd picked up a few pieces of salted beef at Walgra to come north with, but there'd been only mutton down on the Wills. The thought of beef made our mouths water. We could grill the bones, have thick steak sandwiches and juicy roasts – there was no hunger like meat hunger. We could hardly wait to get there and fetch the killer into the yard.

We had to, though, because the blue-black clouds looming behind us meant business. The rain caught us on the last red ridge over-looking the wide plain that fronted old Bimby's hut. Instead of making a dash for it, Sian pulled up and the three of us wrestled the heavy tarpaulin over the load, pegging the edges to make a shelter. We hobbled up in the streaming rain, then hunched under the canvas, listening to it fall. It was just another storm, we thought.

But it wasn't. It was the monsoon.

Dawn came dripping with gusting showers. There was no sun, only low grey clouds. The firewood was wet, the plain sodden, and the track across it a long, unbroken pool of water. Sian stuck his finger into the bucket we'd left out overnight and whistled.

'Three inches at least. We're not going anywhere today.'

It rained, off and on, all day. Five horses went missing, and we found them wandering free, their hobbles having stretched in the mud and dropped off. Then the colts cleared out, and it took us all the next day to get them back. Half a dozen more hobbles had been lost by then, and still the rain fell.

'Dad'll be having a fit,' Judith said. 'We shoulda been there last night.'

Sian was looking at the sky. ''Tisn't gunna stop. We'd better shift while we can. We'll leave the truck, take the swags and tucker on to the hut on the packs. Then we can run the plant down to the paddock – the old man must know where it is by now.'

We were late getting away in the morning. Everything went wrong. The mud slowed us down and the rain kept falling, making the horses hard to pack. And we were out of meat. The last bit of corned stuff had been eaten the night before, so we loaded a carton of herrings in tomato sauce into the packbags. We tied the tarp down over the truck, called the reluctant Larry out into the rain, and headed off.

There was nobody at the hut when we got there. Just a note from Dad saying they were giving Bimby a hand with the cattle, then a bit of a mud map showing where the paddock was. There was a footnote in Patrick's writing: 'Dad sez pull the shoos off the grey be for you bush her.'

'Huh!' Sian said. 'Fat chance! The shoeing gear's back at the truck.'

The horses were jammed into the yard, crowding and kicking each other, as irritable as we were in the cold drizzle. We went through them quickly, pulling the neck-straps and hobbles off. Sian led the shod mare out into the horse paddock.

'She can stop here with our saddlers – better keep a packhorse too.'

It was dark by the time we got back from the paddock. Thankfully we hung our saddles and spread the sodden cloths. There was dry kindling next to the stove and even stretcher beds in the other room. Outside the rain was rattling down again. It sounded good in the warmth, to the taste of herrings and boiled spuds.

Later, lying on the edge of sleep, Judith said, 'Wonder where Dad and Patrick are?'

'Wherever, they won't be shifting far.' I yawned. 'Wonder if it's rained Dajarra way yet?' But Judith's breathing had deepened, and she didn't answer.

Dad got back a fortnight later, riding in with Patrick on borrowed horses during a dry spell. It was the fourth of January, he said – which meant we'd eaten Christmas dinner two days late. It was only fish, anyway. He had a string bag of oranges balanced across the top of his swag, and a letter for me.

The letter was the greater novelty. It had the name 'Len Baxter' on the back.

'Who's he?' I turned it in my hands, pretending not to remember the dark haired young man I'd met back in December. He'd visited one day in company with Pick Willets the drover.

'Somebody heart-shot,' Dad said. 'Came to the camp in Camooweal – didn't you see him making sheep's eyes at you then? Listen, the pair of us could do with a feed – what's there to eat?'

Sian curled his lip. 'Fish.'

It was a strangely different day. Soft and bright, with the sky freshly washed and the clouds white as new wool. The earth steamed as it dried, and the air shrilled with cicada song. Outside the hut, Larry slept with little yelping dreams in the shade of a supplejack, until Patrick pelted him awake with orange peel. We ate the golden fruit and swam in the creek below the yards, and I hugged to myself the contents of my letter – sweet as the sticky orange juice.

No boy had ever told me I was pretty before. I felt as if I'd travelled into another country, beyond the narrow world of that younger Kerry, which I had now left behind forever. I was no longer a child but someone old enough for boyfriends, for love.

Mid-afternoon we got the horses up and yarded a killer. We put the pack on Brandy to carry the meat back to camp. And later, in the smoky hut, with the insects mobbing the carbide light, we feasted on rib-bones and grilled liver. Around us the warm darkness pulsed with frog-sound and the shrill whine of mosquitoes. Far off to the north, heat lightning glimmered soundlessly, like monster firefly lights.

Dad swigged the last of his tea and threw another buffalo chip into the stove to hunt the mossies. He looked around at the four of us, and at the solid walls of the hut stacked with tucker and piled high with gear, and gave a gusty sigh.

'You wouldn't be dead for quids. Would yer?' he said.

TWENTY-TWO

We left old Rambler behind in the spelling paddock where the plant had summered. There was a gloss on his hide still, but he'd more than earned his keep, Dad said. He could loaf for a year or two, and we could trust Bimby Collins to carry a rifle to him when the time came. You owed 'em that much, Dad told us – to not let them go down and die with the crows at them.

There were plenty to replace him. We'd bought a dozen unbroken colts from Bushy Park, trucking them up the bitumen in February, then walking them in during a break in the weather. There were three Constant Star colts, bearing the nasty streak of their sire (Constant Star was Bushy Park's stud book stallion), and a collection of young mares: Sue, Dolly, Beverley, Slipper. Their names came as we caught them after often passionate argument round the table in the old hut. Sian stuck out for Marigold for the big yellow bay he was working, but we wound up calling her Tangerine. He swore she had thirteen legs, she was so rough to ride.

Judith had Caesar, a Roman-nosed bay that Dad had named. He was a kicker, one of the Constant Star line, free-going but touchy. As she was riding out with the boys one day, Caesar's feet scared a bird out of the grass. He dropped his head and threw her and shortly afterwards Patrick came running to tell Dad something was wrong.

'What happened?' Judith asked, but when Sian told her, she stared blankly round at the lancewood rails. She stood in the yard crying, still holding Caesar, and could remember nothing since unhobbling him that morning.

'What happened?' she asked again, and Sian told her again, but still she stared blankly and her lips trembled into another bout of tears. 'Where is this? What happened?'

There was a transceiver in the hut. Dad called the doctor, who diagnosed concussion; he said for her to rest and for Dad to contact him immediately if her pupils became unequal in size, or if she vomited. Neither event occurred, but nor did she regain the lost bit of memory.

~

In March we had two visitors, one of whom brought me another letter from Len. I had sent a reply to his first one when the colts came. He had still been in Camooweal then, but this one spoke of a new job on a place called Morestone. I read it hurriedly while the billy boiled, then rejoined the others because the visitor was a drover and had come to buy horses.

He went off eventually with six, including Starlight and old Dumpy. With Starlight gone, there was just Yerra left out of the brumbies we had taken from Humpy's mob. Only Patrick rode her now, the rest of us had grown too tall. She hid a good stock sense and nippy ease of movement behind a dozy exterior. And our second customer wanted her the moment he saw her.

'Jesus! Anyone'd think it was a horse fair!' Dad said when he got the call on the radio. 'He's the postmaster, an' he wants a kid's pony. He's getting a mate to drive him out here, 'n' he's gunna ride the pony back to the Dip yard this arvo. Sounds like he's buying a shirt or something. Well, here's yer chance to make yer fortune, champ. Sell him Yerra.'

'No!' Patrick leapt to his feet like his pants were on fire.

'Only kidding,' Dad said. 'But get the books out – see if there's anything dead foolproof we can make a profit on.'

Judith, however, didn't need the list of names and descriptions in the horse book. 'There's Collie,' she said.

She was Starlight's daughter, a chestnut, as placid as her dam had been unreliable.

From the moment he climbed out of the vehicle and bounced towards us, it was plain that Warren, the postie, was as green as nine-day grass. He had bought a stiff new saddle and still newer jeans for the occasion. A flat-crowned hat perched uneasily above ginger hair, and below his rolled-up sleeves the skin of his arms and hands was milky-white. He was quite prepared to take which-ever horse we offered, on trust, but Dad got Sian to slide all over Collie and pick up her feet to demonstrate her suitability.

He wouldn't stop for a meal, or even a drink of tea – he wanted to get going.

'Fifteen miles is a fair hike on a fresh horse,' Dad said warningly.

'Oh, I'll trot along. Won't take more than an hour or two,' he said, and Dad blanched.

'She's a bit soft for that. Better take it easy.'

Sian had got Collie saddled by then, and we all watched Warren haul himself aboard. He settled his boots in the stirrups, pulled his chin-strap tight, and picked up the reins – and for the first time in her life the chestnut billy-goated, squealing, across the camp.

He didn't come off. That was the second miracle – the first was how we all managed to keep a straight face.

Dad was shaking his head with a faraway look in his eyes.

'Jesus, Mary and Joseph! 'Cept that he's older, that was you lot, five years ago. I dunno how I ever did it.'

～

We were moving again by late April, heading north up the Gulf through balmy days and knee-deep feed. The owner came out from Martins Creek as we were going by and asked about kids' ponies. He wanted one for his son, something bigger than a Shetland, but reliable. He'd heard the postie in Camooweal had got one – did we have another?

'Maybe,' Dad said. 'What you got to swap? I'm not after cash.'

It was a brown race mare, big-framed and excitable with a kind eye. Not young, and she couldn't breed, but plenty of stock savvy and an easy ride away from the track. She would do, Dad said, adding unexpectedly, 'You can have her, Kerry.'

He did that from time to time, bestowing horses upon us. I had five of my own that nobody else ever rode. He chose a quiet skewbald called Monkey for the swap, and we made the exchange at the station yards, with the plant waiting just outside.

Dad led Monkey over to where the boy was waiting and tossed him up, bareback.

'Look at me,' the boy squealed at his watching parents, but I was too busy staring at the young man bringing the brown mare out of the yard.

'Len! What are you doing here? I thought you were at Morestone.'

He grinned. 'Tending muster.'

He had dark eyes, straight dark hair and a dozen badges pinned to the front of his high-crowned hat. We were about the same height. His nose was straight and shapely, but his ears stuck out. Despite all the imaginary conversations I had conducted with him, I couldn't think of a thing to say. I peeped sideways at him while he cleared his throat and fiddled with the reins.

'I got your letter,' I said at length. 'It was great.'

'Good. Where you heading now?' He frowned. 'I mean, where'll I send the next one?'

'I don't know. Dad's looking for a mob. If we get one, I'll write and tell you, then you can write to the delivery point.'

'That'll do.' His face cleared.

The brown mare shoved at his hat and snorted, spraying him with wet, and we both laughed. It was easier then. We talked about her breeding (Caroset, from a mare called Miss Viola) and Martins Creek, and what it was like at Morestone.

Before I knew it, Dad was there with a saddle over his arm. As her new owner I was to ride the mare away.

I led her out, very conscious of Len's eyes on me, and slipped the reins up. She was fretting at the bit, ears flicking, treading all over me.

I could hear hooves racing down the paddock, and as I reached for the iron she went up, shrilling, and pawing the air, nostrils like great dark pipes, then came crashing down on her flank and shoulder.

'Oh, deary, deary me!' The skinny man who owned the place was as dumbfounded by the brown mare's behaviour as we had been by Collie's.

'Hop on her, boy,' he said.

Len did as he was asked. The mare reefed and danced, sweat breaking on flanks and chest as he trotted her round, watched anxiously by her former owner.

'Just excitable, Mac. Deary me, yes.'

I bit my lip.

'Blue blood. Look, you ain't going far. Johnson's bore, you said? The lad can ride her down. I'll come by and pick him up this arvo.'

'Bit o' luck, that,' Len said ten minutes later as we rode out the gate behind the plant. 'I get another coupla hours with you.'

'Doesn't your boss ever swear? I nearly died when he came out with that "deary me" bit! Dad was glaring like a mad bull, he always knows when Judith and I are getting the giggles.'

'Nup.' Len shook his head and curbed the brown mare's walk

to bring her alongside my bay. 'He as tough as he looks, your old man?'

'You better believe it.'

We never saw Dad's iron visage as unapproachable, but were aware that others did. He had given me a talk about boys during the summer, mostly concerned with what I mustn't do. Girls were in control of relationships, he said; boys were little more than sex fiends. Len didn't look like one, but how could I tell? A phrase I'd heard a shearer use about Dad floated into my head. 'We don't even cook the horseshoe nails he has for breakfast.'

'Well, I don't plan on annoying him,' Len said. 'Hey, you reckon you'll be going to the races at the 'Weal next month?'

~~

We didn't, we went droving instead. Dad got the offer of the Thornton cattle – a thousand head, bound for Merton Downs where the gidyea and downs met, a trip of five weeks. He'd already accepted before we learned of their reputation. No other drover would touch them. Jumpy cattle, everyone said. Rush if the night-horse farted. Dad rubbed his chin with his thumb, pushing his beard sideways so that it showed as much grey as brown.

'Gotta start somewhere. We make a good delivery, we'll have more work than we can handle.'

'And if we lose 'em?' Sian asked.

Dad looked at him like he'd said something indecent. 'We won't.'

TWENTY-THREE

Droving wasn't the same as station work, we all understood that. On the stock route only your reputation mattered, and reputations were built on what you delivered. To lose a mob, or a large part of it, finished you as a drover. That was why the Thorntons' were going begging – nobody wanted the risk while other cattle were available.

The station yards were on a gum flat in the Thornton ranges, with a bit of a creek wandering past at the back, and the bore and horse paddock tucked in behind. Thorntonia Station was mostly hills and scrub. Lancewood to the west, thick as it could stick; and to the east and north, ranges crowned with boulders and raggy eucalypts. There was box and turpentine in the gullies, and spinifex everywhere else except for the bare scree slopes only wallabies could cross. It would take four days to clear the hills, the boss told us. Then once out on the flat country, we'd turn south.

We camped below the yards while we waited to take delivery. A Thornton stockman called Macey pulled out the day we arrived, and Dad hired him. We'd need him, he said, if we had to double watch. He also had a couple of bags of grain sent up on the mail, for the night-horses. If the cattle were only half as jumpy as was claimed, he told us, chances were they'd need it too. The bullocks were mustered into the yards for drafting and dipping, then spent the night there, ready to leave next morning. After sunset the station men came to visit, still in their dirt-stained clothes, with stubble-shadowed jaws. They said the last drover to lift the Thornton cattle had done the lot, third night out. A night-horse had set them off when he pulled away and cantered into the cattle, dragging his reins. The bullocks had split for the lancewood and the drover had lost all but fifty head.

'Musta been a new chum.' Dad was unimpressed.

The head stockman looked put out. 'Skuthorpe couldn't ride in that scrub! That's tough country, Mac.'

'So he shoulda made a better job o' tying the horse,' Dad said. 'Scrub or no, that's pure bloody carelessness.'

That night the cattle ran up in the yard. We heard the brief thunder as they hit the rails, but the bullocks had been spread throughout the separate yards to lessen their impact in just such an eventuality, and the timber held. We could smell the dust drifting over us in the silence that followed the noise, then a beast bawled and Dad, a dark shadow by the dying fire, sank back into his blankets.

At daylight they charged out of the opened gates, pushing the lead riders before them. Patrick and I watched them go, a heaving flood of backs and horns trailing a scarf of red dust. They surged across the gum flat and over the ridge, plunging into the turpentines where only the riders' hats showed. The grey light was flushing to gold behind them and the rattle of galloping hooves on stone rang clear in the cool air.

The first night we camped them in a holding paddock, the trucks side by side between the cattle-camp and the nearest wire. The station men, as was the custom, were seeing us to the boundary. That meant two nights' help with the watching. Patrick, who was horse-tailer, caught Medal, Shuffler, Darky and Rose for night-horses. The station men rode their own — the best they had.

Sian had protested, when we first got the mob, that we couldn't handle it — we had no night-horses.

'Jesus, Mary and Joseph, boy!' Dad said, exasperated. 'We got dozens! All they need is good eyes, good lugs and good legs. Nobody's asking for a bloody pedigree as well.'

It was a quiet night, that first one. The moon, thin as a nail paring, rose late and gave little light, but the bullocks camped like milkers, standing up to stretch and move around at midnight, then settling down again. My rest was fitful, I'd done the early dog-watch on Darky and was too keyed up to sleep. I lay watching the fire, listening to the changing voices of the riders, the sudden spurt of trotting hooves in the darkness, waiting for something to happen. Nothing did. Then Dad was there on Medal calling me, the morning star bright above him, and it was time to get up.

The second night out we camped on Police Creek, on a timbered flat squeezed by scrubby hills. It wasn't ideal but there was nowhere better. I filled the nosebags as soon as I got the swags unloaded, then set about collecting wood and cutting bushes for a fire-break. Everything involving noise and movement had to be finished before the cattle came onto camp.

When Patrick arrived, I helped him hobble up. We put the nose-bags on the second string of night-horses, shivering as the sun dropped behind the hills. Then the bullocks were there, feeding towards us, and the second day's travel was done.

It was another quiet night. Larry caused the only excitement when he lunged to his chain's end, growling at a wild pig snuffling near the camp. Judith, pulling her boots on to go on watch, hissed, 'Siddown!' and he sunk obediently to his belly, still watching the pig, which slipped grunting back down into the cover of the creek.

One of the station men did the morning dog-watch, making it the last time, until the trip ended, we could all stand together round the fire. From now on, at least one of us would always be with the cattle. It was going well, Dad said, rubbing his hands over the flames. Piece o' cake. We'd be out of the hills by nightfall, with the worst country behind us.

The station men were still rolling their swags when Patrick and I were ready to leave. As the truck nosed its way past them, they waved and sang out. The one called Johnno, who had a black hat and a crooked nose, winked and blew me a kiss. The head stockman yelled, 'Good trip!' and I bipped the horn and chugged on down the track, following the mob.

That day the cattle watered, for the first time, in the river. Thorn-tonia was bore country, so they were used to troughs and didn't relish the deep river channels choked with dried burr that rattled against their ribs. Twice the lead fled back into the bulk of the mob before they even reached the water, sending the birds exploding from the trees.

We'd single them that night, Dad said, but keep the extra horses up just in case. We camped on a plain, half a mile out from the river, with a scatter of prickly bushes to provide shelter for the horses. The nights were getting colder now May was ending, and the wind was what Macey called dead tired – going straight through instead of around you.

Macey only had one name. The other was a secret between him and his Maker, he said, and was going to stay that way. He'd never been droving before either. He didn't talk much, but he knew what he was doing with horses. He had Danny in his string, and it was pretty to see him get on the horse without touching the animal's head. The black chucked himself over the moment you tightened the reins.

The bullocks were restless when they came onto the camp that night. Dad stayed out with Patrick, who had the dog-watch, to settle them. I put the camp oven back on the coals to keep his tea hot, and boiled the billy again for coffee. The others were already in bed, and I was pulling my boots off when I heard Brandy's quick shuffle approaching. Dad stopped singing about old Faithful, and I heard him grunt and the saddle creak as he swung down.

It was an hour to my watch, but it seemed only moments before Patrick's voice was calling me from sleep. I pulled on boots and coat, felt my way to the night-horses and freed Blackmagic's reins. In the darkness beyond the truck I waited, whistling softly, for my eyes to adjust and Patrick to come round again.

'Took your time, Kerry.' Yawning, he handed over Dad's belt with the pocket watch on it. 'Wotcher riding?'

'Magic.' I could make out the blaze on his mount and knew her for Tassle. 'Stick a log on the fire.' I reined away, whistling one of Dad's tunes, keeping the black moving and a sharp eye on the motionless outline of the mob.

When my watch was over I called Judith, then sat by the fire to drink coffee before rolling back into my blankets. I slept through Macey's watch and Sian's and came awake to a deafening roar, sudden as the sky falling, as the mob rushed.

The noise was like a cannonade, full of dust and fury. Sian yelled, then we were snatching at boots, running in the dark for the night-horse tree. The noise was fading – not getting less, but going away from us. Cold air, heavy with dust, shocked our faces as we ripped the reins loose and jumped for the saddles. Judith had fallen over the water bucket, so Macey, Sian and I got the horses. When my hands met the hogged mane, I knew I had Socks. The others sprinted away, racing blobs in the confused dark, and the saddle smacked my seat as the bay followed them.

It wasn't a bad rush. Dad had the lead by the time we caught up, but it took us an hour to work the mob back onto the camp. They rang up circling and bawling and pushing at us, unwilling to return. It was almost daylight by then, anyway, the morning star high above the prickly bushes. Dad sent me off to start breakfast and get Patrick away after the horses.

I could hear the bullocks playing up behind me and the thud of hooves on the wind. The rush had been exciting, but now I just felt tired and a little sick, for the dust lay heavy on my empty stomach. I wondered how many head we'd lost in the darkness.

After breakfast Patrick and I caught horses to help count the mob. Nothing was missing, but one bullock – a broken-horned beast with a black head – had been trampled in the rush. He staggered on the tail, one eye pointing south-east and the broken horn dangling. Dad swore at the sight of him, saying he'd never make it. But he was still there at dinner-camp, and again that night. He lay down apart from the others and when they jumped at midnight, he just stayed there, too sick to care.

He was on the camp still at daylight, lurching to his feet, the dangling horn swinging. You could see by the shape of his flank that his ribs were broken. His eyes stared wildly and he moaned as he walked. He couldn't steer a straight course, but he kept on going. We called him Crazy-head and started dropping him off each night near the camp, but not in the mob. Another trouncing would plainly finish him.

By then even Dad had admitted we were riding a tiger. Every night was torn apart by the familiar thunder as the cattle hit their feet. There was no figuring what started them – they'd be camped one moment and galloping the next. They jumped at sunset and daybreak and every hour between. They might run up the length of the cattle camp a dozen times in a watch, or gallop all night, dragging us back and forth like a comet tail, across the map of darkness.

Every morning Dad put on a count, and twice we pulled up while Sian and Macey backtracked to search for and bring in missing bullocks. Once Crazy-head was gone, but Patrick drove him back with the horses. The next night, dropped off as usual just short of the truck, the great brute staggered over to the night-horse tree where Dad ran into him in the dark. He rose up with a snort, slamming his crooked head into Dad's belly and snapping three of his ribs.

Things were serious then. In the dawn light, Dad's face was the colour of clay and every breath hurt. We strapped him up with blanket strips, but he could barely stand, let alone get into the saddle. Sian and I argued with him, while the bullocks carried Macey and the others off camp to graze in a windy dawn under red skies. Dad had to get help, Sian said. But Dad wouldn't leave the cattle.

'You can't even get on a horse!' Sian cried. 'What use are you gunna be?'

'I'm staying,' Dad wheezed. 'A man lifts a mob, he stays with it, even if it kills him.'

'Well, it prob'ly will!' Sian yelled. 'You think you can't die? Do yer? How d'you know you haven't bust your spleen or something?' He was hopping mad but only because he was scared.

'I'll let you know,' Dad said. He coughed, holding his ribs with his big, thick-fingered hands. I could see the missing end Grace had bitten off, and his double thumbnail, and suddenly I wanted to cry. I was scared too, but not for the mob. I didn't care if we lost it tomorrow.

'Stick a feed on for the men, Kerry,' Dad said then. He closed his eyes and lay back in the break and Sian, swearing to himself, jumped on his horse and rode out to the mob.

∾

It was four days before Dad was back in the saddle – and even then he was more ornament than use, Sian said. He rode half-days at first, listing against the pain of his ribs, unable to get out of a walk. Under the blanket strips his body was black with bruising. He couldn't mount unaided, so we shared his watch among us and got used to the sight of him hunched over by the fire as we ran past for the night-horses, or rode wearily back to our blankets.

The bullocks kept rushing. We left the Mitchell-grass plains for red, timbered country where dense swamps of pea-bush grew. Beyond that the land rose to pebbly ridges, where the bullocks' galloping feet struck sparks from the stone, and the scrub went down like pistol shots in the thunder of their passage.

We dropped Blackmagic off in the stone country, carrying a front leg he'd got jammed in the fork of the night-horse tree. We'd pick him up on the way back, Dad said. I drove in to tell them at the station, staring amazed at the orderly world about me, at flowers blowing in the manager's garden, and candy-striped sheets flapping above green lawns.

I had a drink of tea in the men's kitchen. The cook, who was soft and fat with treacly eyes and a big gold hoop in one ear, gave me a box of tomatoes from the garden and a pile of magazines. 'Something to fill your time,' he said. He had a high voice and winced theatrically when he saw my cracked and bleeding hands.

'Nobody's that busy, ducky,' he told me. 'Get a bit of cream into them.'

'It's a Thornton mob,' I said, but it didn't mean anything to him.

Next day, on dinner-camp, we lost Brandy. It happened just as the mob drew off to begin the afternoon stage. We'd started feeding the night-horses at midday, to save time in the evening. The brown gelding, snuffling after the last bits of grain, dropped his head down onto the ashes of our dinner fire, which wasn't quite out. The loose jute folds of the nosebag caught a spark and burst instantly into flame.

The horse screamed as fire ran up his face. He reared and took off, galloping across in front of the truck. Patrick's yell scattered the loose horses. He (Patrick) was stamping and jumping and I saw that little bits of fire were dripping from Brandy's face into the grass. His whole head was alight, his black mane a scarlet banner. He crashed into a tree and fell, and when he got up and galloped on, flame leapt into the branches.

Patrick was screaming at me but it took a moment for the words to make sense. 'Shoot him, Kerry! Shoot him!'

The .303 was in the truck between the seats. It seemed to take forever to get there. I spilled coats and cartridges onto the ground, crashing the rifle stock into the steering wheel while the screaming went on and on. I knew I could hit him if only the noise would stop. I could shoot better than anyone I'd ever met, even Dad, because my eyesight was keener than his. I poked the barrel through the window to use it as a rest, and cuddled my cheek down onto the stock. My hands were shaking, but when Brandy floated into the ring welded around the front sights I held my breath and squeezed the trigger, and the screaming stopped.

Patrick was yelling again, dragging at my jeans. I told him it was a heart shot and not bad for the distance. I said Brandy would have been dead before he fell and he hollered, 'Shut up, Kerry! Forget him!' His eyes blazed above his silly snub nose. 'Jesus! The whole paddock's burning – stop crying and help!' There was fire everywhere, climbing the trees, shooting away through the short dry feed.

We grabbed spare beef bags and beat it until the last scarlet runner died and our arms hung like lead weights from our shoulders. Brandy's body lay in the centre of the blackened ground, but we didn't go near him.

The loose horses had wandered off and the truck still had to be packed. Nobody had come back from the cattle, so Dad couldn't have noticed the fire, or the stench of burning flesh.

'Just as well you can shoot,' Patrick said.

'Yes.' Once, because I'd read about it in a western, I'd stuck a playing card up and shot the spots off it. It was a talent I had. Judith could make horses do anything she wanted, Sian was musical, and I could shoot. I'd rather have played the harmonica, like Sian.

∽

There was no time to write letters. Every spare moment was spent sleeping, but on the rare quiet watch I'd think about things to tell Len when the trip was over. It helped me keep awake.

Things about my brown mare, for instance, whose name I had changed from Miss Caroset to Lady Meg. She'd got excited on camp one morning and almost put me into the windscreen of the truck. Dad had clouted her as her chest hit the mudguard, and she'd spun away and taken off. She was a dream to ride, even when she was playing up.

There were things about the mob too, like crossing the Tick Line. This was an east-west mark on the map below which cattle tick weren't supposed to exist. All travelling stock had to dip at the Line. The stock inspector who came to oversee our mob being dipped had eyes with oblong irises, as startling to me as a second nose. I couldn't believe Dad and the rest hadn't noticed. Sian said I was having them on, and even Dad, whose ribs were starting to improve, looked sceptical.

I could tell him about old Crazy-head's diminishing chances too. He turned turtle in the dip and almost drowned before Sian got a rope on him and pulled him out. And, most important of all, I could tell Len that we still had our numbers, because Dad had got an accurate count through the yard.

We had two night's solid sleep at the dipping yards, because even Thornton cattle couldn't knock down railway iron. Then we went on, back into plains country, treeless, undulating land where the waxing moon rose like a great orange ball behind the cattle-camp. It was bitterly cold. The truck seemed to huddle under the freezing sky and we had only a few pale flames to ward off the dark. Eight more days, Dad said. If we could hang onto the mob for that long, we'd have proved we could cut the mustard with the best of them. Macey said Dad could give him a medal if he wanted, but he, personally, was planning on taking up bus-driving the day after we delivered.

Then, three camps short of the Merton Downs boundary, the strangest incident of all occurred. The route followed Sardine Creek at that point, with no proper track for the truck. It was open country, miles from the main road, so when a blue utility drove towards the camp late that afternoon, we assumed the driver had business with us – until he pulled up half a mile away.

Dad, drinking tea in the camp, waited, and after a while we saw Sian leave the cattle and ride over. He circled the vehicle and pulled up, leaning forward in the saddle. Then he wheeled away and came for the camp at a good clip. There was a man and a blue heeler in the vehicle, he said. The man was slumped over the wheel as if asleep, and the dog was going to have anybody who laid a finger on him or the car.

As usual, he was for doing something about it immediately. Like shooting the heeler so we could get into the car and examine the man.

'Jesus, Mary and Joseph, boy!' Dad said. 'You can't go shooting a man's dog!'

'He coulda had a heart attack.'

'He could be drunk, too.' Dad scratched his beard. 'Be dark in an hour. We're needed here, all of us. He'll have to wait till morning. If he comes round beforehand, I hope to Christ he don't put the mob over the top of us.'

Night brought no change to the car or its occupant. Sian rode back for a last look on dusk and we could hear the heeler's savage snarling from camp. Larry yapped in reply and got kicked for his pains.

The moon, a little past full, rose at the end of Patrick's watch. I could see its light glinting on the distant windscreen of the utility as I rode out. Then the angle changed and the strange vehicle was just a smudge far out on the plain.

I had Shuffler that night. We plodded our endless round, trotting occasionally to turn a wandering bullock back. I shivered and watched the stars wheel in their courses, and was just about to call

Judith out when the lights appeared. Shuffler saw them first. His head stuck up like a startled emu, and his body tightened beneath me. I snatched the reins short, thinking the bullocks were about to jump, and saw the pale discs floating silently towards me. Then Shuffler took off, and with a bang like a bomb exploding, the cattle rushed.

The night raced past me with a noise like a runaway freight train. Far behind I heard somebody yell. The lights curved smoothly across in front of me and blinked out. I couldn't hold Shuffler. His ears were flat, and his terror flowed into me as I sawed and hauled at the reins. The mob thundered beside me and just ahead was a belt of gidyea, solid as a wall in the moonlight. I sweated with horror, watching it rush at me.

Then Sian yelled at my shoulder, the wind tearing at his words. 'Pull off – the – scrub –'

'I can't!' I screamed, panic jolting into sudden rage. Sian was always telling me what to do, as if only he could ever see the obvious. My arms felt weak and useless, and my legs were shaking. Medal seemed to jump and Sian shot ahead of me. His arm went up. It swung again and again, the whip sounding like a volley of pistol shots. Shuffler's stride smoothed and the iron went from his mouth. He swerved in behind Medal, like the stock-horse he was, and we swept around the lead, turning it back from the gidyea with no more than a horse's length to spare.

Macey arrived soon after, then Dad and Judith. Patrick didn't even wake up. We couldn't get the bullocks back to camp, so we doubled them where we were, those off watch lying on damp saddlecloths in the lee of some gidyea suckers. The lights didn't return. When I described them, Dad said this was Min Min country. Queer things happened here. Lights came out of nowhere and vanished again. Such phenomena were often seen – or I could have mistaken the stranger's headlights for a Min Min.

I knew I hadn't – but at dawn the car was gone, and so was old Crazy-head. We never saw either of them again.

Three days later we delivered the mob, counting them over to the Merton Downs stock-camp a mile inside their boundary. We watched them feed away from us, and one of the station men, looking sidelong at me, nudged his horse over to join us.

'How was the trip, then?' he asked.

I kept quiet, letting Sian answer. Dad didn't like Judith or me acting too friendly with strangers. And he'd always told us not to make a parade of our difficulties. The world belonged to can-do people, he said.

Sian must have remembered that too. He yawned, setting us all off. We could have slept for a week, right where we sat.

'Piece o' cake,' he said.

TWENTY-FOUR

On our way back north, we stopped off for the sports day at the Forty Mile Dip. We'd first heard about it from the stockmen at Merton Downs – it was a calendar of gymkhana events and footraces, followed by a barbecue and dance – and Dad, in fine humour after the trip, said we might as well all take a look. Everybody attended these affairs, so you never knew who you might meet, maybe even somebody in need of a drover.

We went full of schemes for scooping the pool of prizes on offer. Sian had got hold of a program, and we'd been practising jump starts and figure eights ever since. The four of us had only ever attended one race meeting, at the 'Dangie, when we'd worked on Walgra, but we'd just been spectators then. This would be our first competitive meeting. We matched horses to events and debated endlessly our chances and the possible competition we'd encounter.

We got to the Forty Mile half a day early and found others before us in a scatter of horse-floats and campfires across the flat. Ours was the only plant, so Dad pulled up across the creek, to give the horses room. We hobbled up, unpacked, and wandered over.

The actual dip yards and bore were half a mile from the racetrack where the events were held. There was a scatter of iron buildings, consisting of the judges' stand, overhead tank, hall, toilets, and the open-fronted shed that served as a bar and refreshment stall. There was a zinc bathtub behind the bar for cooling beer, and a stack of steel posts for the peg events. Somebody had even rigged up a bath-room out of tin sheets between the two stock tanks at the bore, with a sardine tin for a soap holder and a slatted board to stand on.

Dad went off visiting round the camps, so there was nothing for us to do but shine up our gear and wait for tomorrow.

While the boys were bringing the horses in next morning, Dad, speaking through stiff lips as he trimmed his moustache, said, 'How 'bout I shout you girls to the dance tonight? You're old enough for dances now.'

'Except we can't,' Judith said.

'So go along and learn – you'll soon pick it up.' He hummed and executed a three-step, his arm curved around air. 'Some o' the best times I had as a young fella were at bush dances.'

There came to me a memory of my mother's wide-skirted frock. 'We haven't got any clothes.'

'God pity me, girl! It's a bush hop, not the Lord Mayor's ball. There'll be plenty wearing jeans. He pulled a handful of notes from his pocket. 'Here – I cashed a cheque last night. You'll need spending money. There's five bob on the gate for starters.'

When it was time for the events, we mounted and rode across the creek to the gathering swell of sound and movement. I had Lady Meg, Judith had Echo, and Patrick was on Yerra. Sian had chosen a creamy horse called Peso, and Dad rode Trooper. He wasn't competing, he said, but he wasn't walking either.

At the track there was a great bustle of mounted riders and moving vehicles, a swarm of wide hats and bright shirts, and the smell of dust and dung mingled with smoke from the chimney stack at the back of the refreshment shed. A black horse crabbed past with his head on his chest, the silver studs on his bridle glinting in the sunlight.

Judith grabbed my arm as we sat on our saddles, staring about. 'Look, there's Len.'

He was on a short coupled bay with a high head carriage and very straight pasterns. His face lit up as he caught sight of us. He rode over, grinning.

'Hey! Bit of a surprise. How'd the trip go?'

'What?' I stared at him, so bemused by his unexpected presence that my wits had gone begging. 'Oh, it was okay.'

Judith made a noise in her nose. 'Are you crazy, or something? It was lousy.'

She rode off, and I sat there smiling my pleasure at him. 'I never thought you'd be here. Why are you? Where'd you get that dogmeat you're riding?'

'He's better'n he looks.' Len grinned again, patting the bay's neck. 'I'm working down this way now. The boss trucked half a dozen nags across for the boys — the whole stock-camp's here.'

Bent over the bay's neck, he turned his head so that his top ear stuck out above the smooth, brown plane of his cheek. It went suddenly red as he coughed and blurted, 'Come to the dance with me tonight?'

For an instant I couldn't believe I'd heard correctly. Then I felt myself blushing in turn. 'Okay.' I wondered if I needed Dad's permission and decided that I already had it. I felt dizzy and weightless, as if only the reins were anchoring me to the saddle and without them I might soar into the trees. I was awed by the ease with which my first date had come about.

'Great!' His uncertainty vanished and he beamed at me.

'What are you entering?' I asked hurriedly just as he said, 'How's the mare going?'

We laughed together then, constraint gone.

'Everything.' He answered first. 'Hey, what about teaming up for the Gretna? You know, your mare's never been beaten on the track under five furlongs – nothing'll catch her. I'll take out the bending race with this fella, for sure.'

'No chance.' I was positive. 'Patrick's got that sewn up.'

'Wanna bet?' He turned the bay alongside Meg. 'C'mon, let's get our nominations in, they'll be starting soon.'

A short, bandy man with a megaphone and a clipboard had appeared on the track, and we joined the throng of riders heading for him. There must have been twenty at least, and twice that number scattered around in little groups between the rails and stalls. I saw Sian trotting past and an Aboriginal girl on a pretty palomino. She was the only other girl riding. I noticed two skewbalds, several little kids on Shetlands, and an ugly grey pacer ridden by a man in a green shirt.

Patrick was just ahead of us, sitting up stiff and straight on Yerra. Her head hung low, and even in the crowd of strange horses, her eyes looked to be half closed. She was so small in the girth that Patrick had knotted the ends of his surcingle to keep it clear of her feet. I heard him ask for the bending race, and the bandy man, who wore a leather bag on his belt for giving change, took down his and Yerra's name.

'Righto, son. Twelve and under. Who's next?'

Patrick didn't move. 'I want the open race,' he said.

'Go on, stick with the kids,' the man advised. 'Double your chances that way.'

'I want the open,' Patrick repeated, and I had a sudden memory of him at Renmark, in bib and brace shorts, jaw stuck out in the same obstinate fashion.

Half an hour later, having won both heats around the poles, he lined up with the only three men not yet disqualified, and took the race, although he was almost caught by the grey pacer on the run out.

'Holy Hannah!' Len said disbelievingly, and I laughed.

'Told you.'

"'S he going in the figure of eight? Might as well skip it if he is. You want to try thread-the-needle instead?'

So we entered that, and the billycan race, which Sian and Judith won. Sian was actually second across the line, but he had the most water left, so the race was his. The girl on the palomino beat both Judith and me in the ladies bending race, but Judith took the flag race and Meg's speed to the line won me the barrel race.

We broke for lunch then, for sandwiches, steak burgers and hot dogs on paper plates, while the horses rested hipshot in the shade, and trade was brisk at the bar.

The Gretna Green, the first novelty race, was immediately after lunch. Sian and Judith entered too.

'You're mad,' I told her as she lined up beside me, waiting for the starter's signal.

Far up the straight, where our partners waited, I could see Sian waiting tensely beside Len. 'He'll get his fool head kicked off!' I said. Then the signal came and I forgot about everything but winning which included stopping Meg before she ran over the top of Len.

He was quick-footed and neat. As I hauled Meg into a cat-footed turn, he grabbed for the cantle and jumped, landing cleanly astride Meg's rump. 'Go, go!' he yelled, grabbing me around the waist, and in two strides the brown mare had cleared the mêlée of plunging horses and cursing, scattering riders and was streaking for the post. I heard him laugh in my ear, "S in the bag!'

My hat had gone and my hair blew into his face. He leaned forward, clinging to me as the mare tore along, and I knew, right there, between the dust and the yelling crowd, that I would let him kiss me tonight at the dance, if he wanted to.

When the last horse events had been run, the foot races followed, and here and there people began packing up. Horse-floats were being coupled to vehicles and swags thrown onto trucks. Not everybody would stay for the evening. Then when the sun had reached the top of the tallest gum, somebody picked up the megaphone and called Len's name.

He glanced behind him where the horses were tied, then over at the white stock truck backing up to an earthen ramp.

'That's the boss. I've gotta go – we're running the nags back to Bowman's paddock tonight cos we've gotta shift 'em on tomorrow. We'll have a clean-up and a feed an' come back in the 'rover. I'll meet you at the hall door, say, sevenish, okay?'

'Okay. I'll be there.'

'See yer then.'

Hat at a jaunty angle above his prominent ears, he hurried off to collect the bay. The rest of the men were already loading their horses. When the tailgate was shut, the truck drove off with four of them in the front, and Len and another man in the feed box behind the cab. He waved his hat at me as they went past.

～

The barbecue started at dusk. We'd all had a bath at the bore and changed into fresh clothes. I polished my boots and kept Meg up to ride over, so I wouldn't get them dusty. Somebody had started a generator, and there were lights in the hall as well as the refreshment shed. Several men and women were busy there, the women with pinnies tied over their frocks.

My stomach growled hungrily at the smell of frying meat and onions as I slipped off Meg and tied her in an empty stall. The light glinted on her eyeballs and she whiffled down her nose, brushing against my arm.

'Get off!' I brushed anxiously at my sleeve, smoothing the cotton and wishing I'd had some way of pressing it. Everybody except station managers wore unironed shirts so it shouldn't have mattered, but somehow it did.

Over at the food table, somebody yelled, 'Righto, people!' and suddenly the scattered shadows about me were in motion. I moved to join them, then stopped dead, staring in dismay at the girls and women tripping past. Every single one wore a dress – floaty, sleeveless, pastel dresses that swirled like petals about them. The light caught at reddened lips, court shoes and pretty strapped sandals, and I knew it was no use. I couldn't go. Dad had been wrong. Nobody went to dances in riding boots and crumpled shirts.

I turned so suddenly I bumped into Patrick running up behind me. Judith was there too.

'Why didn't you wait for us? Is my hair all right?' She didn't stop for an answer, only looking back impatiently at me as I stood there. 'What's the matter?'

'I'm not going.'

'But –'

'I changed my mind.' I grabbed the reins and swung up before she could argue, and when she called something the words were lost in the drum of Lady Meg's feet.

I had to slow down for the creek. Meg breasted the far bank with a grunt, then fell into her long, mile-eating stride across the timbered flat. Behind were the yards, the bore, our darkened camp, and the faint beat of the generator. I could see lights across my front – a vehicle bringing somebody to the dance. Maybe even Len. My throat felt tight and it was difficult to swallow. I wondered what he'd think when I didn't show. He'd probably be glad if he knew the reason.

As my hands tightened angrily on the reins, Meg broke into her gliding canter. My braid thumped on my back, and I felt the air of our passage on my hot face and smarting eyes. I wished I had short, bouncy curls. I wished I had a lipstick. And I wished, with violent intensity, that I had a dress like the one I had seen, long ago, in my mother's room. Then something moved on the track's verge, and Meg, still cantering, snorted and shot sideways. I pulled her savagely to a standstill. She shook her head, jangling the bit rings as the dust settled, while I sat in my saddle howling for the things I didn't have.

~

It was nearly midnight when the music stopped and the dance ended. I'd ridden back long since and let Meg go. Lying wakeful in my swag in the empty camp, I heard the vehicles start up and leave, then Dad and the others coming back. I pulled the blanket over my head until they'd rolled in, then flung it back and lay for a long time staring up at the glittering immensity of the Milky Way.

Len was just about as distant. I knew I'd never see him again. I had mucked everything up. Even if he still wanted to write, he didn't have an address, and I didn't know where he worked. The memory of his voice was already as faint as the squeaking of bats cutting through the starlit night.

TWENTY-FIVE

Biddy, the red cattle bitch, was given to us twice – because the first time, her owner changed his mind and took her back. Ted had been at Moontah bore when we came over the Territory border. He was a tall, wiry man who'd been living alone there for months. There'd been no feed at the bore so he'd hitched a ride out on the wagonette to the camp that Dad had picked. The red bitch went with him like his shadow. She was a silent dog, watchful and quick, never more than a pace behind him even when he sat by the fire – something Larry would never have presumed to do.

Pumpers were a funny lot, Dad said, though whether they started funny or the job made them that way, he wasn't sure. Ted was no exception, as garrulous as a leaky tap. He was a unionist, and when he got onto the brotherhood of the workers, the dog yawned and crossed her front paws like she'd heard it all before.

Dark came before we'd finished eating. Ted talked on, and Dad reswung the billy for coffee. Sian had kept a couple of horses tied up to take Ted back home, but he wasn't ready to leave yet. He talked about stations he'd worked on and horses and dogs. He gave the bitch to Dad – the pumping job would finish anytime, he said, and when it did he was moving into town. Biddy wasn't cut out for civilised living, would bite a copper quick as a bagman, so she was better out of it on the road with us.

We ate brownie with the coffee, then Patrick and Judith sneaked off to bed. I yawned and lay back in the break, watching the fire-shine on the dog's moving eyes while the old man's voice went on and on. He was fencing and shearing in a constant drone as the red bitch lapped from his forgotten mug. Sian, squeezing a pimple across the fire, grinned at me. We knew what Dad would have done if Larry had so forgotten himself.

The Cross was sinking towards the horizon before Ted was ready to leave, then it took him a few minutes more to frame the words that withdrew his earlier offer.

'You wouldn't think the worse of a man for changing his mind about the old dog?'

'Course not,' Dad said heartily. He didn't sound surprised. Then Sian rode off into the darkness to see Ted home and fetch the horse back, and that, we thought, was that.

Two months later, when we were camped at the Serpentine mustering road bullocks for the drovers, the old pumper and Biddy turned up again. She had a collar on and stood, unsuspecting, to be chained. She was mine, Ted told me. He was leaving that morning with the road mob, and Jimmy Chalmers wouldn't have a dog in the camp, so he was giving her to me. 'Or the old fella – she'll take to him quicker,' he said. 'Leave her tied up,' he called from the saddle. Biddy sprang to the chain's end as he turned his horse, and hung there sulking, then set up a dismal howl that raised the hairs on my arms as he cantered away.

'Don't get too fond of her,' Dad warned us that night. 'He'll be back when the trip's over. She's a mannerless bitch, but she'd cross fire and water for him. A one-man dog's a proper yarra-mun tree.'

'What's that mean?' Yarramun was the blackfellas' word for horse – we often used it – but I'd never known what a yarramun tree was.

'Just something you can't change.' He pulled the short blade of his knife open and dug at the bowl of his pipe, squinting at it in the firelight.

'Why?' I said blankly. 'What's it got to do with changing things?'

'It's just a saying, Kerry. Means fate, I s'pose. Something that don't necessarily make sense, but just is. A sort of contradiction, like its name. Half-horse, half-timber, you can't ride it, burn it, or get rid of it. So you call it a yarramun tree.'

'But how does that make Biddy one?'

He sighed and scratched at his beard. 'Told you – she's a one-man dog, and they stay faithful. She won't forget old Ted, not in five days or five years. He comes back, you'll lose her. Dogs like that give their hearts the once.'

But instead of returning with Jimmy Chalmers, Ted went on a bender at the railhead. His hide must've been cracking, Dad said, after five months on the wagon. We never saw him again. So Biddy, who'd grieved and moped at the chain's end for him, switched her allegiance to Dad, becoming his shadow instead.

She wasn't a nice dog, but she had her uses. Sian called her a sneaking mongrel but that was because she bit him so often. She was sly and spoilt. Where Larry bristled and showed his teeth at a stranger, Biddy would wag her tail until he turned aside, then launch a silent attack. She bit Judith and Patrick and took a particular set against Sian, who didn't like dogs much, anyway. And when Dad wasn't there, she went back to being mine.

He broke her into work, of course. No point carrying passengers, he said. She was good with cattle but a bit savage with horses, taking such a chomp out of Alice's hind fetlock once, back when we still had the wagonette, that the mare ran lame for a week. Everyone on the station quickly got to know her. A man would have to be a nutter, they said, to mess with the McGinnises' camp – that red bitch would eat 'em alive.

She was still with us after we'd delivered the Thornton cattle when Dad bought the transceiver. He'd been a signalman in the war and was keen on radio.

'It'll bring us work,' he said, and he was right. We were shifting a hundred bulls across three properties – a job hardly worth dirtying saddlecloths for, he grumbled – when the first message came through. It was the offer of the Dreyfus Downs bullocks. Eight trips, each of nine days' duration, downriver to the railhead. Eight hundred head a trip.

'Means we'd have to run two camps.' Dad, jotting figures on the flyleaf of a paperback, shot a look at Sian. 'You'd have the second one. With Kerry and Patrick you'd only need two other riders. Think you can handle it?'

'Yeah,' Sian said, offhand, then looked thoughtful so we couldn't see how pleased he was.

After the Thornton cattle, we'd taken spayed cows down to Murchinson Station, then shifted a thousand steers three hundred miles to a fattening depot. It was still only one season's experience, though – not much to produce a boss drover.

'What's the first delivery date?' Judith asked, and Dad rummaged through the truck's glovebox to find the calendar.

'Monday week.' He jerked his head at the bulls around us. 'Get shot o' this lot tomorrow. That gives us the better part o' ten days to pick up some men, shift the plant, sort out the pack gear. Something to pin in your hats – we give good deliveries, we could land a permanent contract here.'

'What if they're as bad as the Thorntons'?' Judith said. 'We wouldn't want one then.'

'Jesus, Mary and Joseph, girl!'

'Well, what if they are?'

'A man couldn't sell you a drink in the desert,' Dad said. He squinted at the sun, then looked at Patrick. 'Righto, champ, you and Kerry can take 'em on this arvo. Don't bustle 'em on the stone. Judith'll fetch the plant – your brother and I have some planning to do.'

∽

Dreyfus was a big place, a company property carrying close to thirty thousand head. It ran to a manager, overseer, and had two stock-camps. Joe Halliday had the bullock-camp, which was mustering our first mob when we turned up two days early at the boundary.

Dad went over to talk to their cook while the five new men got the load off and carted wood and water for the camp. The Mail had brought them out to Dreyfus – two white stockmen and three black ones. Dad told me to keep Biddy chained up till she got used to them. We didn't want them pulling the pin over leg wounds before we even started, he said.

As always, waiting dragged. The nights were cold, and the early mornings, but the days were warmly golden. There was a pink haze above the river when the bullocks came out from watering, the light like oil on their moving hides. It was red country. Pea-bush swamp and coolibah flats that crumbled at the riverbank to gaping chasms laced with tree roots and roly-poly. The water lay thirty or more feet down in paperbark-fringed channels where waterbirds nested and the little crocodiles sunned themselves on pale sandbanks.

It was pretty country, but Dad warned Sian about the pea-bush and the river. You could find trouble in both with fresh cattle. The dry stems of the pea-bush rattled on hides like a stick on iron, and anything could start a mob in the river.

'Jesus! Will you let up?' Sian exploded, then lowered his voice as one of the men looked over to where they stood. 'Either I'm takin' these cattle or you are. And if I am, just get off me back for five minutes. I wasn't born yesterday!'

'All right, boy,' Dad said mildly. He didn't seem to notice how Sian sucked in his breath at the word 'boy', then banged down the saddle pouch he'd been holding before jumping on his horse and riding away. Dad saw me watching then and jerked his head for me to follow him around the front of the truck, out of sight and earshot of the men.

Biddy was chained there. She jumped up against his leg and he pulled her ear, looking at me with serious eyes. 'I want you to listen to me very carefully, Kerry. I need your help with something concerning Sian.'

I felt uncomfortable because they always seemed to be rowing nowadays. 'You don't have to worry about him. Sian's always careful.' It was true – Sian couldn't stand being beaten at anything, so he was never careless. He'd ride every watch rather than deliver a beast short.

'It's not the mob I'm worried about. It's the Mellor brothers – the blokes who use'ta handle these cattle. They've got 'emselves a bit of a name as drunkards and pub brawlers. The talk is they're gonna fix me when the first mob comes in.' His hand went on scratching Biddy's ears, but his face was dark with trouble. 'I wouldn't lose any sleep over 'em, but if they get hold of a kid like Sian – Jesus! the pair of them'll kick him half to death.'

His words shocked me. 'They wouldn't!'

'Don't be daft,' he said tersely. There was a splintery toughness in his gaze and for all my seventeen years I felt a child. He'd killed men in the war, he knew what they were capable of. 'He'd be safe enough this end o' the job,' he went on, 'but the boss wouldn't stand for it. Not handing fresh cattle over to a lad his age. So he's gotta do the railhead, and because I can't be there, you'll have to protect him.'

I gaped at him, then nodded, trusting him to tell me how.

'You mustn't let him out of your sight,' he said, 'down the yards or up town. Be with him wherever he goes. Stand outside the dunny when he's in there, but don't leave him alone. Nobody'll touch him in front of a young girl.'

'I won't,' I promised. 'And it'll be all right because I've just thought – I'll take Biddy.'

He nodded at that, and hearing her name the red bitch turned her head to lick my hand.

Sian wasn't too pleased about Biddy coming with us, but he didn't find out until dinner-camp on the day he took over the mob. We were five days out by then. Dad had turned back with the truck and his plant that morning for the Dreyfus boundary, where he would take delivery of the next mob two days later. By the time he reached his fourth-night camp, we should have trucked and retraced our route to meet him and take over the cattle. We had the pack-camp, with five horses to carry the swags and tucker and a pair of lightweight water canteens.

It was a good mob. They ran up once, on dinner-camp one day, exploding out of the shade trees along the old copper-mine track, with Sailor, the canteen horse, bucking and bolting among them. It was Patrick's fault. He'd taken Sailor down to the river to fill the canteens, then let him jog back without a surcingle to secure the load. One set of rings came unhooked when the horse jumped a log, so that the canteen swung down and smacked him on the shoulder.

'Jesus and Mary, you drongo! What the hell d'you use for brains?' Sian yelled into the dust of the steadied mob, sounding just like Dad. He was angry, windburnt jaw jutting above the grimy blue folds of his cotton shirt. A sparse stubble decorated his chin, and his pale eyes blazed dangerously.

Patrick apologised, shame-faced. There was a hole in one canteen, but we had it mended at Collulah Station, where the cook gave us a loaf of bread and a box of vegetables to balance back to camp.

The Dreyfus overseer should have camped with us on the last night, but he never turned up. It was a poor camp on a bare ridge overlooking a scrubby creek, windy and exposed, with too much cover too close at hand if a beast were to sneak off in the night. The overseer's absence meant we lacked the trucking times, and the bullocks had to be yarded before the train arrived next morning.

I waited as long as I dared, knowing the station master's office closed at five, then jumped on Trinket and trotted down the gravel track to town. It was no more than two miles. I stood in the irons, with Biddy streaking below in the roan mare's shadow. It was a waste of time tying her up, she broke collars faster than you could make them.

The trucking yards stood on a bare flat before the blue metal embankment of the railway line, with the tin shed of the office on the loading platform, halfway between the signals and the yard. Trinket wouldn't cross the line; she reared, snorting, from the shiny steel, her shod feet skidding in the loose metal, and to save time I tied her and walked. There were bottles by the track, and old beer cans. Across a flat glittering with bottle tops stood the pub and a row of shabby fettler's huts. I could see goats wandering between them, a gate tumbled off its hinge, the body of a dead car. Only the yards looked in good repair.

Two men loading bags into an old landrover watched me run up the steps and tap on the little window of the office. I'd just asked for the loading times for the Dreyfus cattle when the nearest man sang out, 'Hey, girlie, come here a minute.'

I pretended not to hear. He was thick-shouldered, with a big belly that strained at his belt and a silly sort of grin showing missing teeth. The station master scribbled the times down, flicking a sideways look at him as he called again.

'Is he drunk?' I was more embarrassed than scared.

'You can bet on it,' he grunted, and suddenly yelled, 'lay orf, Mellor, she doesn't wanter know yer.'

'Wass wrong with me, then?' the man shouted, the red coming into his face. He jumped onto the platform to stand swaying before me, and that was invitation enough for Biddy. He yelled a startled curse and kicked out, which cost him his balance, so she got him on the arm as well, and then the other leg before he tumbled down into the bed of the landrover.

His mate hadn't waited. Biddy's shoulder thudded into the cab door, and her snarl put the hair up on my neck. I called her off and she came slowly, hackles still up.

The stationmaster stuck his hand through the window. He was grinning.

'They say civility costs nothing, Miss, er ...?'

'McGinnis. Kerry McGinnis. Who was that?'

'The Mellor boys.' He chuckled. 'Never knew Harry could move so fast. Prob'ly changed his mind about meeting you, too.'

'Good.' It sounded prim but, riding back to camp, I couldn't keep the giggles from bubbling out of me. Dad could quit worrying. With an example like that to chew on, the whole town would tread carefully around all of us. Biddy had her uses.

～

When the last Dreyfus mob was delivered and the men paid off, we were, as Dad predicted, offered the contract for the following year. And in the meantime, he told us, there was a mob of twelve hundred stores leaving from a property on the Flinders, bound for the trucking yards at Hughendon.

Sian objected. 'The horses have had it. Be September before we'd deliver, then we've still gotta walk the plant back.'

'We'll put 'em on the rail,' Dad said. 'Truck 'em up in a day. The worst of 'em can stay here till we get back; we could buy a bit o' grain for the night-horses, too.'

'Why?' Sian stared at him. 'We've had a full season. What's this all about? We don't need the work.'

Dad tossed the dregs from his pannikin and looked the three of us over. Patrick was up on the load hunting something. 'Where're you, champ? You're in this too,' he called.

When we were all there, he said, 'It's about a base for us. Somewhere to bush the plant and hang our hats in the off-season. There's a place called McGraths. A red gravel paddock running down into Flinders grass. It's got a dam and an old shack, a bit of a yard. Going for a song. We could just about swing it with some extra cash. Something like another mob. It'd be a home – if you want it.'

'Where is it?' Sian spoke before I could.

'Just outside one o' those two-pubs-and-a-store towns,' Dad said. He puffed at his pipe, looking innocent. ''Bout halfway between here and where those steers are waiting. We could look it over on the way.'

Which was how we came to be on the road again in late August, heading south as the days warmed up, through good feed and a plentiful supply of gates. Cocky country, Dad called it. Paddocks you could canter across in half an hour, phone lines looped slackly above the fences, and stubby little troughs fit only for watering sheep. The steers were Brahmans, sleek and big-eared. They strode out like a regiment, long legs eating the miles, muzzles lifted to the questing wind.

It was crowded country. Sometimes you could see the roof of the next station before the last one was out of sight. Or hear cocks crowing during the morning watch. Pulling into the homesteads brought sheepdogs yapping about the truck until Larry or Biddy flew off the load. The kids were always next, running out to stare at the plant passing. This happened at a place called Farquar Creek too, but the boy there, blowing from his run down the paddock, had a message.

'Tell him he can't come in! Quick, before he opens the gate!' He waved at Patrick who was struggling, head down, with the cumbersome barrier, reins over his arm and the loose horses waiting behind.

'Course he can,' I told him, 'it's the stock route. And there'll be twelve hundred steers right behind him, as well.'

'But we've got the stallion in here!' His eyes blazed with urgency, he was almost yelling it. 'Mum said to tell you – he's dangerous. You can't ride through his paddock. Tell him he's gotta go round.'

'He's got a whip.' I didn't take the boy seriously. Even though it was a public stock route, most of these little places objected to drovers crossing their country.

Patrick was mounting, the gate closed again behind him. He trotted the plant into a bunch and moved them off, tails blowing in the wind.

''S okay,' I began, then the stallion charged out of the scrub like a thunderbolt, ears flat and crest high, making straight for Patrick.

The horses split in a terror of squeals and rasping snorts. Some hit the fence, some went over it, the rest fled. Patrick's mount, Danny, plunged sideways, forelegs clawing at the sky, just as his rider swung the whip. He must have got the stallion's eyes, or the tender bit of his nose, because the horse flung up his head and ran past. Danny was bucking in circles, trying to bolt. The stallion wheeled and went for him again, screaming with rage, and then the dogs reached him.

Larry got a hind leg; Biddy, being faster, a front one. The pain and weight of the attack broke the stallion's stride, and when Patrick hit him again he threw it in.

Biddy streaked at his head – you couldn't teach her not to – and he stabbed, lightning-quick with his forefoot, tumbling her into the grass as he galloped away. The whole thing lasted barely three minutes.

Danny's shoulders were lathered. He kept jumping about, twitching his ears. He was snorting with fright, the white showing in his starting eyes.

Patrick himself was bone-pale, his boots rattling in the stirrups. 'That bloody horse wants civilisin'.' His voice was high and aggrieved. 'Or shooting. He's done for your dog, too.'

It was true – she lay sprawled, the snarl still in place, her tough skull shattered. I crouched beside her, stroking her ears, while Patrick went after the horses. The boy was watching, bug-eyed, and I could hear a vehicle coming down from the house. It was no good crying – I knew she'd never really been mine.

I left her there for the birds to dispose of and walked back to the truck. We'd have to mend the fence. And rooting the pliers out of the toolbox it suddenly occurred to me that the reason Biddy had greeted so many men with a wagging tail, then bitten them, was because none of them had ever turned out to be Ted.

TWENTY-SIX

It was a good summer, that first one at McGraths. The paddock was tucked away off the edge of Miranda Downs which lay south-east of Normanton. We had three months before the rains started, which was time enough to patch the roof on the old shack and pour a new concrete floor. Sian cut the posts and rafters to build a shed to house the camp gear, and we roofed it from an old building the council was demolishing in town.

We did up the fences too. The paddock held about twenty miles of country, with the shack and dam built on the red gravel end next to Escape Creek. There was a good big hole in the creek, the water stained brownish-red, like the dam, from the clay in the gravel, but it had been dry in October when we came, and couldn't be relied upon, Dad said.

The Wet season lasted for months. We had never seen so much

rain and were thankful not to be sitting it out under canvas. Day after day the clouds poured in from the north, shedding their load on the land, and when the horses tired of the boggy lower ground, they moved up onto the gravel along the creek frontage. The insects ate them alive. Lying under our mosquito nets in the humid darkness, we'd hear them trotting and cantering all night. The flies ate into the softened flesh below their eyes, too, leaving areas of raw flesh you couldn't cover with your hand. As Dad said, nothing came free, there was a price even for green feed.

In the end Judith and I fuelled smoke buckets for them and they learned to stand in the drifting smudge of these, out of their tormentors' reach.

'It's not like the desert,' Judith said.

'No, it's better.' It was late March. I looked at the creek sparkling under the curve of soft blue, the sweep of nodding green, heavy now with seed, the black shade of ebony and wild plum. 'Deserts're only meant for lizards.'

The boys patched the old yard (we'd tear it down and put up a decent one next summer, Dad said), and Sian caught the half-dozen breakers we had. The four of us worked them.

Dad was getting a bit slow for it now. There was very little brown left in his beard, and his back was a source of constant trouble; some days he could scarcely straighten and walked inclined forward, as if studying the ground. It was no cause for worry, most ageing stockmen we'd met did the same.

By May we were on the road, having mustered the plant (fatter than they'd ever been) and slung our swags onto the truck with the rest of the camp gear. There was a bolt fitted to the outside of the shack's only door, which Dad slid shut. Nobody would enter in our absence, he said, unless they really needed shelter, in which case you couldn't deny them.

We weren't leaving much behind, anyway. Just some of the pack gear – which as we'd bought another vehicle to use in the second camp, we no longer needed as a means of transport.

It was good to be on the move again. We'd only been at McGraths – which we'd renamed Redwater – six months, but I already thought of it as home. We'd do up the shack into a proper house one day, I thought, and grow a garden with marigolds and big shade trees, and keep hens. But not yet. Not while the road ran on through country changed to strangeness by the Wet, the stirrup-high grass rippling like the back of a moving beast, and every creek-bank a blaze of vivid flowers blue as the sky above.

Judith jumped bareback onto Socks to take the plant down to water, and when they poured over the bank in a thunder of tossing heads and flashing heels, the bay farted tremendously and threw her. She landed on her feet, yelling passionately into his dust, 'You'll be sorry for that, you old villain!'

Next day Patrick came tearing out of the grass, legs working like pistons, with a Downs Tiger on his heels. Only a foot of the snake's body was on the ground, the rest was reared up and going for Patrick. Dad, who was holding a pair of hobbles, flung them at its head just as Sian grabbed the axe and threw that. It cut the snake clean in half, and I watched in cold horror as the head end whipped in the bloodied grass, biting itself.

'Mother o' God!' Patrick shuddered. 'Thought he'd get me for true.' He flopped down in the piled bushes of the wind-break about the fire as if his legs had died on him, and one of those big grass-hoppers with plated head and sides leapt out of the foliage to thud against his arm. He yelled and jumped clean across the fire. We laughed ourselves silly, but that night none of us turned in without making dead sure our nets were well anchored under our swags. The only thing worse than being bitten, Judith said, would be waking in the night to find a snake in bed with you.

We took a mob of twelve hundred spayed cows from Dolomite Station down to Jundanelly, finishing up in time to trek back north-west to Dreyfus to take delivery there.

The cows rushed the first night out, wrecking half a mile of fence, and crippling Sian's horse, Hunter, which, galloping blind in the dust, also hit the wire. Sian was unhurt, but the bay's chest was ripped open and we had to leave him behind.

Next day one of the cows calved, though her dewlap was slit, like the rest of the mob, indicating she'd been through the spaying bail.

Dad was cranky about it. 'That bloke calls himself a cattleman and sends a man off with calvin' cows! A couple of yer better get out there an' grab the calf.'

'You gunna kill it?' Patrick asked.

'How long d'you think we'd hold the cow then?' Dad rasped. We're gunna carry it. Make a bit o' room on the truck, Kerry. And let's hope it's the only one.'

There were actually two more. It occurred, Dad said, when cows culled for spaying happened to be already pregnant. All three mothers soon got used to the arrangement and would come bawling with full udders onto the camp, looking for their young. I got fond of the little heifer and hoped her new owner wasn't going to knock her on the head, but when we got there I didn't ask.

We delivered on a Wednesday at noon, and by Friday night were forty miles along the track to Dreyfus, the calves, the crippled Hunter, and other incidents of the trip, already fading memories of the season.

Joe Halliday still had the bullock camp. We pulled into our old position under the bent coolibah, and Sian took a shovel to the grass where the fire had been last year. You couldn't see the middle wire of the fence for feed.

Joe rode over, grinning, on a jumpy bay whose chest and thighs were creamed with lather. He squatted on his heels at the camp's edge, holding the reins and chewing on a grass stem.

'Some season, hey?'

The horse shied, snorting as Patrick came in with a log for the fire, and Joe growled at it. 'You'll be fourth down the route – the Kelverton bullocks have gone, bloke called Chalmers with steers from the border, and old Alec Rawson went through yesterdee.'

'Saw his tracks,' Dad said. 'Mob be ready on time?'

'Fact is, we're a bit short-handed.' Joe's wide mouth turned down. 'I lost a coupla men – the horses're too good for 'em. Or they ain't good enough. So I'm a day behind meself. If I could borrow a coupla your lot – one day should do it.'

'You could give him a hand, son?' Dad looked at Sian, who nodded. 'Judith'll be free too. I'll be at the station to pick up me men. If the Mail's on time an' I get back early we'll knock a killer. We're just about outa meat.'

'Right, thanks, Mac.' Joe stood up, and the bay backed, snorting.

He passed the split reins under its neck, growling softly as it began to plunge and rear, then vaulted lithely into the saddle, settling his boots and sketching a wave as the horse crabbed sideways, fighting the bit.

The Dreyfus bays were all Red Rocket's progeny. He was a studbook sire the station had kept eight or nine years back. They were good stock horses – but there wasn't one not touchy about the head. The station men were used to the problem, but Dad maintained he wouldn't have one of their nags as a gift. There were plenty of other ways of getting killed, he said.

Next day, while Sian and Judith rode off with the stock-camp, Dad and I drove into the station. We'd left our second vehicle, a tray-backed landrover, there with a flat tyre before taking the Dolomite cattle. It had suffered a blow-out on the trip down but there hadn't been time to mend it then. While Dad repaired it, I discovered the battery was also flat.

We had lunch in the kitchen, picked up some spuds from the store, and then the new men, one of whom was so drunk he pitched out of the cab of the Mail truck and lay giggling and making swimming motions in the dust.

Dad looked at him in disgust. 'Chuck him up the back,' he told his two companions. 'He falls off, yer needn't bother stopping me.'

He had to tow the landrover to start it, and again at the gate with the gully when I stalled it there. The sun was westering by the time we reached camp, where Judith and Sian sat drinking tea, their still-saddled horses hipshot in the shade. Patrick was off taking the plant to water, and at a little distance through the coolibah were the mustered bullocks, tailed out by the station men.

'We'll have to look sharp to beat the dark,' Dad said. Grabbing the rifle, he sent Sian and Judith off to cut a small mob out of the herd and drift them over beneath the tree he'd selected. It was a coolibah, lumpy with burls for easy footing.

Dad thrust the rifle into the crotch and hauled himself up, sitting quiet among the branches while the two riders pushed the cattle towards him. I chucked the knives, steel and axe into the tray of the 'rover. One of the new men, seeing what we were about, was breaking bushy armfuls off a whitewood to serve as a bed for the meat to rest on. His name was Charlie, he said. He had a black hat, and a big silver belt buckle.

'Been on the road long?' he asked, dumping the last load onto the vehicle.

'Years.' I was watching Judith's mare, Echo, who was playing up. Maybe she could see Dad in the tree, bringing the rifle to his shoulder. A roan beast beside her pushed his muzzle up, scenting the air, then the rifle boomed. Echo seemed to stagger and crumple, Judith fell, the cattle took off, and I stared in disbelief at the shaking branches of the coolibah where Dad was no longer visible.

'Jesus!' Charlie said on a high note. 'He hit the mare.' As if to disprove it, Echo lunged upright and bolted down the paddock, ears flat and reins flying. The sight did not reassure me.

'Judith!' I screamed, and ran. She was flat on her back making funny, strangling noises through her wide-open mouth. There was blood on her teeth, but my frantic eyes could find no other injury. 'Judith, are you all right?'

'She's had the wind knocked out of her,' Charlie said behind me. 'Sit her up, so she can breathe.' He helped me pull her into a sitting position. She whooped, speechlessly, holding her chest. There was grass stuck in her plait, and her hat had rolled away. Charlie picked it up, then held it, staring.

'He did hit the mare.' The brim was splashed with blood, and so too, when I looked, was the grass all about it. I remembered the shaking coolibah foliage, and the way the cattle had split around the trunk as they took off.

'He must've been pulling the trigger when the branch gave way.'

In my mind's eye, I saw the lifted face of the roan bullock, a target too inviting to ignore.

'Jesus and Mary!' I sprang to my feet. 'He's prob'ly thinking he's killed her.'

By the time I reached the coolibah, Sian was already there, bent over Dad who lay unconscious under the .303. He'd smacked his face in falling – on the broken branch or the rifle, we couldn't tell – but there was a swelling lump on his temple to prove it. The bullocks had been over his legs. From the knees down his jeans were smeared with dust, but it was probably the fall that had broken his hip. We didn't find out about the second break, just above the ankle, until word came back from the hospital next day.

We used the wireless to call the doctor, then Sian and Judith drove him to the homestead, waiting there until the plane came. I stayed at the camp – there was still Patrick and the men to see to. Joe rode over while I was cooking tea, knocking his hat up politely and speaking from the saddle.

'Sorry about old Mac, Kerry. My blokes are getting a killer for yer now. Anything else we can do?'

'I dunno, Joe – maybe drive the 'rover back to the station tomorrow? If we're still lifting the cattle, I mean.'

'Why wouldn't you be? Sian can take the camp, can't he?'

'But we'll only have one without Dad. He won't be riding for months if his hip is broken.'

'The trucks are booked,' Joe said. 'Yer want my opinion, one camp's better'n none at all. Tell Sian I'll take coupla the new men, if he don't want 'em. Here's yer meat coming now.'

Dad was taken to the Mt Isa hospital where we expected him to stay, but two days later he was flown to the coast. For specialist treatment, we were told. The bullocks, in trampling him, had not simply broken his leg but shattered it. The surgeon would be putting a steel rod in the leg bone itself, a pin at the ankle. Given the patient's age, they said, convalescence would be slow.

In fact, it took the whole season because infection set in after the operation, and when that was cleared up and he was due to return to the Mt Isa hospital to begin therapy, he caught pneumonia.

'How can you get sick after you go to hospital?' Patrick demanded. 'They're supposed to make you better, not worse!'

'He's a tough old bugger, he'll weather it,' Sian said, but on watch at night, whistling Dad's travelling song to the cattle, I was not always so sure.

~

We took five of the nine Dreyfus mobs that year, while Jimmy Chalmers, whom we'd known back on Walgra, handled the rest. We'd just trucked the last mob when Sven Jansen, the Queensland

Meat Exports cattle-buyer, pulled into the camp for a drink of tea and passed on the news that Watson River was selling its herd.

'They'll be looking for drovers,' he said. 'How's your old fella getting on, by the way? Back on his feet yet?' The last question was directed at me because Sian was already leaving, heading for the Station Master's office to see if he could contact Watson River by phone.

We landed a six-week trip down into the basalt country, pushing a thousand head – cows, weaners, calves, bulls and steers. A dog's breakfast of a mob, Dad would have said. Charlie, who'd been fifth man in the camp all season, had left us at the railhead, so Sian put on an elderly blackfella he found in the pub. His name was Duke. A tall man wearing black glasses, with cataracts growing on his eyes. He could ride straight past a beast without noticing, but Sian used Larry to help push the mob along, and the dog always gathered in those that Duke missed.

Towards the end of the trip, the feed cut out and it became a struggle to keep the weakest cows moving. The owner paid us a visit, saw how things were and agisted a small paddock for two hundred of the worst of them. We pushed on again then, losing a bull and another cow in a boggy dam, and gaining a pair of newborn calves.

'Godalmighty! Just what we need.' Sian rolled his eyes. He was tired – we all were. And so, by then, were the horses. There'd been casualties among them too. Joss had got sick and been left behind, Ford had a wire cut across his wither. And Sian had sold Echo – the first time anyone but Dad had disposed of a member of the plant. She'd been useless since she was shot. The bullet, which had gouged a furrow across her rump, seemed to have addled her nerves for good. Any sudden sound set her bolting. The only way she'd be safe, Judith said, was to stop up her ears. Sian reckoned it was simpler to sell her.

Dad was home before us. He came limping out from the shack to watch as we drove up – Sian driving the truck and me behind in the landrover. Larry flew joyously off the load to greet him, but I stared in dismay, taking in the stick and the loose hang of his shirt. His beard was shorter than normal, silvery white in the sunlight, and he had carpet slippers on his feet.

His appearance shocked the others too. We told him about the season and the plant, about the different trips, trying to ignore his lurching progress between the table and stove. Until Patrick bluntly spoke the question in all our minds: 'How long you gunna need that stick, Dad?'

'Just till me hip takes up a bit – could be a month, or two.' He lit his pipe and puffed at it. Even his hands looked different, soft and pale from the months inside. It wasn't the broken bones causing the problem, he said, they'd mended. It was the arthritis that had set into his hip joint.

'Same as old Ben, at Dreyfus,' Patrick said before anyone could kick him silent. 'He can't even ride now.'

'I'll manage.' Dad's eyes hardened, and there was a snap to his tone. For the first time that evening he looked and sounded like himself.

For all that, it was well into summer before he could walk unaided. He smoked in his cane-bottomed chair on the verandah, shifting restlessly about to ease his hip, fashioning hobble-straps and mending saddles. He drove the few miles to town when the roads were dry to pick up mail and news, coming home from one such trip with the nose of a red cattle pup poking out of the neck of his shirt.

'A dog's comp'ny 'bout the place,' he said.

'Pups're a damn nuisance on the road, though,' Sian objected, which was true enough.

In March there was a letter from Delroy Downs in the Territory, offering us twelve hundred steers, leaving in mid-April and bound for a fattening depot in the Channel Country.

Sian got the map to work out the distance and time.

'Walk it in,' he said happily. 'We could take half the horses and spell 'em after delivery at Dreyfus. We'd still have time to come home for a fresh plant before they were ready – Dreyfus never sends its bullocks till late June.'

'Better let 'em know you'll take 'em then,' Dad said. 'The letter's a fortnight old already. Be a shame to miss out.'

Sian looked at him as he fussed with the kettle, his beard, grown out again, spread fanwise across his shirt. He hadn't thrown the stick away yet, it hung by the door, and on mornings when his hip was extra bad he'd still use it for a bit.

I jumped up then, grabbing the teapot. 'I'll make it, Dad.' It gave me a chance to turn away as Sian spoke.

'Why? Won't you be doing it?'

'Can't.' Dad was at his most laconic. 'Got meself a job. I'd wire 'em today if I was you.'

There was silence then while I placed the tea and the pannikins on the table. I couldn't think of anything to say, and neither, apparently, could Sian.

Through the open door I could see the saddles Patrick had been greasing, and a rail full of buckled hobbles. And beyond them Judith, a score of neck-straps on one arm, chasing horses about in the new yard. Dad had ridden on maybe three occasions throughout summer. Short excursions only and each had plainly been an effort.

'Stand *up*, you cockeyed old hussy!' Judith yelled then, and Dad smiled faintly.

'You can leave three of me quiet nags here. Diamond, an' old Ben I guess, and Rose. And the 'rover. I'm the new pannikin boss o' the town common – and that's mostly sitting on yer arse at the yards. Three horses'll be plenty.'

'Right,' Sian answered, when it was plain Dad had said all he meant to. 'I'll get off a telegram to Delroy then.'

∽

Five days later we started out under a sky brushed with feathery wind clouds. The plant, with Patrick in the lead, raced skittishly from the yard, each horse with its neck-strap and hobbles and freshly pulled tail. There were a couple of shin-tappered colts paddle-footing it on the wings, still sore from the breaking yard, while Judith and I rode behind. Sian, Larry and the truck had already left – Sian had fuel, groceries and the hired man to collect in town before catching us up.

Dad stood by the yard wing, leaning on his stick as the horses streamed by, the red pup tucked under one arm. It scratched and wriggled to be free amid the flying hooves, until he growled, 'Bide!' then it licked his hand and lay with hanging legs, slobbering onto his shirt.

I reined Shuffler beside him, though the black was dancing and champing at the bit, mad to follow his mates. Dad just stood there, saying nothing. I wished I could talk to him, but I had never been able to – not about things that mattered. I wanted to say that he was neither too old, nor too lame to come with us, but I knew I couldn't. He had settled the matter in the only way he knew, and he wouldn't go back on it now. He never did. Granite would change sooner. Tears smarted under my lids as I looked at him. There was nothing to say.

'See you then, Dad.'

'See you, Kerry.' His eyes were sad, and hard, and wise as he fondled the panting pup.

Shuffler sprang, snorting, into a canter. I stood in the irons, foam from his bit spattering over my hands. Up ahead Judith's whip cracked, her voice ringing clear above the hoof beats: 'Git *over*, Pluto!'

When I looked back, Dad, made small by distance, still stood there, like a rock. Like the yarramun tree – alone in the landscape under a windblown sky.

EPILOGUE

Dad died in December 1992.

When the call came I caught the first bus down to the nursing home in Charters Towers and trod anxiously behind the sister through the wide hallways with their handrails and skid-free floors. There were chairs everywhere, the smell of lemon cleaner, and a tape-deck playing a collection of forties music.

'In here, dear.' The sister pressed my hand, as if I were still seventeen. The doctor, professionally gentle, was just leaving. 'He's very tired. But he has lucid spells, so he might wake. You can stay with him if you wish. Ring for Sister if there's any change.'

It was peaceful sitting beside him with my hands resting on the white coverlet. I didn't attempt to take his – he had never liked being touched. The rasp of his breathing mingled with the faint melody from the hall – Vera Lyn with 'We'll Meet Again', followed by 'The White Cliffs of Dover'. His hair was white, his scalp showing pinkly through. It was hard to equate the man he had been, the giant of my childhood, with the frail, shrunken figure in the bed.

'Dad? It's Kerry. Can you hear me?' The music swelled as if a door had been opened, bringing 'Bluebird of Happiness' into the room. His lids flickered.

'Sky-eyes,' he said quite strongly.

'What, Dad?' I bent above him.

'My dear wife,' he said, then something that sounded like 'song'. I touched his lips with my fingers and the words came out on a sigh, 'My blue lass.'

They were the last he spoke.

～

When the doctor and sister had gone, I stayed with him for a while, holding the hand he could no longer pull away, and examining his gift. Perhaps it hadn't been meant as such, or specifically directed to me, but there it was, just the same.

For sitting alone in that quiet room I saw her then, more clearly than at any time since her death. A young woman, little more than a girl, dressed in a shimmery frock, her eyes like pieces of blue sky. My mother.

INDEX